HUMANOID ENCOUNTERS

THE OTHERS AMONGST US

1990-1994

ALBERT S. ROSALES

Triangulum Publishing.

Copyright © 2016 Albert S. Rosales

ISBN-13: 9781519547101

ISBN-10: 1519547102

Book designed by Ash Staunton.

Central image from cover art used with permission by David Chace

Figure 1. One of my early sightings in Santa Clara, Cuba, 1965?

Humanoid: *adjective* hu·man·oid \'hyü-mə-ˌnȯid, 'yü-\

Having human form or characteristics.

"Why?" You ask. Why do I go on, compiling events from worldwide locations and sources, why do I continue the struggle? Will this catalogue of uncanny events, someday be as important as I think it is? I hope so.

Humans are arrogant and this arrogant behavior has doomed this once beautiful planet. We have been warned on numerous occasions, about our war-like nature, our disregard for other species, destroying the environment, ignoring the writing on the wall, etc. There are indeed 'others' amongst us, perhaps they share this planet and are trying to prevent its destruction, perhaps they are remaining descendants coming from the future to warn us, or yes, wayfarers from distant stars concerned about our destructive and arrogant behavior, and even more likely visitors from other dimensions that co-exist with ours.

These visitations, encounters, abductions, whatever the case might be, have been occurring for perhaps thousands of years, I will never be able to collect each one of them, and many have gone and will go to their graves with their secrets and encounters that forever changed their lives.

This has never been an easy task, my obsession, if you will, has cost me dearly, relationships, financial hardships, etc, but I keep coming back and trudging on. I always thought that writing a book about a compilation of humanoid encounters would be impossible, too much

7

information and too little time. But with the encouragement of several fellow researchers, I will attempt to show events that have been mostly ignored or ridiculed, events that I believe are the key to the survival of humans on this planet.

Of course it would be impossible to include all the cases, but included are some 'highlights' of the period 1990-1994. Many of the most interesting cases reported.

The wave of sightings and encounters which began in Eastern Europe, Russia and all its territories in the fall of 1989, continued on without respite in 1990. The amount of cases reported in the region for 1990 was a record high. Close encounters, abductions and contacts dominated. Every former Soviet republic was involved, especially the Ukraine. The wave of encounters began to diminish towards the end of 1991 but it did not really end until 1997. I must give thanks to researchers like Ukrainian Anton Anfalov for assisting me in collecting a lot of this data which otherwise would have forever remained unknown in the west. Russian researchers like Alexei Pryma, Gennady Belimov, Mikhail Gershteyn and others, collected and investigated hundreds of unbelievable cases.

The wave continued on in 1991 however to a lesser extent, as other incredible cases were being reported elsewhere in the world, especially Puerto Rico which was in the throes of a wave which had commenced in 1987. Dozens of close encounters were reported on the island. Other amazing cases were sprinkled throughout the world, Spain, Argentina, Brazil, Australia, U.K., etc.

1992 delivered an apparent increase of encounters with other worldly creatures around the world. 1993 brought forth what was termed by Israeli researcher Barry Chamish, "the return of the giants" or of the mythical "Nephilim." The focus was definitely in Israel, where bizarre incidents were a common occurrence during 1993. Activity sort of eased down towards the end of the year and into 1994 which was slower and with fewer cases of interest.

1994 was sort of preview year of the madness that was about to come in 1995-1996. The return of the so-called "flying humanoid" was widely reported in Italy with numerous incredibly cases. It would also herald the coming of a strange cryptid creature that was soon to be known to the world as the "Chupacabra" Read on and see what took place during that incredible period in UFO/humanoid history.

It would be impossible to mention each and every researcher and person that has helped me amass this incredible amount of information. I have been reluctant in writing a book with all the latest compilations. Many of them have used my research which is free for all to see on-line, they know who they are. Without the encouragement and assistance of fellow researcher and experiencer Ash Staunton, I would still be debating this issue, I thank him.

I also received encouragement from many others, to name a few, Alexander Rosales, Jaime Brian, Wade Ridsdale, Hank Worbetz, Gerardo Macias, Sue Demeter St. Clair, Gladys Gonzalez, Daniel Garcia Ramos, Robert Lesniakiewicz, Patrick Moncelet, Alejandro Barragan, Kay Massingill, Franck Boitte, Jean Sider, Freddy Soisson, Donald Cyr, Annie Theriault, Edwin Joyce. Way too many to name here, but they also know who they are. I wish all the best in the future that is to come, sooner than later.

Albert S. Rosales

<u>TYPES OF CE (Close Encounter) CLASSIFICATIONS</u>:

- **Type A**: When an entity or humanoid is seen inside or on top of an object or unidentified aircraft.
- **Type B**: When an entity or humanoid is seen entering or exiting a UFO.
- **Type C**: When an entity or humanoid is seen in the immediate vicinity of a UFO.
- **Type D**: When an entity or humanoid is seen in the same area where UFOs or unknown objects have been reported.
- **Type E**: When an entity or humanoid is seen alone, without related UFO activity (Example: bedroom visitation).
- **Type F**: When there is a psychic contact between entities or humanoids, but a humanoid is not necessarily seen.
- **Type G**: When there is direct contact or interaction between a witness or witnesses and a humanoid or entity; either involuntary, as a result of a forced abduction, or as a voluntary contact.
- **Type H**: When there is a report of an alleged crash or forced landing of a UFO with recovery of its occupants, or when an anomalous entity is captured or killed either by a witness or military personnel.
- **Type X**: When the situation is so uncanny that it doesn't fit any of the previous classifications. A new classification, there are several such cases in the files already. I would call these cases "extremely high strangeness events."

1990

Location: Near Esso, Kamchatka peninsula, Russia.
Date: 1990.
Time: Unknown.

Several strangers or humanoids wearing "spacesuits," were observed in this remote region, the most pure ecological area on the Kamchatka peninsula. The humanoids were very tall and were dressed in tight-fitting metallic silvery spacesuits.

Local legend and folklore tells that in "ancient times" a flying boat had crashed (or landed?) beyond the low mountain of Ulegendy and since then the area had been visited regularly by numerous UFOs. On many occasions while local reindeer breeders slaughtered their herds in the village of Anavgay, five or six disc-shaped objects would hover over the location for hours.

Locals were reportedly accustomed to seeing fiery globes in the sky, purple colored hazes and humanoid creatures. Also what appeared to have been holographic images were seen in the sky over the region.

HC addendum.
Source: Kamchatka Ufological group, Lubov Timofeeva, 'Anomalia,' Saint Petersburg #11, June 1-15, 2001.   Type: D

Location: Kiev, Ukraine.
Date: 1990.
Time: Unknown.

An elderly male witness, Valentin K. was reading a book in his room while his wife worked in the kitchen. Nobody was near him at that moment. Suddenly he saw several flashes of light, which circled the air around him. In the next moment, he appeared in a quite different and unknown location. The place was like nothing he had ever seen before. He saw a huge meadow of bright green, trimmed grass. There was a river nearby, filled with transparent, clear water. Beyond the river he could see sloping hills. There were no visible trees. He could see several humanoid figures walking around in the distance, and nearby suddenly appeared a strange semi-transparent humanoid figure, like an orange cloud.

The witness thought that it was all a dream and at that very same moment the nearby silhouetted assumed a dense nature becoming non-transparent, it seemed to materialize in front of the witness. The figure was human-like, but not completely. Its face, hands and clothing were dull orange in color. The strangest detail was the face, instead of a nose, there was a small dark opening, instead of a mouth, also a round opening, resembling that of funnel to pour water through. Ears were totally absent. The entity's eyes were large, yellow-brown in color, which stared at the witness intently but with "kindness."

The alien came closer to the witness in a strange floating gait, almost floating in midair. It wore totally bizarre clothing; the front section resembled that of a screen. Suddenly two other similar entities appeared nearby, which differ only in height, the first and original one was as tall as the witness, the second smaller and the third was taller than Valentin. The witness still thought that he was dreaming, but the humanoid closest to him somehow read his thoughts and answered via telepathy, *"No, this is not a dream, I am real, Give me your hand!"* Mechanically the witness obeyed the humanoid and stretched his hand. The alien gave him its hand. Valentin shook the alien's hand, which felt normal like that of a human, hot, with five fingers.

"Where are you from?" Asked the witness, overcoming his sense of fear. Instead of an answer, the "shield" located on the alien's chest, began emitting bright colors and soon the witness saw images of "galaxies," constellations, planets. After that the witness remembers nothing. He came to his senses again in his bedroom. He felt somewhat torpid and his hand was hot. His wife apparently had not notice him missing; she remained in the kitchen all the time, and apparently the whole "adventure" lasted only several minutes.

The witness, who was an accomplished artist, drew portraits of the scenes he witnessed.

HC addendum.
Source: Anatoliy Zubkov, "Molod" Ukrainian newspaper and "NLO—(UFOs)-Liaisons of the Universe?" Lugansk, Ukraine #10, October 1993.
Type: G
Comments: I believe the witness was somehow and momentarily transported into another dimensional world, or parallel Universe.

* * * * * * *

Location: Vladivostok, Russia.
Date: 1990.
Time: Unknown.

Aliens apparently abducted a 32-year old metal worker named Victor. Under hypnosis he was able to remember being in a white square room with round windows. "Galina" a being that looked like his wife but was not, apparently brought him to an area, blasted him with something, and he fainted, later he came to in the strange room.

There was another entity there, a small man, dressed in black clothing. They questioned Victor, and urged him to reveal something he did not know. Then a humanoid that was different from the small man approached Victor. They probed his torso and he fainted. Later he woke up in the same room. Victor was missing for several days, and when he returned home, his real wife informed investigators. Victor was tested, and strange cross-like marks were found on his body where the beings had touched him. Victor disappeared twice more. Later when hypnotized again, he recalled alien beings, screens and tentacles touching him. He remained under medical care for a while.

HC addendum.
Source: Paul Stonehill, The Soviet UFO Files.   Type: G

* * * * * * *

Location: Outside Madona, Latvia.
Date: 1990.
Time: Unknown.

One of the local residents living outside the hamlet who had never believed "neither in hell nor in God or UFOs" at one point reported experiencing a series of strange events. He reportedly came upon a landed disc-shaped object and began contacting the alien crew on a regular basis. He was later visited by an "unearthly being" twice and even stranger still once a month a powerful humming sound was heard under his wooded cabin, even his window panes shook as a result of the hum.

The witness attributed this part of the phenomena to underground Soviet military activity in the area. According to the source there is possibly an underground alien base in the remote region amid the forests of eastern Latvia.

HC addendum.
Source: Pavel Muhortov 'M-skiy Triangle' Riga. 1990.   Type: C or G?
Comments: Unfortunately there is no detailed description on the humanoids.

* * * * * * *

Location: Izmail, Odessa region, Ukraine.
Date: 1990.
Time: Unknown.

A local female, Valentina Lisina reported communicating "three times" with visitors from another planet. She reportedly kept a diary of the events. The humanoids were very tall, about three meters in height, slender, very beautiful in appearance with blond hair and were dressed in long white robes.
The visitors informed Valentina that they had come from the "6th dimension" and showed her a strange map. The witness also reported seeing the flying craft in which the aliens arrived. No other information.

HC addendum.
Source: 'Interesnaya Gazeta' Kiev, D-block #11, 1996.   Type: G?

* * * * * * *

Location: Moscow region, Russia.
Date: 1990.
Time: Unknown.

Five young men had gone out for a picnic outside of Moscow. They were enjoying nature and resting in a picturesque meadow near some woods when suddenly they all saw a "flying saucer" or disk shaped metallic object approaching them. The object approached the group, stopped its flight and began hovering above the group. Seconds later a beam of light was projected from the object and two of the men were engulfed by the light. And in moments both men were taken onboard the object through the beam of light, the beam then vanished and the object departed. The three remaining men quickly reported the incident to the local militia. But the police did not believe them and accused the men of murder. (!) The militia believed that the three men had killed the other two and had concocted the bizarre "saucer" tale. A criminal investigation was opened and the public prosecutor opened a case. Two other men were arrested. Happily for the men during the investigation while inspecting the scene of the "crime" with the militia the two missing men suddenly appeared. The criminal investigation was quickly terminated. The two men could not remember where they had been all the time, they appeared confused and surprised as to the stir they had caused. Once hypnosis was used on the men it was revealed that they had appeared in a room inside the hovering UFO. The room had smooth walls, ceilings and floors which emitted a very brilliant light. Under further regression both men recalled an awful abduction experience in which they were in great fear and paralyzed by several humanoid entities resembling biological robots who experimented on them without regards to their feelings. After tissue samples were taken from them both men blacked out and later woke up sitting in the same meadow where they had been removed by the beam of light. No other information available.

HC addendum.
Source; Col. Ret. Marina L. Popovich, Moscow.   Type: G

* * * * * * *

Location: Moscow, Russia.
Date: 1990.
Time: 3:30 a.m.

A local female resident living near Militia Police station #27 reported a strange encounter with two humanoids that appeared on her balcony. She suddenly woke up and after seeing two silent flashes of light she saw a glow appear behind the windows. When she came close to the window, she saw a disc-shaped craft approximately 10-12 meters in diameter. The disk disappeared behind the house and soon a large figure appeared from that direction. The humanoid figure was floating in the air in a vertical position; flying towards her house, then descended to the ground and began walking among some trees. Sometime after that, this entity zoomed up and approached her balcony. The entity was very tall, about 2.5 meters in height.
The humanoid was dressed in a dark-grayish spacesuit and was standing, with its head bend looking down to the ground from the balcony. A second figure, smaller in size, about 1.5m in height, now appeared in sight, it stopped within sight of the witness and pulled her helmet backwards and the witness saw the face of a girl with very white skin, with large eyes emanating warmth, good will and intelligence.

Unexpectedly the witness felt back to her sofa, her eyelids became heavy and she quickly fell asleep. She awoke in that same position only at 7:00 a.m.

HC addendum.
Source: Vladimir G. Azhazha, PhD, 'The Other Life' Moscow, 1998.
Type: C

* * * * * * *

Location: Curitiba, Brazil.
Date: 1990.
Time: 5:30 a.m.

The witness was awakened by the cries of her young daughter and upon opening her eyes she found herself already sitting in bed and she was cradling her young daughter against her chest that had already stopped crying, she couldn't remember getting up from the bed and taking her daughter in her arms. At this point she was sitting with her back to the wall.

She turned to look at the wall and was stunned to see only about two meters from where she was sitting with her daughter a bizarre humanoid figure levitating about 1 ½ m from the floor. The humanoid spoke to the witness without opening its mouth, which was slit-like, she did not see a nose, and told her not to be afraid. The witness attempted to scream but no sound came out she then tried to move but was totally paralyzed. She tried to call her sister who was sleeping only a few feet from her but was unable to utter a sound. But gradually a type of calming effect took hold in her mind. The humanoid was still there sitting in midair, his legs crossed just like Oriental lamas. The humanoid was bizarre in appearance, from his head protruded a sort of long horn-like protrusion resembling a twisted tube, his skin color was light green, mixed in with a silvery tinge, which seemed metallic and scintillating but not shiny, the eyes were similar to humans but larger and slanted almost touching each other in the center of the forehead, she did not see any ears. Its chest and arms were much larger in proportion to its crossed legs. According to the witness the humanoid appeared to be inside some type of square "compartment" about 1/2m in length, the humanoid's long and delicate looking hands appeared to be moving very fast as if using some kind of unseen keyboard. He wore clothing that appeared to be the same color of its skin.

A few minutes before 7:30 a.m. the humanoid vanished in plain sight, just like a holographic image, the witness thinks she spoke with the humanoid by using telepathy or some type of "silent language." The only movement she saw from the humanoid was its fingers, which appeared

16

to be five. The humanoid gave the witness his name and told her several other things which she unfortunately 'forgot' soon after the encounter. Soon after the encounter the witness became an environmental activist.

HC addendum.
Source: Portal UFO Genesis, visitor tales.   Type: E

* * * * * * *

Location: Reutov, Moscow region, Russia.
Date: 1990.
Time: Morning.

A local woman named Polina N. was on her way to the local railway station when she suddenly heard an "inner voice" that said, *"We want to talk to you."* She turned around and saw two humanoid figures standing near the trees, dressed in a uniform that reminded her of those used by soldiers from a nearby military unit. Afraid, Polina tried to escape but her legs did not obey her. Meanwhile the figures approached. At this point she realized they were wearing not uniforms, but streamlined black & silver spacesuits and it seemed to Polina that the humanoids were female. *"We want you to come with us"* she heard the strange inner voice speak again. One of the alien figures then put her hand on the back of Polina's head. Immediately she became calmed and "indifferent."

The female humanoids then grabbed Polina under her arms and she felt herself quickly levitating and flying above the ground. She returned to her senses in an empty room evidently onboard a UFO. She could see a large white screen in front of her that reminded her of a projection screen. One of the alien females gave her some thick sour tasting liquid to drink from a cup that was made of some strange material. The screen then became lit and Polina suddenly saw what appeared to be her inner organs displayed on it. She had the impression that she was looking at her body from inside.

Then she heard the alien voice in her head again, *"Can we take information from you?"* Polina became frightened of this alien request and refused. And then Polina heard the alien voice once again, *"You haven't lived yet. This is not your real life. Here, look at who you really are."* With those words she saw the image of an old man, and the aliens added, *"This is your real inner self."* The image then dimmed, became smoky and then vanished. Two very tall female humanoids then appeared and came to Polina. These aliens had small heads, narrow chins, and narrow slits instead of mouths. While talking their thin lips did not move (all communication with Polina was telepathic). Then they placed Polina inside of some type of "capsule" and she lost consciousness.

17

Later Polina returned to her senses sitting on a lawn near a row of houses. She felt very dizzy and nauseated. She turned around and could not understand where she was. A man approached her and said, *"Well honey, look how drunk you got!"* and continued walking away. Polina gradually recuperated her strength and upon seeing two women ran to them asking them where she was and could she get to the Reutovo railway station. Apparently she was now about 15km away from the railway station. Polina could not remember anything more about her abduction, so the leader of a local Ufological group proposed that she underwent hypnosis. She agreed, and under a state of hypnosis she was regressed back to the point when she was walking to the railway station. Apparently the humanoids in spacesuits had brought her to a field somewhere outside the hamlet.

There was a huge spacecraft sitting on the field, with two rows of windows. Like an orange segment, one sector separated from the hull and descended to earth, creating a passage into the object. Polina was then carried inside and then the sector ascended, closing the opening. During hypnosis, Polina saw the aliens again, but now according to her description, these were different looking aliens. She described them as looking like ancient Greeks (Hellenic), with white curly hair. She understood that the other aliens she had previously encountered were merely biological robots. She remembered that the alien leader had told her that they had come from another star system, where exactly she wasn't able to understand.

As they told her, their civilization (not only theirs) conducts observations on life on earth and had being doing so for thousands of years. The aliens told her that the Earth serves as a sort of base for many civilizations that visited there. Events that occurred on Earth reflect on the life of other worlds and that's why humans saw UFOs so frequently. But they only observe over humans having no right to interfere in the affairs of humans.

HC addendum.
Source: Vladimir Ivanovich Pogonov, Regional Moscow club for the Research of anomalous phenomena.   Type: G

Location: Gornyak state farm, near Tashkent, Uzbekistan.
Date: 1990.
Time: Morning.

A group of schoolboys which included Vitya Lavrentyev and Roma Lipak were playing football in an empty field during a cloudy morning. Suddenly something appeared in the sky remotely resembling a helicopter. Immediately the boys began running in the direction of the object. It became evident that the object was not a helicopter.

The boys saw a "cosmonaut" at the beginning of the encounter. The humanoid was tall, more than two meters in height, with a strange head and antennas jutting from top of its head. The alien had elongated "wavy" eyes and a round opening in place of a mouth. It wore a light gray diver's suit. Lavrentyev then attempted to alert other boys but suddenly the alien disappeared in plain sight. Another witness, Roma Lipak, reported that he saw a group of boys ran to an irrigation ditch to see the "extraterrestrial" and filled with curiosity he ran after them. Suddenly a strange feeling that was hard to describe came over him, he stopped turned around and saw a humanoid figure looking at him. Roma couldn't run or move, his legs disobeyed him.

According to Lipak's description, the alien was tall with a globe-shaped head, triangular green ears and a black dot in the middle of its face. This alien wore a luminous yellow suit. On the breast area there was a red triangle. It had strange hands that hung down to its waist. Then a globe shaped object appeared, descended and a ladder came out of it. The alien then ascended up the ladder and the craft flew away. Roma suffered from pains in his eyes and a severe headache. Lavrentyev saw an alien spacecraft and described it in detail. It was a large "saucer" or disk-shaped object about 30-40 meters in diameter. The spacecraft stood on three curved landing legs and was emitting light. The light was red in color on the left side and yellow on the right side. Some type of device hung down from the bottom of the saucer, suspended by three wires or cables. Lavrentyev thought that the device was some type of lifting platform or elevator which allowed the aliens to exit and enter the craft. A curious fact was that the incident occurred during a heavy rain, but amazingly the rain did not fall on the spacecraft as if the ship was surrounded by some kind of invisible energy shield or field.

HC addendum.
Source: V. Sidorkin - correspondent, 'Nedelya' newspaper, Moscow, 1990.   Type: B & C

* * * * * * *

Location: Shilunoi, Lithuania.
Date: 1990.
Time: Daytime.

A local resident of the hamlet, an aged pensioner named Usiliene was watching clothes in her house with the door to the yard open. It was a sunny warm day. Suddenly she heard strange voices coming from the yard, someone or something speaking in an unknown language; the speech was very bizarre without vowels. After hearing the strange voices the witness turned the switch of the washing machine on and it did not work. At that very same moment the witness felt someone touching her shoulder.

She turned around and was confronted by a bizarre sight. There was a "screen" floating in mid-air in her yard. She could see a sun, alien worlds, numerous stars, and also what appeared to be thin humanoid figures and two-legged animals. All of these images were shown on the screen.

After the "demonstration" the screen vanished. She could not tell for how long she had been watching the screen; she then became frightened and became emotional and cried. Later after calming down she went to the yard but saw nothing, and the electric appliances in her house began to operate normally again.

HC addendum.
Source: A. Kuzovkin, N. Nepomnyaszhiy, Moscow, 1991.   Type: F?

Location: Los Zazos, Tucuman, Argentina.
Date: 1990.
Time: 4:00 p.m.

Goat herder, Flores de Mamani, was walking her animals back to her ranch along an isolated hillside when she suddenly felt paralyzed, completely unable to move. She was leaning back against a rock when she saw, a hovering sphere very close to her position. The normally fierce dog remained quiet and the goats remained very still. A door like opening became visible on the sphere and two little men came out. They wore brown diver's suits, and had what appeared to be backpacks on their backs. The witness attempted to scream but could not.

The beings were about four-feet tall, heavy set and there appeared to be some stripes on their shiny brown suits. They wore helmets with a glass-like visor. She also noticed what appeared to be two antennas coming out of their suits. They seemed to glide just above the ground. The sphere was described as shiny and silvery with several multi-colored lights around it. One of the little men then approached the witness grabbed her arm and tied a rubber hose around it, and then he proceeded to extract blood from the witness arm using a syringe like instrument. She felt no pain.

The other little man then proceeded to milk one of the goats that remained completely still. Soon the little men glided back to the silvery sphere and went inside. The sphere then shot away at tremendous speed. Below where the sphere floated the ground turned white and nothing grew there for a long time.

HC addendum.
Source: Pablo Villarrubia Mauso.   Type: B
Comments: Interesting case encompassing a wide range of phenomena: trace effects, sample taking, and paralysis of both human and animal, gliding ability of the aliens.

* * * * * * *

Location: Cargo Muchacho Mountains, near Yuma, Arizona.
Date: 1990.
Time: 2-3:00 a.m.

The witness had gone four-wheeling with a friend in the area and in the late afternoon their Jeep broke down. They sat in the Jeep and waited for the next vehicle so they could get a ride back to town but it was too late in the day and no one showed up, it was clear that they would have to spend the night there and wait for the first vehicle in the morning. They were not worried since they had food and water.

Around two or three in the morning they both woke up to a hissing sound. It didn't sound like a vehicle or helicopter or anything else that could get up there so they were curious. They got out of the Jeep and walked towards the sound; it came from behind the first bend in the road. They rounded the bend and saw a disc-shaped object sitting there on the road right in front of their eye. They both ran behind the bend and decided to take a very careful look at it. They snuck up as close as they could behind the rocks by the roadside. They found a good spot to spy on the object.

They then saw three alien creatures entering the disc through a door on its side. They were about six and a half feet tall, with very long arms and legs and small torsos. Their heads seemed quite normal size. They were very human-like, just out of proportion. The object was about twenty feet across and was wider than the road so it was sticking out on the slope side of the road. It was shaped like a giant old-fashioned hubcap.

After the three aliens entered the object it took off up and sideways with the same hissing sound they heard before. They didn't sleep the rest of the night and at sunrise they went back to the landing site to investigate but there was not much to see. It apparently left no traces as far as they could tell.

HC addendum.
Source: http://www.ufosentinel.com/ Type: B

* * * * * * *

Location: Moscow, Russia.
Date: 1990.
Time: Night.

Ex-military officer Moskalenko was walking with a friend, Major Oleg Belomestnov when a sudden powerful blow in the back knocked Moskalenko down and flung him off the road. Belomestnov helped him to his feet, shaken by what he saw, he accompanied Moskalenko home. Moskalenko was in pain and confused, he saw visions, vague and hazy landscapes. Suddenly they were ordered to stop and a short lean, unkempt man, clad in black, warned him that there may be another "energized strike." The man in black communicated by using telepathy. He paid no attention to Belomestnov, who was shouting at him. The man told Moskalenko that this was a warning.

The stranger then squatted down and touched Moskalenko swollen leg with the palm of his hand. It instantly got hot and the pain vanished as well as the pain in the rest of his body and the delusions and apparitions that had been bothering him from time to time since a previous UFO encounter. The stranger in black then asked several pertinent questions related to that UFO incident and moments later disappeared.

HC addendum.
Source: Paul Stonehill, The Soviet UFO Files.   Type: E
Comments: Another report indicating curative powers in the part of aliens or humanoids.

* * * * * * *

Location: Zaporozhye, Ukraine.
Date: 1990.
Time: Night.

A young Tatar-Muslim woman Aihsa, a resident of the city, reportedly entered into a series of contacts with extraterrestrials. One night while she was alone in her room she suddenly saw a strange light coming from an unknown source, and then several humanoid entities somehow entered her room despite the fact that the door was locked. The aliens were tall, about two meters in height, and were beautiful in appearance, with charming faces, and slender proportional figures which emanated light. The aliens had long, shoulder length, light colored hair. All were dressed in very shiny, metallic overalls, which were tightly fitting. They approached the witness and she somehow understood them, as she could hear their words straight in her head, evidently these aliens were using telepathy. They began to transmit information into Aisha's brain. The contact lasted for half an hour or so.

Beginning with this initial contact, Aisha's contacts continued. Later she was visited and contacted on a regular basis by another type of humanoid which were dark skinned and came from the IR-SHIIR star system in the Big Bear constellation (Ursa Major) planet NIASU and of the SAINA race. These aliens told Aisha that the light haired humanoids that had first visited her were from the planet "GISSAMERA." This planet is part of the union of several star systems called "O-NAVAIL" (The Great System). Aisha also encountered numerous UFOs, including some at the "Varvarovka" anomalous area which emitted blinking lights.

HC addendum.
Source: Elena Petriv in: 'Mriya' Zaporozhye August 3, 2000, and Dr. Anton Anfalov PhD.   Type: E & G

* * * * * * *

Location: Simferopol, Ukraine.
Date: 1990.
Time: Late night.

In the summer 1928, a teenager from Yalta was loitering in the mountains of the Ai' Petri plateau walking among the rocks and crags when suddenly he noticed a strange light emanating from a "karst" (shaft) on the ground, being curious he approached closer and kept watching the unearthly light from coming out of the shaft. Sometime later he was suddenly seized by fear and ran home.

Many years later (1990) the same witness (now an adult) was in his bedroom at night when a very tall woman suddenly appeared in his room amidst a strange circle of light. The woman communicated by using telepathy and said: *"Do you remember when you were a young boy, you saw the light from the place we live in the shaft?"* The man was stunned since he had not told anybody about his previous experience. She told him that they live in an underground city under the Ai' Petri plateau with an approximate population of 2,000. She said they traveled in UFOs.

HC addendum.
Source: Viktor P Sikilinda, Anton Anfalov.   Type: E

Location: Kyrgyzstan (exact location not given).
Date: 1990.
Time: Various.

Shepherd Omusha's wife reported seeing a strange Yeti type creature not far from the pasture. The creature was standing on a high rock. She started pleading her husband to leave the horrid place and go to another pasture. The man did not agree, although he was anxious about it too. He began searching for the creatures; he found their tracks, but never saw a living one.

One evening he heard his wife screaming very loudly. He grabbed his rifle and rushed outside. The wife was lying on the ground, almost unconscious. She was speechless and could not say a word. She could only point her finger in the direction of the rocks. The shepherd gazed in the direction that she was pointing and saw the silhouette of a running man. He did not hesitate and fired his rifle. In the morning the shepherd found blood spots on the rocks. Omush thought that those creatures would not come back to their pasture anymore.

Several days later he found his son dead. There was no trace of violence on the boy's body, only a little wound on his neck. Omush was sure that a Yeti killed his boy. He swore revenge and waited for the creature to return. One night he fell asleep and when he entered his house in the morning, he found the dead body of his wife. Again, there was only a small red wound on her neck. Out of desperation he went into the woods searching for the creatures. Shepherd Shapak took care of Omush's sheep. One day he suddenly saw the sheep becoming very troubled and excited. They were bleating and rushing from one side to another. The animals were apparently frightened with something. Shapak could only see a silhouette of a man covered with thick fur disappearing amid bushes and trees. Then he saw another man on the ground. Shapak ran up to him and recognized Omush. The shepherd was already dead, blood was leaking from a small wound on his neck.

HC addendum.
Source: Dmitry Sudako, Anomalia.Ru   Type: E
Comments: Fatal human-humanoid encounter, in this the humanoid was a type of aggressive Yeti variant. It is interesting to note that in some of the animal mutilations deaths reported, a small incision is also found on the unfortunate animal. It appears in this case that three humans were the victims.

Location: Meadow Lake, Saskatchewan, Canada.
Date: 1990 (approximate).
Time: Late night.

The witness, a child at the time, was woken up in the middle of the by what he feels was some type of telepathic impulse. He looked out the window and saw a tall bright white human-shaped figure that soon disappeared. In the morning the witness and his family went looking for tracks. They found some strange tracks on the mud which looked human except there was an additional toe in the footprint. Several neighbors and friends came to see the print. That same weekend other neighbors reported unexplained cattle mutilations.

HC addendum.
Source: Direct from the witness, asylum75@telus.net   Type: E

* * * * * * *

Location: Chernovtsy, Bukovina, Ukraine.
Date: 1990.
Time: Late night.

V. V. Ustyuzhanin was returning to his native village from a regional center in his car when suddenly he noticed the landing of some strange craft nearby, bluish in color. After that, a second smaller craft separated itself from the larger one. After that a thin ray of light became visible between both crafts. Startled, the witness looked at his hands and the steering wheel of his car and noticed that both were emanating a bluish light also.

Soon he saw a human-shaped alien figure standing in front of the craft, and then he soon saw what appeared to be geometric figures inside the alien and then on a screen like projection he was amazed to see an image of himself performing all the day's chores, but in a reverse sequence. (!) Everything he did that day he was able to see in reverse order.

HC addendum.
Source: Anton Anfalov, quoting local press.   Type: C?

Location: New Town, Edinburgh, Scotland.
Date: 1990.
Time: Late night.

A man named Brian Wilson was working the late shift one night at a local Pizza Parlor when a pair of "rather small" adults, who had a somewhat "lopsided" look about them, approached the counter, raised their right hands, and announced; *"Hi, We're Americans!"* *"What would you like?"* Brian asked them, to which they countered, *"What do you make?"* *"Pizzas"* replied Brian. *"What are pizzas?"* enquired the supposed Americans.

The couple watched Brian intently as he prepared two cheese and tomato pizzas. All the while, the male "kept looking around the shop like he'd never been in a pizza parlor before." Then the female pointed to a bowl of green peppers and asked what they were. By now, Brian's colleague Doug had also noticed that there was something rather odd about the pair, and the two chefs exchanged glances of disbelief as Brian carefully explained what a pepper was. *"Do they taste nice?"* wondered the female. As the pair waited in silence for their pizzas (complete with green peppers) to cook, other customers came in and out of the shop as usual. Once their order was ready, the extraordinary Americans settled their bill. Each took a single bite out of their pizza then threw the remainder into the bin outside the shop.

Brian entertained a suspicion that his visitors may have literally been from another planet *"I had read stories on the subject of aliens masquerading as human beings,"* he told investigators. *"These two individuals came across as acting as humans, but not doing a very good job of it!"*

HC addendum.
Source: Ron Halliday, UFO Scotland.   Type: E?
Comments: Hybrids or somebody playing a joke?

* * * * * * *

Location: Urgench, Uzbekistan.
Date: 1990.
Time: Midnight.

A 15-year old school boy, Alisher Sabirov was returning home from a regional center along a dark road when he suddenly noticed a light in the darkness. The light appeared to originate from the sky. He first thought it was a meteor was a bright light suddenly illuminated him, he then heard a voice inside his head; *"Will you fly with us?"* Without hesitation he answered *"yes."* Then something started descending over him. It was

27

a triangle shaped craft with smooth corners, a large bright light and a huge central opening.

The alien craft landed several meters from the witness. It was about eight meters long and three meters in height; it ejected three landing props as it landed. On one side of the object a panel moved aside soundlessly and a ladder was lowered down. Then a tall alien woman appeared on the opening. She was taller than the average height and had long hair down to her shoulders. She was dressed in a silver cone-shaped dress down to her heels. Alisher heard the soft female voice in his head again that asked him again if he wanted to fly with them. He was then asked a myriad of questions about himself and his hometown all telepathically.

The woman took the boy's hand and accompanied him to the ladder. She ascended first and then Alisher. Inside the UFO it was easy to breathe, the air was light and aromatic, somewhat sweet-smelling. It was light inside, like daytime, but he could not see the source of the light. The light was soft and pleasant to the eyes. They went through a corridor about five m long, which gradually widened and turned into a spacious square room.

In this room another alien sat on an armchair near a large control panel. The chair was apparently floating in mid-air, not standing on a prop. A second chair nearby was empty. The boy noticed a large color screen that was changing images (by sequence) displaying, bridges, canals, etc. The woman ignored the boy's questions about the functions of the buttons on the panel. She only turned the lever on the right corner of the panel and said: *"We see and study the world using this."* When the woman spoke, interestingly she spoke in the ancient Russian (Slavic) language, which the boy barely understood.

Then she took him by the hand and led him to another room, almost the same size as the previous control room. It was empty, there was only one alien sitting on a chair in it. This alien was different; he had only one eye (Cyclops) and large hands. The eye was without pupil. The cyclopean alien immobilized the boy for about fifteen minutes (apparently scanning him). After that the alien woman took him out of the room. They went back to the ladder and Alisher descended alone. Using telepathy again, the woman said that they would meet again. The panel then closed. The landing props of the UFO then retracted and the craft hovered still about 1.5 m from the ground.

Alisher then walked under the hull and banged on it, he heard a hollow sound. He also saw three large lights on the corners of the triangle and managed to insert his head on the large hollow hole on the middle. After that he felt heat and the craft vanished.

HC addendum.
Source: A. Melamed, 'Mysterious Alien Tashkent.' Type: G

Location: Bexleyheath, Kent, England.
Date: 1990.
Time: Late night.

One night Carol and her husband (involved in many other experiences) had forgotten to draw the curtains and on lying down she saw a little being with an oval face, pale skin and big bug-like eyes just float past the window, next from the other direction, one entity with a very crinkled looking skin also floated past. She heard a voice saying 'you should not have seen us, it was a mistake', at this she went into a total state of shock. Unable to move, unable to get up and go to the toilet, it took her ages getting over it.

HC addendum.
Source: Margaret-Ellen Fry, 'Who are they?'   Type: E

* * * * * * *

Location: Khabarovsk, Russia.
Date: 1990.
Time: 10:30 p.m.

A. Pashayev, a cadet at a local police academy watched a fiery sphere that emitted a whistling sound descend towards the ground. The sphere suddenly stopped above a rocky outcrop and a bright light became visible. Inside the light appeared what resembled a large glass corridor. A woman walked out of the corridor carrying in her hands what appeared to be a portable radio. Soon two hatchways opened on the sphere and two platforms were ejected and on each platform rested a small "flight vehicle" black in color.

That same evening another resident was lying on her sofa watching TV when the door of the balcony suddenly was opened and a very long, seemingly improbable thin foot entered then the entire body of an extremely tall and thin humanoid. The figure was extremely thin and silvery in color, with a large ball shaped head, without a nose and a slot-like mouth. The humanoid waved his hand in the air and the witness felt extreme gravity and lost consciousness. She does not remember what happened next.

HC addendum.
Source: UFOZONE Russia.   Type: B & E

Location: Ashgabat, Turkmenistan.
Date: 1990.
Time: Midnight.

A local man Alexander Ataev (Turkmen by nationality) reported seeing a saucer-shaped object land near his home, a hatch opened and several men wearing silvery suits came out of the object. The aliens approached Ataev and told him that they had come from a planet called "*Tron.*" From conversation with the aliens, Ataev understood that contacts or alien meetings were premeditated and not just by happenstance. He could only vaguely remember the rest of the conversation, he was told that their visits to earth were not of "idle curiosities" but were made in order to have direct influence on people.

HC addendum.
Source: Alexey K. Priyma, 'Unknown Worlds' Moscow, 1996.   Type: B

* * * * * * *

Location: Ryazan, Russia.
Date: 1990.
Time: Various.

Mrs. I. Nazarova reported claimed that she was an "alien missionary" and was in contact with an alien civilization from a planet named "RAMGA." As she told, the aliens on the planet were also humanoids and there were both males and females, and had a bluish color aura or biological energy that is rarely found on Earth. Reportedly their usual practice was to send the souls of their "missionaries" to various planets in order to "reincarnate" on those planets in the bodies of the local inhabitants. Nazarova claims that she is one of those reincarnated aliens from the planet Ramga inhabiting a human physical body. She also claims that unlike humans, the souls of the reincarnated aliens are able to remember their entire previous lives on their native planets and are very conscious beings. Basically these particular aliens were trying to spread their humanitarian missions through our part of the Galaxy. Nazarova obtained alien messages through the so-called "psychograph" method from distant interstellar communication, and drawing various symbols and pictures that her fellow aliens transmit to her on a regular basis (telepathy?).

HC addendum.
Source: Pavel Khailov, Bezhetsk, Tver region, Russia.   Type: F

Location: Near Manaus, Brazil.
Date: January, 1990.
Time: Unknown.

In an isolated area witnesses saw a bizarre humanoid described as tall, hairy and with one huge single eye in the middle of its forehead. No other information.

HC addendum.
Source: GEPUC Brazil.   Type: E
Comments: Was this creature the fabled 'Mapinguaray?'

* * * * * * *

Location: Yebra, Guadalajara, Spain.
Date: January, 1990.
Time: Morning.

Brothers, Tomas and Francisco Vireda wee out hunting with their dogs in an isolated area when suddenly a bright light illuminated some trees ahead of them on the trail. Approaching the site the dogs acted as if someone unseen was hiding in the bushes. Concerned, the brothers moved back to see a disc shaped craft encircled in small yellowish lights rising up slowly. Both men returned to their homes without telling anyone what had occurred.

The next morning Cirilo Gomez was walking along some fields and while resting against a fence he noticed a figure observing him from a nearby hillock. At first it resembled a woman but then Gomez noticed that the figure was extremely tall and was wearing a black flowing robe. After shouting at it several times the witness was stunned to see it glide over the field at very high speed. Terrified he ran panic-stricken from the area. That same night at a nearby village a witness saw a large unknown object fly at high speed above the roadway.

HC addendum.
Source: Iker Jimenez, Encuentros, La Historia de Los Ovni en España.
Type: D

31

Location: Yebra, Guadalajara, Spain.
Date: January, 1990.
Time: Noon.

Farmer, Juan Barco encountered a strange humanoid wearing a bronze metallic outfit and a flowing robe that walked clumsily over some fields. It was over two meters in height and appeared not to have any facial features. Terrified he ran to town in order to obtain additional witnesses, but no trace of the humanoid was found. The next day two disc shaped objects were seen splashing into the Sacedon marshes.

HC addendum.
Source: Iker Jimenez, Encuentros, Las Historia De Los Ovni en España.
Type: D

* * * * * * *

Location: Kupchino, Leningrad, Russia.
Date: January, 1990.
Time: Unknown.

24-year old Konstantin was walking by the local dump when he suddenly saw a huge figure standing about fifty meters from him. At first he took the figure as a man dressed in a large fur-coat. But the fur coat was strange, it was shaggy and spiny. Thinking that it was some kind of homeless person Konstantin approached the figure and to his amazement realized that the "homeless" person had transformed into something very strange, covered either by feathers or thorns.

Then next to the "cactus-like" humanoid a second creature stood up, straight out of the dirt pit. The second creature was quite thickset, solidly built, but not quite as tall as the first one. It wore something resembling a cap on its head. He now noticed that the "fur coat" creature had what appeared to be "feelers" or small horns on its head and were moving around in different directions. Then the strange creatures began to walk among the heaps of trash. Their manner of walking was quite strange, very different from humans. Their legs did not bend, but became elongated or shorter just like telescopic antennas. The witness only heard a strange rustling and crackling sound.

Then Konstantin saw the UFO from where the creatures had come from. It reminded him of a large cake, a low broad circular craft with vertical edges, like a hockey puck. Both aliens were seen to enter the craft and after emitting a whistling sound the craft momentarily rose up into the air and hovered at a very low altitude above the ground.

The craft had a dome on top encircled by luminous lights. It then ascended into the sky leaving a thick cloud of smoke behind quickly disappearing from sight.

HC addendum.
Source: 'Anomaliya' Newspaper, Leningrad, 1990, #2.   Type: B

* * * * * * *

Location: East Kalimantan, Indonesia.
Date: January, 1990.
Time: Late night.

A witness driving a car along an isolated road in South Eastern Borneo saw a kind of metallic robot like figure the size of a four-year-old child in his headlights, walking along the side of the road. He quickly drove away and did not stop.

HC addendum.
Source: Patrick Moncelot, quoting 'Antara News Agency.'   Type: E

* * * * * * *

Location: Toquila Valley, Colombia.
Date: January 9, 1990.
Time: Late night.

Deontologist, Ivan Naranjo, and two passengers were traversing a lonely valley when their vehicle, a Nissan jeep, began to experience engine trouble. The vehicle soon ground to a halt by the roadside as its electrical system went dead. Stranded in the middle of the Andean foothills, Naranjo was doing his best to get the vehicle in motion again when one of the passengers gasped involuntarily at what was taking place in the night sky.

In the horizon, headed their way, was an amazing interplay of red, green and yellow lights, which did not correspond to any atmospheric phenomenon, they could identify. They watched in sheer astonishment as the array of colors lit the sky and grew closer, increasing in size as it closed the intervening distance. Within seconds a huge disc-shaped device, was hovering unsteadily in the blackness over their heads. The object was out of control, and to their horror, about to crash land right on top of them.

Naranjo and his passengers found themselves paralyzed by what he characterized as "muscular sluggishness." Then suddenly out of nowhere, another massive disc-shaped craft appeared. Gliding into a

33

space immediately above the dangerously wobbling craft, it fired a dense beam of white light at the vessel, stabilizing its erratic motion immediately.

The surreal event became even more so as they both landed and two humanoids emerged from the larger craft to ostensibly perform repairs on the now stabilized saucer. Soon the repaired saucer began spinning furiously on its axis, vanishing in a thick fog. The "rescue" ship also vanished amid a powerful whirlwind that stripped earth, rocks, and dust from the surface below. Exhausted by the ordeal, the shocked witnesses spent a night of fitful sleep in the wilderness.

In the morning they were stunned to see a landscape that gave the appearance of having been blasted by divine fire; water ponds adjacent to the highway had been turned into grim puddles of mud, and the carcasses of small desert rats and lizards littered the landscape, roasted by some form of radiation. One of the passengers would later die of an unknown malady, possibly related to the strange energies released by the alien vehicles over the valley.

HC addendum.
Source: Scott Corrales, UFO Files #1.   Type: B

* * * * * * *

Location: Odessa, Ukraine.
Date: January 14, 1990.
Time: Night.

Gennadiy Kosushenko was watching news on television when suddenly everything in the room seemed to slowly dissolve away in plain sight, cupboards, couch, etc. Frightened he tried to grab the back of a slowly vanishing chair but his hands seemed to go right through it. A milky fog then enveloped his whole body.

Soon a male entity appeared amidst the fog, standing only a couple of steps from the witness. The man was quite normal in appearance, nothing special. He appeared to have been about forty years of age. He looked at the witness smiling. Inexplicably the witness became calm and was no longer frightened. He felt a strange tranquility inside him.

The alien man began speaking directly into the Kosushenko's mind, which could hear the voice but could not see the stranger's lips moving. The "alien" told the witness that he constantly controlled his behavior and then said, *"We are your brothers and you are not a real resident of earth, but an agent for an extraterrestrial civilization."* The alien then added, *"How do you feel in that unsuitable terrestrial body?"* The witness answered that he felt fine that everything was normal.

34

At that, the alien man vanished and the milky fog surrounding the witness slowly melted away. The room had now returned to normal.

HC addendum.
Source: Alexey K. Priyma, XX Century, Chronicles of the Unexplained, Moscow, 1999.   Type: E

* * * * * * *

Location: Volzhskiy, Volgograd region, Russia.
Date: January 15, 1990.
Time: Unknown.

Local schoolboy, teenager Sergey Ilyin reported another contact with aliens since his original contact on October 1989. During meditation while training in Eastern single combat philosophy, Sergey felt his "astral body" separating from the physical one. He suddenly then appeared high above the earth and then he saw a sort of "pipe" shaped object made from single cells or rectangles, like a computer graphic. At the end of this "pipe" (or cylinder?) he saw a disc-shaped craft. Then there was a flash and he (or his astral body?) appeared inside the object. There he saw the same alien "man" he had met in October 1989, but this time the man was not wearing any goggles. Sergey then heard a voice in his mind, *"We would like to show you something."*

The alien invited Sergey to sit on an armchair near a screen. The room around him was filled with different types of instruments or devices, very different from anything on Earth. The room appeared very spacious, there were about 15 other aliens in the room and all seemed busy at some sort of task. Not far from Sergey sat one of the aliens near what appeared to be a "computer" (or something that remotely resembled a computer). The alien "man" appeared to stare vacantly into the computer. In general the faces of the aliens were emotionless, their skin was grayish. Sergey could not remember how their eyes looked like and according to his opinion these "aliens" appeared to be "bio-robots" but some were probably living beings.

Once onboard the spaceship Sergey reportedly flew to a planet by the name of "KHAAN-K" and then to the planet "CINTORI." On the computer screen the aliens showed Sergey how the transition into different dimensions occurs, in particular travel to the 7th dimension. *"Are you from planet TRON?"* asked Sergey. *"Yes"* the aliens replied (Soviet newspapers published several articles about UFO contacts with visitors from the planet Tron in 1990). The aliens were apparently able to read his thoughts and answered his questions before he could ask. Soon Sergey returned to his body ending this interesting if not bizarre contact. Later Sergey was to have numerous dialogues with representatives of an unknown extraterrestrial civilization and experienced several unusual astral-flight journeys to unknown and even some known planets, like MARS. According to Sergey he noticed that Mars, according to his impression, was inhabited, deep under it surface there were numerous alien scientific laboratories and the inhabitants therein were similar to human beings. Soon Sergey refused to talk anymore about his contacts and turned to religion to seek answers.

HC addendum.
Source: Gennadiy S. Belimov, 'Alien visitors among Us' Moscow, 2003.
Type: G or F?

* * * * * * *

Location: Donetsk, Ukraine.
Date: February, 1990.
Time: 1:15 a.m.

The witness a 68-year old pensioner named Ivan Nikanorovich who lived alone in a house at the edge of a large meadow woke up one night when his dogs began to bark furiously. He got up from bed, dressed and went outside. In the yard he noticed several very tall "people" about three meters in height.

Upon seeing the figures the terrified Nikanorovich attempted to run but fell to the ground. Soon he fell under apparently hypnotic control of the "aliens" and began walking towards them, leaving his house and poultry pens unlocked. As they walked in the garden next to the kitchen, the aliens spoke among themselves in strange squeaking sounds resembling that of dolphins. At the end of the garden the witness saw a round object, shiny as the moon and about twelve meters high and around ten meters in diameter. The witness was so frightened that he did not notice any details on the object. Entering into the craft by ladder, he could see that the craft was bluish in color.

Inside the craft he noticed a strong "violet" smell. When he first saw the aliens standing near his wicket fence, they were wearing spacesuits but as they entered the spaceship their suits were automatically peeled off, and Nikanorovich saw two males and two females wearing sports style suits, made out of a strong wrinkle free material. The alien faces were human-like, but their noses were flat and protruded downwards. They had no bridge for their noses. Their eyes were large, round with eyebrows; they had small mouths and ears smaller than those of humans. Fine, sparse hair covered their heads. The faces of the female aliens were beautiful, with grayish color skin and short-cropped hair.

Two alien females approached the witness, took his clothes off, and examined him thoroughly. When they touched him he felt as if their

36

bodies were of same makeup as those of humans. They had five fingers in each hand. Still, the witness felt mortal fear, afraid that he was going to be taken away forever and not survive their "experiments." The aliens examined him, listened to his heartbeat, etc. Soon the aliens placed some metal clasps on his body that emitted clicking sounds. The witness could see red dots or lights appearing on the instruments in the room. Most of the clamps were placed on his fingers and then they measured the volume of his legs, chest. Soon they placed what appeared to be electrodes on his chest (EKG?) he could see on a circle-shaped device his internal organs. The aliens did not place any instruments on his head. When the medical examination was over they dressed him and by gestures made him exit the craft.

In the meantime the aliens communicated among themselves in high-pitched voices. The doors of the spacecraft opened and Nikanorovich was descending down the ladder when the aliens pulled him up by his shirt collar and back into the spacecraft. Resigned to his fate Nikanorovich was led into a room with a couch like object, where he sat down. Moments later he felt the spacecraft apparently rising slowly from the ground. They invited him to come and look out an oval-shaped window and he saw the earth from a very high altitude with thousands of small specks of lights scattered beneath, apparently cities. But the whole marvelous panorama vanished in a few seconds.

They were now flying in space at unbelievable speed, but strangely no one in the room felt any effects. He was able to stand up and walk about the room. In the room he could see what appeared to be a main control console with two screens on one of the walls. One screen was about 3 x 5 meters, the second smaller. The craft seemed to approach many planets (probably in our Solar System), and minutes the small dots in space suddenly transformed themselves into huge bodies in the sky, he could see all this in the large screen that seemed to be more active than the other one. He saw a container with transparent liquid, which tasted like ordinary water. They explained to him by gestures what buttons to press if he would like to have a drink. At this point Ivan's fear had vanished, as he realized that the aliens meant no harm and apparently had good intentions.

Gradually, he began examining everything around him with interest. Besides the main control panel in the room there was another panel in the room where the male aliens constantly sat around. He could see many devices installed on the walls and on the ceiling. Most of the equipment was covered with "panels" which moved aside as any of the alien crew attempted to check something on it. All the rooms inside the spacecraft emitted an even bluish light, and some buttons and levers shone so brightly that it was difficult to look at them. Ivan was amazed by a meteor "catching" system onboard the alien craft, when they encountered huge rocks in space the craft was able to evade them easily while the smaller rocks were collected in a special container that opened and closed automatically, during the flight, Ivan counted five such captured "meteorites."

Most of the flight Ivan remained in that one room, but he was allowed to visit other areas in the craft, even the special crew compartments. At one point he fell asleep and was suddenly awakened by one of the aliens and was called over to one of the screens. On the screen Ivan could see an endless desert with many scattered rocks, and deep craters and fissures on the ground. Apparently that was the first planet he saw. They passed by it at high speed without touching down. He sat down on the "couch" and soon sensed the spacecraft smoothly landing. The aliens then placed a spacesuit on Ivan, which was completely hermetical with many tubes jutting out from it. Three windows were present on the window for viewing purposes. The aliens had spacesuits of a different design, with one glassy window-like opening. Ivan moved out following the aliens thinking that they wanted to leave him there.

Outside Ivan could see small humanoids, standing on a meadow and by a river. These small humanoids were not afraid and did not run away. The faces of the little men were round, good looking and child-like. Their bodies were covered by fuzzy hair and they had wing-like protrusions on their backs, commensurate to their height. Their maximum height was about 1.20m. Their wings were feather-like, slightly tilted upwards. They had doll-like faces. Their color was mostly white with brown patches. These small entities also possessed hands besides the wings, and legs. However none of them were flying as Ivan arrived; they were walking near the river. Ivan watched the strange humanoids for a while until he was guided back into the spacecraft by the aliens.

While on the spacecraft Ivan felt rejuvenated and energized, he moved around easily and his chronic leg pain had completely vanished. When it was time to eat, the aliens invited Ivan to a table where two alien females and a male were sitting. The food was prepared by the females, which consisted of many tasty dishes inside cans, plates, etc. The food was very tasty and resembled terrestrial cuisine. All meals ended with very tasty drinks. After eating Ivan usually felt drowsy and usually sat and rested on the couch.

He visited a second and then a third planet which was very rocky, with stones resembling gold, silver and precious stones that covered its surface. The aliens again put a spacesuit on Ivan before walking onto the planet's surface. He did not see any living creatures on these planets. Ivan thought that possibly this planet was used as a resource for the aliens to build their spacecraft. He did not touch anything on the surface. Their stop on the planet was very short and soon they continued their flight until Ivan was again called to the control room where he saw a new planet, entirely covered by water. He then sat on the sofa again and sometime later the aliens called on Ivan to come to the screen again where he saw a surface covered with smoke and fire and was difficult to discern.

They soon landed (twice) on a fifth planet where Ivan saw terrible sights and thought that if humans did not change their ways this type of future was awaiting them. Ivan saw a destructed city without a living soul around, he saw numerous bones scattered around. None of the houses had any doors or windows and there wasn't a bush or blade of grass around. He also saw the bones of great huge animals, no less than five elephants in size.

Later they again landed twice on a sixth planet, which was a complete opposite of the previous one. They exited the spacecraft without donning the spacesuits. Ivan was surrounded by indescribable beauty, dense forests, rives and a sea visible afar. He could see many animals but no people. He thought that maybe this planet was like a "farm" for the aliens. So Ivan asked, *"Do you have animals resembling those we have on earth?"* He was told that they had animals similar to the ones on earth but also many with substantial differences. The next planet, number seven, was the alien's home planet.

The alien females exited the spacecraft there and Ivan did not see them again, he was accompanied only by the two alien males, in the alien planet, Ivan felt youthful and agile and was easy for him to walk. The smell of lilac was present in the air similar to the smell onboard the spacecraft. At first the aliens led the aliens into what they called a church or place of worship. Inside the church he saw several elderly men standing side by side with young men. He could hear a chime a loud melodic choral singing. All seemed to be praying. The church appeared remotely like a terrestrial church. But the living quarters or buildings were radically different from those on earth. All buildings were topped with cupolas. Every resident of the planet had its own flying apparatuses; Ivan did not see any other kind of transportation there. The inhabitants only used their flying machines for long journeys and enjoyed walking more. Everything in the planet was beautiful and well groomed (like Disneyland?). Everywhere Ivan went to, he was greeted with calmed restraint. There was no apparent excitement. All the humanoids in the planet were tall, about three meters in height. He felt like a Lilliputian among them. He received the impression that the average lifespan in this world was very long, but that they eventually perished. Ivan was then taken to a beautiful cemetery. He also noticed a common practice among the aliens, one that consisted of each one giving each other food gifts. He was given a big beautiful fruit resembling an apple. He attempted to hide this apple-like fruit and bring it back to earth as proof but the aliens did not permit it. He was made to eat it in view of them.

After church Ivan was taken to an excursion at a "production" plant. At this particular plant, he saw mountains of something that looked visually similar to cheese and butter. At this plant only one alien seemed to be in charge by pressing certain buttons, the rest was done automatically. After the short visit Ivan was brought back to the spacecraft, which was still at the same location.

While returning back to earth, the spacecraft performed a short stop. They left the ship clad in spacesuits, and went out into a place enveloped by a dense fog. Through the haze Ivan could see bright white lights all around, their source unknown. Later when he entered the craft he heard someone calling his name. The sound was very clearly heard through the helmet of his spacesuit. He turned around and saw his two sisters, both who had died many years before, Zina and Nadya. They both looked very young. They gave Ivan pastry and guiding by their hands took him aside where they told him that his father and grandparent still lived. Ivan wanted to go and look as his relatives but his alien guides did not permit him to do that. Ivan also saw his neighbor who had died recently. He appeared to be carrying some pieces of wood or boards. The figures of his sisters seemed semi-transparent but upon touching them they felt like normal humans. They had normal colored pink skin. Ivan then saw a large beautiful meadow where his father and grandfather were pasturing sheep. At this moment the meeting with his dead relatives was over, the aliens did not allow Ivan to have a detailed conversation with his "dead" sisters. From there he was taken straight home.

When the spacecraft silently landed, Ivan at first thought that they had landed in another planet, but as soon as the hatch opened he noticed his native country immediately. They then brought him to the same place he was originally taken from.

Ivan does not remember how he got back home but without realizing how, the aliens were already gone. Later, Ivan noticed that the snow had melted in the place where the spacecraft had landed, and a dark spot approximately three meters in diameter was visible. For three days after 'returning,' Ivan did not eat anything, and became very ill. His whole body ached, including his muscles. He remained in that state for a long time. At one point he thought he was going to die. In a month he developed a severe itch in his skin.

HC addendum.
Source: Gennadiy Ya. Leszshenko, 'At the Edge of the Unknown or What is Behind the Curtain' Donetsk, 1994.   Type: G
Comments: By far the most incredible story out of the former Soviet Union in that incredible year of 1990. For a simple Russian peasant it was almost totally impossible to imagine something as fantastic as this story. Apparently the author personally investigated the case.

Location: Punta Indio, Buenos Aires, Argentina.
Date: February, 1990.
Time: 6:00 p.m.

Emilio Cabot along with Marcelo, Graciela & Nancy were meditating in an area known for its paranormal phenomena when they heard footsteps behind them. They stopped their meditation and noticed what appeared to be a dome of light settling over the nearby river. As they all sat down to chat they suddenly noticed two pairs of shiny eyes in the nearby woods. They shone their flashlight at the eyes and saw two gnome-like figures about 90 cm in height.

The figures appeared to have gray wrinkled faces and wore pointy hats, gray pants with a very large belt and a large shiny buckle. The moment the witnesses spotted the short figures they felt no fear and a sense of peace came over them. The two "gnomes" appeared startled and seemed to jump head first into the brush. The witnesses were able to determine that the humanoid had human-like eyes that were very shiny.

Before encountering the "gnomes" they had seen the dome of light over the river and inside of it they remembered seeing building like structures. There is an old legend of a submerged city in this area of the Rio de la Plata. They searched around for the gnomes but failed to find anything.

HC addendum.
Source: Proyecto CATENT, Argentina.   Type: E

* * * * * * *

Location: Lipa City, Philippines.
Date: February, 1990.
Time: Evening.

In the Granja district of Lipa City locals saw a white luminous outline of a female entity in prayer appear on one of the leaves of a tall coconut tree. It was seen several times and was visible only in the evenings. No other information.

HC addendum.
Source: 'Our Lady, Mediatrix of All Grace.'   Type: E or F?

Location: Dzhambul, Kazakhstan.
Date: February, 1990.
Time: Near midnight.

Vasiliy Ivanovich Latsemirskiy a lathe operator at the Dzhambul super-phosphate plant was fishing on the brushy banks of a by-pass canal, in a quite location far away from any crowded place. When suddenly his dog began whimpering and whining and hiding behind Vasiliy's legs. The dog had never done this before. There was a sudden flash of light and when Vasiliy looked down at his dog it appeared to be sleeping soundly. Surprised he turned around and was stunned to see a huge globe or sphere which emitted multicolored lights hovering at about ten steps from him. The witness then felt as if his brain had been totally cleared of all thoughts as if his head had been somehow emptied. He just stood still contemplating the scene with complete indifference. He saw an opening or door suddenly form on the surface of the luminous globe and then a short ladder was lowered to the ground.

Soon two young female figures walked down the ladder, the females were dressed in silvery tight-fitting shiny overalls. They had long loose flowing silvery hair. They did not approach the witness but he suddenly heard their words inside his head, *"Would you like to fly with us?"* they asked. The words had sounded very loudly inside his head and without knowing why, he obediently agreed to go and followed them to their craft. The circular craft was about twenty-meters in diameter and was shaped like a flattened globe, it stood on four landing props, positioned about five meters from each other, the craft had multicolored flashing lights, positioned all around its perimeter.

When the witness entered the cabin of the craft the first thing that attracted his attention was the control panel, near this panel a male humanoid (pilot) was sitting with his back towards the witness. He did not move and the witness thought he was a robot. The cabin was rhomb-shaped and composed of rhomb-shaped thin slabs of yellow color. The alien females invited the witness to sit in a specific chair. The young females then sat opposite to the witness and began to stare at him intently. The silence inside the cabin was total. The witness felt no movement or indication that the craft had taken off, of flight or landing. The cabin had numerous portholes or illuminated screens around its perimeter, but the witness felt no curiosity and sat with his head looking down at the slabs on the floor. Only once did he dare to raise his eyes and look at the non-talkative females aliens sitting in front of him. The alien women had bulging lips, large slanted blue colored eyes without pupils, their breast were very small, thought Vasiliy and at the same moment he detected what appeared to have been smiles on their faces.

The witness could not remember how long they had been flying or even if they were flying at all, when suddenly he heard the loud voice in his head again telling him to, *"Get out."* When Vasiliy walked out of the craft he saw an indescribable beauty surrounding him. There were many flowers, including totally unearthly, non-terrestrial types. He did not see grass, bushes or trees, just flowers. He had never seen such flowers in his life. There wasn't a soul around and only at a great distance did he see several small houses resembling small cottages. There was neither a moon, nor a sun but the 'sky' was very light, which seemed unnatural to the witness. The air was fresh, but seemingly artificial, but was easy to breath and it felt very pleasant. Again he was suddenly interrupted by a telepathic message asking him, *"Would you like to stay here forever?"* And only at this moment did Vasiliy thought about his beautiful grandson back on Earth and how he could live without him, once he thought of that another message flashed in his head, *"All is understandable."*

The witness was then returned back to Earth the very same manner. The strange male pilot or robot never moved. The craft then stopped in midair and began to hover exactly over the very same spot where Vasiliy had been fishing earlier only at an altitude of about thirty meters. Vasiliy then step out of the opened door of the craft and seemed to slowly descend to earth like in a parachute, not experiencing any fear. That same night other workers at the phosphate plant observed a UFO that emitted light. Later Vasiliy began to experience problems with his health, he got terrific headaches, and his body temperature seemed to drop. He spent 26 days in a hospital. He was eventually released by the doctors but he felt no better.

He then went on vacation. At the site of the UFO landing a clearly defined circled about twenty meters in diameter could be seen months afterwards where the grass would not grow, though the vegetation all around it was abundant. Within the circle the deep imprints of the landing props could be still seen. Vasiliy remembered one more detail, as he left he had asked the female aliens to provide him with proof of the event and was told that they would be glad to do so, but that their 'proof' or present would disappear on Earth.

HC addendum.
Source: Stebelyev V. Aizahmetov, 'Flying with the saucers' In 'Znamya Truda.' Local newspaper, Dzhambul, August 1-3, 1990. Also Vybornov G. in 'Leninskaya Smena' newspaper, Alma Ata, August 11, 1990.   Type: G

Location: Near Korbach, Germany.
Date: February 18, 1990.
Time: 6:30 p.m.

The witness was out walking with her dog in the Waldeck hills, when of all the sudden her dog lay down on his back and started to whimper. The witness had to carry the dog. At first she heard a low him, which ceased after about thirty seconds. A large round object, whose diameter measured ten to twenty meters, was floating above a clearing and suddenly began to glow with an incredibly bright light, lasting about twenty to thirty seconds. After that, its light dimmed and now it had a metallic appearance. The bottom of the oval craft glowed in a dark red color (like glowing charcoal) and the object lowered itself silently to the ground.

In the meantime, the dog had escaped. The witness, who was completely blinded, wanted to run away, but was hit by a "blue ray of light," which paralyzed her. She was short of breath, tried in vain to call for help, and was completely wet with perspiration within thirty seconds. Then "there was a voice" sounding female and somehow metallic, which said: *"Don't be afraid, nothing bad will happen to you."* Actually, though, the witness became even more afraid and nearly panicked. The ray of light changed to green and her breathing improved. All of the sudden two entities were standing in front of her, both of them between 1.4 and 1.6 m in height, with baldheads and gray skin. They had normal human like eyes and noses. They wore dark green overalls. On the chest they carried a strange symbol, which resembled this; "^C L." She did not understand their language. They soon returned to the craft, which was standing on four legs about 1.5 m high. The green beam vanished and the witness sank to the ground in a faint. It was 9:30 p.m. when she woke up again. She took a few steps and vomited. Which she repeated after reaching home, where her dog was already waiting for her.

HC addendum.
Source: Ulrich Magin and Illobrand Von Ludwiger.   Type: C or G?

Location: Graham Bell Island, Franz-Joseph Land, Russia.
Date: Spring, 1990.
Time: Daytime.

A frontier guard, a private of the air defense radar unit noticed a UFO hovering in the sky. Soon a senior officer joined in the observation. The object, which was visible in the sky hovering over the military radar installation was giving off a brilliant light and was slowly rotating. It then suddenly stopped and a yellow beam of light descended to the ground from the object.

A humanoid figure wearing a silvery overall descended within the beam of light. The humanoid figure walked for some distance on the ground and then zoomed up into the object in the same manner. The object then began to rotate slowly and gaining speed quickly disappeared from sight. As a result of the distance of the object from the observers no additional details were observed.

HC addendum.
Source: Vladimir Sinitsyn "M-ski Triangle" Anomalous News Bulletin, Riga, Latvia, 1990.   Type: B

Location: Near Cooperstown, New York.
Date: Spring, 1990.
Time: Late afternoon.

The main witness, Dee, and a girlfriend had decided to take a walk in the surrounding countryside. While they were taking a rest near a large outcropping of rocks, there was a 'humming' sound coming from one of the nooks. His girlfriend stood and started walking toward the noise. Though it was late afternoon and they were in heavy tree cover, there was enough light to see into the rocks. As she got closer, she said that the sound was coming from inside one of the large boulders. Dee began to walk toward her and the boulder to listen for himself.

They stood there for about five minutes when they noticed the boulder seemed to 'shimmer' like water. They quickly stepped back as the shimmer grew and change to a greenish hue. Then, suddenly, two small beings emerged from the shimmering portal. The beings walked towards them as they tried to move away but were paralyzed and unable to talk. These beings were about three foot in height and had green colored clothes that looked like overalls.

The faces and body features were human-like though. They also had long blond hair and very dark, large round eyes. Their hands had four distinct fingers and were very rough textured. They took each of the witnesses by the hand started pulling them toward the rock. They both quickly regained their ability to move and broke away from their grasp. As they ran down the hill, they could hear them running behind them. A minute or so into the chase, Dee felt something hit him on the back and realized one of the beings had thrown a stone at him. He stopped and looked back, but they were gone though he could hear voices from a distance that sounded like there were more of these beings and the sounds were getting louder.

They were both shaking when they arrived home. They agreed not to tell anyone about the incident. He never had another encounter with these beings but he felt that they knew where he lived. One morning, he found a small pile of stones on his patio picnic table with a small four-fingered muddy hand print beside it.

Dee recently moved out of the area, but his girlfriend still has the feeling they know where he is. One evening, while sitting in his office at home, she heard voices outside. She looked out the office window and caught a quick glance of something darting into the bushes.

HC addendum.
Source: http://naturalplane.blogspot.com/2010/01   Type: E
Comments: I feel that this type of entity is interdimensional in nature and has paranormal abilities.

Location: Santiago, Chile.
Date: Spring, 1990.
Time: Afternoon.

Businessman Federico Rojo Feria provided the source with a truly amazing story. During the spring of 1990, while at the Torre de Santa Maria building with a female co-worker, he found himself watching a human-looking flying entity from the 19th story of the building. His account of the facts states that the vision was so surprising and shocking that both coworkers were paralyzed for almost two minutes, the uncanny experience's duration.

Raul Nuñez interviewed Mr. Rojo and kindly conveyed the report to our *Bestiary*. The witness re-stated his experiences of the time, saying that a flying entity passed only a few meters away from the large window at which they were located, engaging in a wide elliptical flight maneuver, gliding over the Mapocho River before climbing away toward the Cordillera. The wings were like those of a giant bird, but the other parts of the body were configured like a human's. He was unable to make out the arms clearly, as they blended into the shape of the large wings. The witnesses were traumatized for several weeks by the encounter. One of them became so panicked that he refused to speak of the subject again and his behavior toward his coworkers changed. To date, it has not been possible to find this last witness to hear their version of the events stated in this report.

HC addendum.
Source: Sigrid Grothe, NOUFA (Noticiero Ufologico Autonomo, Chile) and Raul Nuñez.   Type: E

* * * * * * *

Location: Ivanovo, Russia.
Date: Spring, 1990.
Time: Late evening.

Mr. Veniamin Kurochkin, a professional artist was resting in a hotel when suddenly three humanoid entities entered his room, directly through the wall. A female entity stood in the middle of the group and the alien men were positioned to the right and left of her. All were tall, dressed in tight-fitting suits, similar to knitted sports suits. Their suits were smoky-ash in color. One of the aliens looked to be fifty years of age, the other man was about thirty years old in appearance and the woman was very young. The most amazing feature was that all three figures were transparent; Veniamin could see everything in the room through them. The alien trio silently approached the witness, who was frozen with fear.

47

Veniamin asked who they were; *"Tron"* answered the fifty-year old man. *"Tron?"* asked Kurochkin, concentrating his stare on the man. Kurochkin then asked again, *"Is this your name?"* The aliens answered, *"No, We are TRON. We all are Tron,"* said the alien man. The alien woman then bends down and stretched her hands towards the witness, Kurochkin felt enveloped in a bluish fog. The next day he could not recall what happened to him inside the bluish fog. He could not remember despite all attempts. Every attempt for him to remember ended in a strong headache.

HC addendum.
Source: Alexey K. Priyma, 'Unknown Worlds,' Moscow, 1996.   Type: E

* * * * * * *

Location: Donetsk, Ukraine.
Date: Spring, 1990.
Time: 11:00 p.m.

Irina Vladimirovna M. suddenly saw an opalescent cloud appear in her room, it appeared to have a "screen" on it. At first the screen was blank but the image of an alien being appeared on it. He seemed to have stepped into the screen. The alien was completely unearthly looking, with a large round head, long neck, and sloping shoulders. He resembled an aged man with brown bumpy skin. His eyes were very big, slanted, darkish and without pupils. He wore a long folded cloth, of a slightly bluish tint. He stood and gazed upon her fixedly. Afraid, she asked him "mentally" who he was but received no answer.

After twenty minutes the screen blacked out. After this first "contact" Irina saw another TV-sized screen in her room, in it, she could see different equipment and technical devices. After that she could see an earthly panorama showing a beautiful sunset. She then saw a "pod" with eight figures standing on it. The pod then made a steep turn and vanished, a beautiful landscape then became visible and then she saw a huge lighted globe. One other night around 4:00 a.m. Irina saw in her room three alien figures, one with his back to her, and the two others standing away from her and not clearly visible. She heard them speaking an unknown language, which resembled curt speech, abrupt, similar to birds chirping. The sound was clear and distinct. Suddenly the alien standing closest to her glanced at her and all the figures turned towards her and at that same moment she lost consciousness.

HC addendum.
Source: Gennadiy Y. Leszshenko, 'At the Edge of the Unknown, or What's Behind the Curtain,' Donetsk, 1994.   Type: E or G?

Location: Mahachkala, Dagestan Republic, Russia.
Date: Spring, 1990.
Time: Around midnight.

The witness M. characterized as a sober minded and respected individual after returning home saw a strange bright green coin-like circle hovering in the air above the refrigerator. At first he thought it was a portable flashlight accidentally left switched on by his wife, but when he asked her, she denied that. M. looked again at the green coin-sized light and noticed that it seemed to be increasing in size, and becoming more intense. Suddenly the object began to move in the air, it made circular movements and it began flying around the witness in a complicated trajectory. The witness felt heat coming from the light and also heard a whistling sound. The green light then expanded more and transformed into a human-like head. The witness thought that he was going crazy and turned his face to the wall and began praying to Allah.
However when he looked back over his shoulder, the image was still there, despite his prayers. The image had now transformed itself into a humanoid shape, with arms, legs and a body that was totally covered with dense fur, like an ape.

The humanoid appeared to be a cyclopean with only one eye in the middle of the forehead which emanated a red beam of light, like that of a flashlight. The neck was absent and its head was set squarely on a pair of powerful shoulders. The entity's height was more than two meters and it was very muscular. The intruder began floating in midair just above the floor, moving forward towards where M's children were sleeping. M. hurried and rushed ahead of the entity towards his children, covering them with his body. At this point he began to pray again asking Allah to save him and his children from the hairy monster. The creature floated towards the bed and covered M and his children briefly picked them up and then dropped them back down immediately on the bed, without harming them. The creature then stepped back as M still covered his children, his body now facing the strange entity. The entity stood motionless at some distance from the bed. The humanoid did not make any threatening moves. Trembling in horror M hid his head under the bed sheets and continued praying in earnest. Soon the doors creaked and there was a loud slamming sound, this awoke M's wife, which confirmed her husband's story, emphasizing that he had never experienced any hallucinations. After the encounter he always worried about the creature returning and abducting him and the children. In due time the family moved into another apartment.

HC addendum.
Source: Aleksey K. Priyma, "UFO Witnesses to the Unknown" Moscow, 1997.   Type: E

Location: Es-Suveira, Syria.
Date: March, 1990.
Time: Unknown.

A local boy named Mahmud Midzhor reported to the correspondent of the local "As-Saura" newspaper that he had arrived from the far "red planet" named 'DIZO.' He stated that the aliens there were 1.5 times taller than humans, or about 2.5 meters in height, "they possess unnatural powers and magic capabilities."

According to the boy, he had arrived in a spacecraft and awaited directions "from above" to start purifying the Earth from the bad and vicious people. Mahmud named several planets of the solar systems including numerous planets unknown on Earth that surrounded his native star system.

HC addendum.
Source: Vadim Szennikov 'Echo of the Planet' Moscow #4-5, 1990.
Type: G or F?

* * * * * * *

Location: Primorskiy kray, Far East Siberia, Russia.
Date: March, 1990.
Time: Unknown.

Two privates from military unit #26870, Sergey Medyelyaev and Nikolay Kudryavyi, spotted a UFO hovering in mid-air above the territory of the military camp. It was oval in shape and white. A violet beam of light emanated from the object and then hovered in place for about six seconds and then it seemed to dissolve in mid-air.

Around that exact time a meteorology observer from the same unit, private Kravtsov encountered a strange entity in doors while coming out of the washroom. He immediately stepped back in fear and the humanoid appeared to have done the same thing, gliding away very quickly floating just above the floor.

The entity appeared to be globe-shaped, but it had a "head" and one thick "leg" beneath. The witness did not notice any arms. This incident lasted for about 20-30 seconds. After the encounter, Kravtsov had difficulty speaking and stammered.

HC addendum.
Source: Valeriy Dvuzhilnyi, Dalnegorsk and Andrey Pavlov, 'Komsomolskaya Pravda,' Moscow, December 1, 2000.   Type: D

Location: Minsk, Belarus.
Date: March, 1990.
Time: 2:00 a.m.

I.N. Fyeodorov a local resident, had been watching television late at night and when the broadcast ended he had gone out to the balcony to smoke. He had been standing in the balcony for about five minutes, when he suddenly heard a hissing sound. At the same time the area around him began to be covered by a thick foggy veil.

Moments later, Fyeodorov saw standing to his left, a humanoid entity dressed in tight-fitting golden attire, with what appeared to be antennas jutting out from its head. Its face was covered by a dull mask. The entity had apparently descended from somewhere above in the sky.

The witness was now terrified but then the entity spoke in a female voice that said, *"Do not be afraid!"* The witness noticed a slight mechanical accent in the voice (possibly caused by an automatic electronic translator). The witness then asked, *"What's going on? What do you want?!"* The entity then answered, *"We would like to examine you and take you to our ship."* The witness answered, *"What ship? Why is it not visible, I have read that they are luminous."* The female entity answered, *"We have more than luminous ships only. Walk to the ship, it is just next to the balcony."* Having passed through the balcony as if it was invisible, the witness and the female alien came to a narrow aperture of an entrance hatch.

As the witness walked into the ship, it seemed to slightly rock under his weight, the object was evidently hovering. The woman then followed him into a cone-shape compartment where she sat him on one of the seats placed in a circular position.

She then vacated the room with these words, *"I will be in the other compartment watching you."* The witness then asked, *"And what will you be watching for?"* She answered, *"You need not to worry, all will be alright, after a while you will be returned to the same location."* Soon after she left the room, the witness heard a hissing noise again and like he was in a floating boat, as though they were flying upwards.

During the flight, from time to time the witness heard the woman's voice, which regularly inquired about his state of health. She would ask, *"How do you feel now? And now?"* The witness felt anxious with the constant questioning but answered them promptly. The woman then added, *"It is of interest for us to observe your reaction and make sure that you are feeling well."* *"How do you feel now?"* she asked again. Somewhat annoyed the witness then asked, *"And why do you ask this question again"?* She replied, *"Because we are now very far away from Earth, in the area of Altair."*

This news suddenly caused great worry on the witness, but she soon calmed him, saying, *"Don't worry we will soon take you back."* And

51

indeed, soon all the phases of the flight soon repeated themselves in a return sequence, and they arrived soon at his home.

The witness thanked her for bringing him back. She then said, *"Normal humans are frightened of us, but we are not so bad. Tell all your people not to be afraid of us."* She then added, *"We shall meet again."*

The man then exited the room and into his balcony, looking back the alien woman was waving goodbye to him. When he looked at his watch he realized that he had been absent from his apartment for about 1.5 hours.

HC addendum.
Source: UFO-COM (Byelorussian UFO web-site) and researcher A. Shamma.   Type: G

* * * * * * *

Location: Rostov-on-Don, Russia.
Date: March, 1990.
Time: Late evening.

30-year old Dmitriy Naumenko (involved in a previous contact in November, 1985), was in his bed attempting to fall asleep when he suddenly heard someone calling his name. He jumped up in amazement, because he had been alone in the house.

He then saw a beautiful young woman with a head of amazing white hair sitting on a chair near his table, while the whole room was lit in a surreal, dull bluish light. He immediately recognized her as the same woman he met back in 1985, "from another world" as she had said at that time. While in the previous encounter she had been dressed in a normal terrestrial dress and boots, this time she was dressed in a shiny seamless overall, apparently metallic in nature. *"I have come to visit you again,"* Said the beautiful alien woman, smiling. She then added, somewhat irked, that Dmitriy had totally forgotten about her those five years.

At this moment Dmitriy heard a male voice coming from the kitchen, the voice said, *"What is this?"* another male voice answered, *"It is tea, let's drink."* In a whisper, Dmitriy asked the alien woman who was talking in the kitchen. She answered that they were her "friends" and not to worry, *"they will not cause you any harm."*

At this point Dmitriy felt his mind wandering, sensing a ringing sound inside his head and a strange reddish gloom in front of his eyes, like a smoky cloak, this cloak completely covered the alien woman. The alien woman then vanished, at the same time the strange dull bluish light almost disappeared.

52

In a confused state, Dmitriy dressed and went out to his front yard. He then saw a large cigar-shaped object hovering in the sky near the Rostov City tower. The object had a greenish halo around it. Several beams of light shone down from the object and strangely the ends of the beams did not seem to reach the ground, they seemed to be cut off at about twenty meters from the ground. The cigar then started moving and slowly floated away, soon disappearing into the night sky.

Two days later the local newspaper, "Molot" (Hammer) published an article detailing the fact that several locals had seen a huge cigar shaped object hovering near the television tower apparently the same night of Dmitriy's encounter.

HC addendum.
Source: Alexey K. Priyma, 'Unknown Worlds,' Moscow. 1996. Type: D?

* * * * * * *

Location: Barrio Borinquen, Atravesada Puerto Rico.
Date: March, 1990.
Time: 10:00 p.m.

The witness was alone at home meditating, when she suddenly found herself transported to her backyard. A silvery disc-shaped craft then approached from the mountains and began hovering nearby. From under the object, a tall human-like figure emerged, the being floated towards the witness.

The figure was described as having fair white skin and blond shoulder length hair. He wore a white uniform with a bright red belt and red gloves and boots. He approached the witness and extended his hand. The witness attempted to run but the being grabbed her by the arm and held her. Four needles now emerged from the man's glove and were inserted into her arm. She then felt powerless and "controlled." She was taken to where the object hovered and was told telepathically that "they" would return to contact her again. She was then taken back to the house and released.

HC addendum.
Source: Jorge Martin, Enigma #37.   Type: B
Comments: Translation by Albert S. Rosales

Location: Near Nerekhta, Kostroma region, Russia.
Date: March 8, 1990.
Time: Night.

Doctor Filaret Korovkin heard the air steaming over his head as he walked along a field and looked up to see a flattened sphere light gray to violet metallic in appearance. No windows, hatchways or doors were evident. From below the object a semi-transparent tube descended to earth, through this pipe he was pulled into the object.

Inside he found himself in a rounded room, with two doors and escalators going up. It was impossibly much larger than what appeared to be from the outside. The walls were completely covered with different signal panels, screens and some instruments.

The human appearing occupants told him, that in respect of time, in the terrestrial sense, it did not exist. Furthermore they did not use "fuel" to travel; they somehow had mastered gravity and used "null space" and "zero-channels" to travel. They predicted that in the course of time the inhabitants of earth would discover such methods of energy.

HC addendum.
Source: NLO-7-1996.   Type: G

* * * * * * *

Location: Riga, Latvia.
Date: March 20, 1990.
Time: after 6:00 p.m.

High school student Maris M (involved in a previous encounter) disappeared on this date sometime after 6:00 p.m. He could only remember going out of the house, visiting the Palace of Culture, a hobby shop and coming to his senses outside the town of Panevezhis in Lithuania. For a long time he could not understand where he was, only knowing that he was not in Riga, he was wandering outside of town alone at the edge of a forest. But soon something resembling a reddish fog unexpectedly appeared high in the sky; it seemed to become denser, getting smaller until it vanished. Moments later from the same area of the sky an alien spacecraft appeared.

The craft landed in the nearby forest. After running towards the direction of the landing about 300 meters away, Maris saw the spacecraft. An illuminated entryway was open, with a stepladder reaching the ground. While walking towards the craft, Maris noticed a strange robot-like creature walking towards him. The "robot" had large eyes, and bizarre looking protrusions, which confused and frightened the boy, causing him to stop in his tracks. But the robot suddenly seemed to decrease in size and transform itself into an exact replica of Maris, even dressed in the same clothing. The "robot" now made friendly gestures and invited the boy inside the spacecraft. Inside, three aliens sat near a wall opposite to the entryway. They were sitting in deep armchairs, but all were of amazing height.

A woman sat to the left, and unlike the two men she had thin lips. All the aliens had round ears, four fingered hands, snub noses with two openings and egg shaped (elongated oval) heads. Staring at the alien female, Maris noticed a hint of eroticism in her dress. Part of her thighs and breasts were visible. Her suit was fit snugly and covered the other parts of the body. The two alien men wore low-necked (décolleté) suits. It soon became apparent to Maris that all three aliens were "telepaths."

All three smiled in a strange way. Maris could not see their teeth; there was only a slit-like opening for a mouth. The alien in the center, which was the largest and most robust of the three, did most of the talking. The stunned witness was somehow able to understand as the alien invited him to sit down. Not believing his eyes Maris touched the chair to make sure it was real. The robot then sat on the opposite chair and was fastened by two seatbelts.

The robot began speaking to the young witness, bragging that he knew almost half a million languages including all the languages on Earth. The robot was indeed very talkative and loquacious, telling the boy not to be afraid and trying to calm him down. The robot was now speaking in the Latvian language, and asked the boy several personal questions, age, where he lived, etc. Maris felt slightly awkward as the other three aliens glanced at him, examining him very intently.

During the conversation the boy asked three times, what was the meaning of a strange hieroglyph on the buckles of the alien's belt but did not receive an answer. In the meantime the robot told Maris that their extraterrestrial civilization selected people for contact from time to time, though the contacts were numerous. The extraterrestrial civilizations reached those people that were able to "understand" them and even named the specific declination in the physical construction of Maris's organism. Suddenly the robot asked Maris if he wanted to see how the other planets looked like. Maris promptly agreed.

After that, everything around Maris began to assume a strange transparency, but he could not see anything outside the spacecraft, the lights became lit in a strange matt white light, which hindered any view beyond them. There were no windows in the cabin. Soon a transparent line about two meters wide could be seen along the perimeter of the spherical room. Maris could see a forest outside. By the movement of the craft, Maris understood that the craft had taken off. Out of fear Maris looked at the roof, the robot apparently understood his concerns and said that everything would be corrected. Maris soon became more relaxed and became very curious about his surroundings.

One of the aliens pushed on a pedal on the floor and the speed of the craft seemed to increase. Then one more pedal was pressed and in moments everything became dark and the light inside the craft became a reddish white tint. Maris looked at his hand and it was the same color. Maris perceived the scene around him like a photonegative; the former dark spaces became light, and vise-versa. This lasted for about five minutes. Then in two-three seconds, everything returned to normal. When the speed decreased, the walls became transparent and the boy could see a red-blue planet afar. But the destination of their journey was not that planet as the craft was already landing on a "green" planet, which they were quickly approaching. The robot advised Maris that the landing site had been specifically select for him. At the moment of descent Maris saw a dark mountain in the distance. But the descent was swift and a foggy green atmosphere worsened the visibility.

They soon landed on a meadow, amid a jungle area. A small door opened and the alien crew exited. The aliens were almost three meters in height, but somehow were able to exit through the small door without bending down. Maris head almost touched the top of the doorway. The plants and flora outside looked very much like the ones on earth. He saw several animals, one resembling a common dog, another a parrot and another animal resembling a four legged snake which ran by meters, about one meter in length. The animals or entities were not afraid of the humanoids or aliens. It was very light and easy to breathe outside. When Maris walked he felt very light almost as if floating.

Strangely, he saw several curved armchairs standing on a spacious glade. The humanoids then ceremoniously sat on the chairs. Maris also sat down. The complete conversation was difficult to remember but Maris remembered that the name of the planet was "EMSA." It contained three super-giant cities on its surface and the rest of the surface was virgin nature or woodlands. Besides EMSA, there were six other planets in that system. One, reddish-blue, which Maris had seen from the spacecraft, was lifeless. Then another huge planet called MENPLURIYA, which was without oxygen in its atmosphere, another planet was called EMSA-3, which was inhabited, and contained one huge city on it. Another planet was called Aires in which the aliens told Maris they used for experiments with new "life forms." The last was the smallest and remotest and was called EMSA-2 with two small towns in it, with concentrated technocratic and research facilities.

According to Maris, the planet MENPLURIYA was the most closely resembling Earth. It was a small planet literally swarming with predators. It had once contained a city, which was abandoned because of changes in the planet's atmosphere; only one outpost or station remained there. The glass-like robot, which had visited Maris in Riga apparently, lived on that station. But the main reason that the city was abandoned was because of the growing aggressiveness and potential psychological and physical deterioration of the planet inhabitants, which was constantly changing, just like the earth's atmosphere.

Further conversation revealed that the aliens were convinced that Mars was inhabited but did not give any specific information why they thought that, apparently their capabilities were also limited. The aliens mentioned that the distance between their star and our sun was about 26700 parsecs, which seemed wrong and too large. Their star is not visible even with the most powerful telescopes. It is similar to a G-class star or sun. Interested, Maris asked the aliens if there were civilizations located closer to the earth. The aliens answered that there was a star in the area of Polaris, which had three earth-like planets and were inhabited by living organisms.

During those conversations, Maris was suddenly distracted by a strange entity that ambled out of the forest. It somehow resembled a terrestrial chicken walking on almost one-meter long thin legs. The "chicken" looked at the aliens and the boy with large eyes and began slowly moving away on the road leaving the glade. This did not cause the slightest impression on the aliens (similar type creatures had been reportedly seen around 1937-1939 near Aluksne and Pechory). Soon after that a two-meter tall being with a bucket-like cowl on its head appeared on the glade.

Maris watched as one of the aliens promptly grabbed a tube-like weapon from his belt and shot a dispersed blue ray of light towards the strange entity. The uninvited alien guest then retreated back into the thicket the robot had stood between the shot and the strange entity and had partially hindered the shot. They all looked in the direction for a long time and then the owner of the shiny tube dropped it on the grass.

They then resumed the conversation with Maris, talking about the earth. They pointed out that a super-calamity would not endanger the earth until at least 200 years (that's refreshing), but added that, *"planets, grow, live and die."* Maris then asked the robot if everything is programmed and could be predicted. The robot then explained to Maris (already a young atheist) that a scientific "team" under the leadership of a superior entity called the "Professor" began the colonization of the earth using at first, bacterium. But the higher the civilization, the more difficult the "operations," and there was more energy consumption. Humans on earth now were sufficiently developed and at times were not under the control of those aliens who conducted the experiments or operations.

Apparently humanity was at the edge of its Rubicon and was about to enter an intergalactic community as a young member or "brother," and "experimentation" on earth will resume. The term Apocalypse, which no one knows precisely when it would occur, had shifted to the distant future. With every new arrival of the "Professor" or creator, humanity receives a new injection of ideological and scientific creativeness. Such visitations have been reflected in ancient epochs depicted in many ancient rock carvings and paintings. There had been a total of forty visitations to earth. Arrivals from this specific civilization were more frequent but less significant in scale. The next arrival (41st) will be of special consequences for humans. According to the aliens, the entity called the "Professor" has been worshipped on earth as a God, and was of evasive character. Maris soon realized that the less he knew about that enigmatic character the better for him, he felt that if he knew too much about the "Professor," he would be destroyed.

The aliens then invited Maris to stay in their green planet (EMSA) which he politely refused. Then he asked the aliens to show him the cities on EMSA. But apparently that would be too hazardous for him. The abundance of light, energy and radiation on the cities was very harmful on human organisms, though similar influences were experienced by humans in certain areas on earth (example, Bermuda Triangle). So they showed him the lighted cities from a remote location. The city was brightly lit, radiating all the colors of the rainbow. The city stood within a mire, or swamp. It contained enough residents to make it a small country.

Numerous different small animals inhabited the mire. Apparently the animals were very aggressive but this did not worry the residents and tragic encounters with the animals or "monsters" were rare. There was a tall cylindrical tower in the center of the city, narrowing at the top. There was a platform with a large sign on in, the same symbol the aliens had on their belts, the symbol somewhat resembles the letter "T" with an additional line of its right side and the letter "m" beneath. Circling the air above the city, Maris noticed several blue globe-shaped objects flying in different directions. The robot, answering the boy's question, drew a picture of the inner structure of the flying object on a screen that suddenly appeared from nowhere. Their capabilities were not restricted to the atmosphere; the inhabitants of the green planet have found a way to remove gravity when traveling about.

He added that similar discoveries await humans in the future. One of the components of the fuel used by the alien craft was called "mortozya" a very active and aggressive substance. The reagents of it are so-called "heavy spirits" and ionized atomic hydrogen that transforms to deuterium and tritium in a sequential manner. The energy of controlled thermo-nuclear reaction or more exactly the energy of atomic nucleuses is transmitted to envelope the globe. Depending on the amount of transmitted energy, the top epidermis as well as the whole globe, begins to manifest outside matter (?) and the visible flight in space is just temporal movement. The necessary trajectory of the movement, depending on the energy expenditures, defines the curvature of space, necessary for the pending maneuver. Factually, the globe flies in a straight line but in a curved corridor of the host planet or "world beyond." Transition into that world occurs instantly just like turning off an energy source. (!) The upper part of the globe is the specific "accumulator" which collects the products of the radioactive decay and solar energy that then is transformed into "light stream."

Soon, Maris and the aliens were onboard the spaceship again and in two minutes, the same sequence of red-white photonegative switch occurred again. Apparently caused by the jump "through zero space" on the other end of the Galaxy, which did not take much time at all. The walls of the craft became transparent again; he saw the sea and a small island beneath.

The robot then explained to Maris that they were flying through an area known on earth as "The Bermuda Triangle" that the flight would last about twenty minutes. Maris asked the aliens to be let out in Riga and the robot explained that he knew exactly where (which proved to be wrong). They soon appeared above a large city and flew above the rooftops and then descended near an unfamiliar monument. Maris then noted that the contrast of the gamut of colors had been distorted again, but not as much as when using interstellar "jumps." Apparently, in such situations the UFO is invisible. The distance from the ground was about two meters and the boy jumped straight to the grass. An aged female street-cleaner that was sweeping the street saw him, jumping out of nowhere, straight in front of her eyes, an amazed look remained on her face.

After walking the unfamiliar streets for a while, Maris realized that he was not in his native city. They did not understand his Latvia language and then he began to speak Russian, in which he was then clearly understood. Maris had apparently landed in Minsk the capital of Belarus. Apparently the aliens had somehow mistaken both cities. Maris had no money to return home. He then asked for help from a local militiaman. He then lied to the officer telling him that he had a friend in Lithuania and had taken the wrong train. He asked to be sent back to Riga. The policeman complied and using normal protocol logged the incident in his journal. He was then taken to an underage detention facility and a telegram was sent to his parent in Riga. Soon Maris grandmother arrived and took him home. Apparently the boy had taken a previous journey in which the aliens had originally dropped him off near the town of Panevezys in Lithuania, but those details had apparently been completely erased from his mind.

HC addendum.
Source: O. Burak, "I Believe in the Green Planet," M-Skiy Triangle, Riga, Latvia, #5, 1990.   Type: G

Location: Dnepropetrovsk, Ukraine.
Date: March 24, 1990.
Time: Night.

Several locals reported encountering a tall robot-like creature in the outskirts of the city. The creature was close to two meters in height, strongly built and possessed a bright circle of light on its chest from which, bright beams of light emanated. It walked in a strange mechanical way. And it had a huge head resembling a flattened saucer, two long devices jutted from the alien's head, resembling antennas or horns, with lights which appeared to blink. The front section of the alien's head emanated a sort of greenish steam, very foul smelling. The frightened witnesses fled the area on foot.

HC addendum.
Source: X-UFO Russia, Yaroslav Sochka, UFODOS.   Type: E

* * * * * * *

Location: Yerevan, Armenia.
Date: Beginning of April, 1990.
Time: Daytime.

About two weeks before the main encounter, an 11-year old local boy named Spartak told his classmates about an unusual dream he had: An alien robot, had warned him about his arrival, asking him not to be afraid. The robot predicted that when he would be playing with five other boys on the school yard, he would come and talk with them.

Soon after that a group of five boys were playing soccer on a field behind the school and after the game was over two boys ran to get some water and the other three stretched out on the grass, looking towards a nearby vineyard. Suddenly they saw a UFO descend towards some wasteland near the vineyard. The globe-shaped twinkling object was made out of a shiny material and landed about 300 meters from the schoolyard. The UFO was no more than 5-6m in size (about 10-15 m in diameter according to estimation) and seemed to split up in two halves like a "tangerine." Other witnesses later reported that the UFO a small protrusion on top that seemed to be a dome, which had an opened hatch. The UFO was encircled with yellow and red lights and had a row of six circular windows or portholes which emitted light, positioned on the rim around the center.

After splitting open in front of the stunned witnesses, three or four humanoid robotic creatures about 3-3.5m in height exited the UFO and began to walk around the object, all in different areas. The humanoids figures were exactly the same in appearance and two or three of the

60

figures periodically bended down to the ground apparently looking and collection soil samples. One of the alien figures began moving towards the schoolyard and the stunned witnesses. The robot easily crossed the wire fence around the vineyard which was about 1.5m in height, but couldn't cross the taller fence surrounding the school. So the stunned witnesses watched as the "robot" transformed itself into a large blue globe of light less than one meter in diameter and then began to roll like a ball upwards along the fence and then down on the other side. Once it had reached the ground it transformed itself back into the robot figure, and continued walking towards the boys. At this point the two other boys returned and now all five boys were witnessing the event exactly as the robot had predicted on Spartak's dream.

The robot approached the boys, which were frozen with fear and unable to move. They described the robot's skin as grayish metallic in color. There was a circular helmet that covered the robot's head with two visors in front and two small vertical antennas on top. The robot had a light source of its forehead area and had what appeared to be a control panel with buttons on the upper part of his right leg and a smaller panel with just one large button on the same area of his left leg. The legs were encircled in something that resembled knee-leggings and ended in broad "feet" or horizontal elongated oval-shaped platforms, like props. The children couldn't remember how many fingers the robot had but they thought it was three or four which were sharpened and thick.

One of the frightened boys attempted to run but the robot struck him with a beam of light that knocked him to the ground. A red burn mark was left on the boy's hand and was still visible in October that same year. Local doctors could not diagnose what kind of burn it was.

Then a conversation between the boys and the robot ensued. The boys spoke out loud while the robot's answers were displayed on the shiny screen on its chest area. The robot appeared awkward, heavy set without any human facial features, somewhat frightening in appearance. The boys had been so stunned about the whole encounter that they couldn't remember how long they "spoke" with the robot. They saw different types of inscriptions and images display on the robot's screen. Some appeared to be symbols which the schoolboys could not interpret. To their surprised they were able to see their own names written in the Armenian language on the screen.

Every time one of the boys spoke, his name would appear on the screen. The talk was mostly about the future of Armenia. The boys remembered one phrase most of all, *"Now your country is in big difficulty but we will be helping you."* After that moment the boy's recollections became mixed and fragmentary. According to the boys, they felt hypnotized and sleepy and apparently the robot was somehow scanning their minds and studying them in sequence. The boys distinctly remembered that the robot projected a beam of light from its forehead causing one of the boys to start levitating up into the air; another boy attempted to hold his friend down by grabbing him by the legs but was also levitated up into the air. Both hovered in midair for several seconds and then fell to the ground.

Later for some time the robot walked around the schoolyard, periodically bending down collecting stones from the ground, the robot apparently scratched one of its hands while doing this and the hand assumed a strange reddish tint (right hand). Soon the robot returned to the field exactly the same way it had come to the schoolyard, transforming into a rolling blue ball again in order to climb the high fence and then walked towards the landing craft which he then entered. The object then closed assuming the globe shape again it then it propelled itself up like a "spring" and after hovering for a moment above the schoolyard it flew away.

When questioned about the other humanoids or robots the boys said that these remained near the object all the time picking items from the ground. According to researchers the grass turned a different color at the location of the landing, and apparently the UFO did not exactly land but hovered very close to the ground. Numerous footprints apparently made by the robots were found these were 20cm in diameter and about 5-10cm deep. Other ground disturbances or traces were found by using the method of "bio-location."

HC addendum.
Source: A.G. Tonakanyan, T.E. Arutunyan of ASUNI or Armenian Section of Ufology and tradition ways to transmit information. Also Sergey Oganesyan Chairman of the Abovyan Section for research of anomalous phenomena (AP), Tatyana Faminskaya & Stanislav Yermakov, Moscow members of AP, Commission of SNIO in "Anomalia" Moscow January-March 1993 & Oct Dec 1993. Robert Lesniakiewicz.
Type: B

* * * * * * *

Location: Tosno, Leningrad region, Russia.
Date: Early April, 1990.
Time: Night.

The witness, Ekaterina Mikhailovna Rumyantseva, a former doctor's assistant and a very religious Orthodox woman, liked to pray at nights watching the sky since early childhood. On this night she had gone to the balcony and on her knees began to cry and pray the following prayer, *"God, make me powerful like a magician. I would create order on earth. We have too many murders, robberies, lewdness, depravity and violence."* After she ended the prayer she stood up and walked back into her room. As she entered her room she heard a voice inside her head, *"Go out in the street, bring him home,"* immediately as if guided by some type of unseen influence Ekaterina walked outside her home not even bothering to close the door or switching the lights on. She only took with her a small lit candle. She stood outside her home on the street wondering who she was supposed to bring home.

The next moment she saw a reddish "dog" looking up at the sky. The witness also looked at the sky and saw a strange cloud with a dark center and edges that were emitting light. She stared at the strange cloud for some time and then said to the dog, *"Are you sick? Come into my home."* As soon as she said that the strange cloud began to move silently above her. Ekaterina and the dog entered her home; she closed the door but did not switch on the light. She then heard the strange voice inside her head again, *"Bring me water."* She thought to herself, *"what kind of water should I get, boiled or not?"* As soon as she entered the antechamber she saw standing about a meter from her a small dwarf-like man or gnome, no more than 30-40cm in height.

Surprised, she yelled, *"We don't have people like that!"* The creature answered, *"I am not a person, I am a sky warrior."* The witness then asked, *"Are there many of your kind?"* The creature said, *"Yes, our kind is large in numbers."* The witness then asked, *"And why do you visit us?"* The creature answered, *"Your Earth is ill and is sending out impulses to the Universe warning that she is dying. You should not take oil and gas from the Earth because is like taking blood from a living human organism,"* the alien added, *"The kernel of Earth is losing its specific weight."* (?)

The witness then said, *"We have very wise scientists and they would like to enter in contact with you."* But in disdain and scorn, the alien answered *"No! We will never enter in contact with your scientists. You don't have scientists, they are all insane, criminal and depraved (corrupted) they don't know what they are doing. This is not for your mind to comprehend the mystery of the 'Black Star.'"* (?)

"And what is that?" asked Mrs. Rumyantseva. *"That is your nuclear power, which humans don't know how to control and contaminate the earth and themselves, changing their DNA structure, causing criminal behavior in humans. All the children will be 'cripples.' If you wish to clean up your soil, water and air from radiation we are ready to help you. We are concerned about this. If the Earth 'explodes' (!) your Moon would also be destroyed, and we are not indifferent to that"* (does this mean that they have bases on the moon?).

The woman then asked, *"Do you have your own planet?" "Yes,"* the dwarf-like alien answered, *"We have two planets on the opposite side of the Sun."* (?) The witness then asked, *"Do you have females?"* The creature answered, *"We have them. But we do not have sex with our*

63

females." The witness then asked, *"And how do you obtain children (procreate)?"* She received a strange answer, *"They are programmed in our kind. Females have the girls, men the boys. We visit all the planets; we need warriors."* He did not elaborate on that.

He then added, that humans don't die, they just transform their outlook in a spiritual manner. The human body is similar to a caterpillar from which the butterfly hatches. He then added, *"And remember, all humans live according to a 'program' that was established in advance. Your kind lives as you wish, but in the Universe are only that would remain in accordance with the 'program.' You would judge yourself. We will accompany you. A planet is prepared for you in the "Fiery Rings." But not all of you will go there, only the people with the 'good program.' The people with the 'bad programs' will go to the "Quasar Windows." Your planet must pass through the fire, because it is polluted. Your scientists have created numerous harmful microbes and bacteria, which have been buried deep into the oceans and earth's crust in special containers, but these containers are rupturing, soon everything will leak out into the surface. The Universe would not tolerate that. The Earth will be like a decayed painful tooth on a human, and will be removed. So the Earth and your kind will pass through the fire. All the good will remain, and all the bad will vanish (or will be destroyed). The selection process is occurring now. Over the entire Earth, earthquakes will occur and the waters will inundate the earth."* That was the end of the alien gnome's speech.

Suddenly the alien's eyes began to pulsate, a clicking sound was heard and over the alien's head a fiery ring appeared. The creature began to be covered but the fiery ring and warned the witness not to touch the ring, because it could scorch her. The witness then realized that the entire conversation with the humanoid had been telepathically. When she glanced at her watch it showed the wrong time.

That same night a fiery globe was seen hovering over Tosno, over several nine story apartment buildings. In the morning the witness met a female neighbor who told her that she had seen a small globe-shaped object flying out of Ekaterina's home, the small globe then joined a larger globe and they both flew away, the neighbor's did not sleep the rest of the night fearing an explosion. E. M. Rumyantseva remains puzzled as to why she had been visited by aliens.

HC addendum.
Source: Witness story recorded by S. Shumkin in 'Tosnenskiy Vestnik,' a local newspaper from Tosno, February 5, 1992.   Type: E
Comments: A bizarre and convoluted tale that probably "lost" a bit in the translation. I am puzzled as to why an "alien" would visit an elderly pensioner in an obscure city and imparted all this puzzling information to her.

Location: Khoper Nature Reserve, Voronezh region, Russia.
Date: April 4, 1990.
Time: 2:15 a.m.

A stoker named Alexander Nazarov was carrying out slag and coal outside the furnace area and had gone out of the workshop. As he opened the gate he noticed a huge humanoid figure suddenly appear in front of him.

The strange entity was about three meters in height, and stood with its back to Nazarov. The humanoid had a "small head" that seemed to jut out of its shoulders, uncommonly long arms, very thin legs and wore a broad copper-color belt on its hips, which connected to its legs by a strip of the same color. The humanoid was dressed in a shiny light blue overall. A crescent-shaped symbol, which emanated red light, and resembling the half moon, was seen on the humanoid's left hand.

Nazarov was suddenly seized with fear and rushed back into his workshop garage and attempted to phone his boss V. Gavrilov, but was unable to make a successful phone connection, he then returned to the same location.

The humanoid was no longer around, but a white beam of light was shining over the forest, about fifteen meters from the witness, inclined at a 45 degree angle. Nazarov also noticed that the telegraph poles were also lit up in a bright white light and a strange gas-like cloud was now distinctly visible at the place where he had originally seen the humanoid. The "cloud" floated at about ten cm above the ground.

Alexander attempted to approach the location but his legs became paralyzed and he had the unpleasant sensation of being pierced by hundreds of "tiny needles" in his hands and stomach area.

That very same night there were reports of mysterious fires along the railway and inside the reserve area. Two electric pumps were apparently shut down by an unknown force. Electronic watches also reportedly malfunctioned in the area.

HC addendum.
Source: Olga Kostenko, local press, Vladimir Lebedyev TASS and Vladimir Yeletskih, 'Behind the Brink of the Miraculous,' Voronezh, 1992.   Type: D?

Location: Near Bishopville, South Carolina.
Date: April 16, 1990.
Time: Afternoon.

A woman was fishing at a local pond when she heard loud splattering in the water. She thought a long had rolled over when suddenly a gigantic humanoid jumped out of the water.

The terrified witness described it as huge, green, and scaly. It seemed to skim over the water. The witness ran from the area.

HC addendum.
Source: Mark Chorvinsky, Fate, August, 1990.   Type: E

* * * * * * *

Location: Troitskaya, Krasnodar region, Russia.
Date: April 19, 1990.
Time: Night.

Victor Molchanov noticed the landing of a strange object close to his yard on the outskirts of the village. Next, he was confronted outdoors by several tall aliens who invited him to visit their planet (apparently some kind of mental or psychic influence was used on the witness by the aliens). The witness returned briefly to the house and told his wife about the aliens. She brushed him off without taking him seriously. He then went back outside and entered the landed UFO.

The aliens were very tall, 3 or 3.5 meters high, their skin was grayish, their eyes were big, slanted, cat-like and dark, covered by black lenses (like contact lenses). They had narrow bodies, sharply cut light hair (some, maybe females, had long hair). The hands had three fingers with reddish webbing; they also had long arms that hung down below their knees. According to Molchanov the object was globe shaped. It's crew consisting of six aliens, including his alien guide.

He entered via a door that opened up like a "water-melon" and up a short ladder. He was then made to sit on a high armchair. As the craft moved away, Molchanov was able to see through an opening, his house, then the village, and soon the whole planet earth, apparently from space. He did not sense any acceleration whatsoever.

At one point, bright sunlight entered the craft and he was told by the alien not to look since he could be blinded. The alien spoke about different planets that Molchanov had never heard of and was told of a coming warming trend to the earth starting in 2002-2005, which will cause natural calamities. The aliens communicated among themselves by using mental telepathy and exchanging glances.

Soon they landed on their planet and Molchanov noticed that the sky was pink in color and the air was extremely fresh, clear, aromatic and balmy. The aliens told him that the earth had once eternal spring in the ancient past. He noticed other craft around, some cigar shaped, others oblong and oval shaped.

The dwellings had some kind of golden crux-like device on top. The flowers were remotely similar to terrestrial peonies. Next two robotic creatures (metallic ones and cold to the touch) entered the open craft's door. These "robots" had square heads, two hooks on the hands, instead of fingers, they performed different tasks on the craft, pressing some buttons and bringing in some boxes.

Before being returned to earth, the witness was told by the aliens that they were going to return to visit him on April 19, 2007. He was also told that the planet he had visited was in the Orion constellation, near the belt of Orion. According to additional research by Anfalov and Larissa Chora these aliens are from the planet "URU," most likely located near the double star Hipparcos 25240 in the Orion constellation, 189 light years distant.

HC addendum.
Source: Boris A. Skuin & Anton Anfalov & Alexey K. Priyma.
Type: G
Comments: Molchanov was told of a "coming warming trend of the Earth starting in 2002-2005, which will cause natural calamities. The temperature will rise 15 degrees Centigrade and approximately one third of humanity will die because of drought and floods, especially in the northern regions.

Location: Near Patterson, New York.
Date: April 23, 1990.
Time: 10:00 p.m.

The witness, a thirty year old man computer programmer named Sam, was driving home on Route 164 in Patterson from a friend's house in Fishkill. This particular road is very dark at night, as there are no street lights and very few homes. As Sam drove along the dark, winding road, he began to feel uneasy, like something bad was about to happen. He slowed down and looked into the woods on both sides of the road, expecting a deer or some other animal to dart out in front of him. Sam often got feelings like this in the past, and on more than one occasion, he would listen to this inner voice and take the appropriate action, only to nearly miss what could have been an injurious accident or otherwise unpleasant encounter.

On this night, Sam noticed a solid glowing object on his left, just above the tree line. The object was pulsating, and was yellow-red in color. The lights seemed too low to be a plane, and appeared to be several hundred yards away. The pine trees along the road partially obstructed his view, so he continued to drive, but slowly. He came up a clearing and stopped his car and noticed that the object had gotten much closer to him. As he watched, the object moved directly over his car. Sam rolled down his car window and watched the object for about a minute or so.

He decided he wanted to get a better look, and stopped the car and got out. He sat on the hood and watched this object, which he described as about the same size as a "minivan" and about a hundred feet above his head. The object changed in shape from an oval to a perfect circle. Sam reported feeling heat coming from the object as well. He was surprised to see five small figures gathering around the edges of the light as if they were looking at him. He got the impression that this object was some type of window, and although he saw only silhouettes, he was certain they looked humanoid in shape. The object dipped lower and seemed to grow in size. Eventually, it became so large and low that it blocked all of Sam's view of the sky. The object then began to move very slowly, and Sam was amazed that something of that size could move so slowly and be as silent. Sam's amazement gave him the sense that the object "was not part of our universe and was peering in from another dimension."

Then something strange took place, the next thing Sam remembered was driving down the road, the object completely gone. He did not remember getting back into the car, seeing the object completely pass over, or finding the road again.

When Sam finally arrived home, he discovered it much later than he had thought. He estimates the entire sighting was under ten minutes, yet the trip home took him three hours. He had a difficult time sleeping that night and felt as if something was watching him from the dark corners of

68

his bedroom. For the next week, he woke up in the middle of the night feeling very confused, in a cold sweat, his heart pounding.

HC addendum.
Source: Rosemary Ellen Guiley & Phillip J. Imbrogno, 'The Vengeful Djinn,' pp. 155-157.   Type: G?

*   *   *   *   *   *   *

Location: Krasnodar, Russia.
Date: April 30, 1990.
Time: Early morning.

An elderly pensioner named M was working in the vegetable garden in his plot of land near the airport, when he suddenly noticed what appeared to be clouds or fog forming above the nearby potato field without any visible source. A globe-shaped object about 4-5 meters in diameter then floated out of the mist. The amazed witness saw three humanoids exit the object, two males of average height and a "miniature" woman no higher than 1.3m in height. *"Come here dear,"* said the woman in a pure Russian dialect. Obeying the command, the stunned witness stepped forward.

The aliens then led him into the globe. Everything inside was of a yellow-orange color, numerous screens were visible along the perimeter of the cabin. The woman then asked the witness about how his life was like and what did he do on a daily basis. The witness spoke in a murmur while the alien trio silently listened to him. When he finally stopped the alien woman asked, *"Would you like to go with us and learn about life on another planet? We invite you as our guest."* The witness refused the invitation. The alien woman then bade goodbye, but the before they left the witness asked them to give him something as proof of their visit. He added that he would like to have confirmation on his hands. *"On your hands?"* Smiled the alien woman. *"Yes on my hands,"* answered the witness. The only woman then commanded, "Give me your hand," she grabbed the witness palm and he lost consciousness.

Later when he woke up, he found himself laying on the ground in his garden. The glob-shaped object that had hovered above the potato field had vanished. The witness then felt a strong pain in his hand. He looked and saw a half-moon (crescent) shaped mark on the back of his palm, similar to a mark made by a hot branding iron.

HC addendum.
Source: Galena Sobolevskaya and Alexey K. Priyma and Alexey K. Priyma, XX Century, Chronicles of the Unexplained, Moscow, 1999. Type: G

Location: Pesaro, Italy.
Date: April 30, 1990.
Time: 10:30 p.m.

An anonymous witness watched a luminous object shaped like a helicopter cabin descend diagonally from the sky and land on the road ahead of him. It was about five meters in diameter. A man-like figure exited the craft and approached the witness and then spoke to him in perfect Italian. He wore a shiny transparent coverall.

He spoke with the startled witness for about thirty minutes touching on different subjects, including humanity's negative influence on earth, and the existence of a supreme being.

Soon he walked back into the craft, which rose up, again diagonally and disappeared into the distance.

HC addendum.
Source: Archivio SUF, Tambellini.   Type: B

* * * * * * *

Location: Petrovskoye, Paninskiy area, Voronezh region, Russia.
Date: April 30, 1990.
Time: 1:30 a.m.

A local resident named Sergey Ovsyannikov had arrived at the Babay pond near the above village in order to do some fishing. However there were no fish yet, so he just sat down and waited. At 10:00 p.m. he saw five dots of light moving over him, and one appeared straight over his head and increased in size.

Just after 1:30 a.m. feeling very cold, the witness decided to walk to the nearby hamlet of Pereleshino in order to spend the night there. Near the dam he saw a lighted disk on the opposite side of the pond, beyond a narrow strip of forest. Several humanoid shaped figures, which seemed to emit light, were near the disk. Sergey's curiosity was strong so he approached the area and saw two objects hovering over the ground.

Everything was lit up around the objects, like daylight. The luminous entities were moving over the fields, not touching the ground, floating low over the ground. The figures seemed slender; approximately three meters in height, their heads, bodies, hands and legs were distinctly lighted. In total there were six to eight humanoids.

The witness then began to shiver as he saw three more similar entities to the left of him. Immediately he ran back to the pond and began inflating his rubber boat in order to leave the area quickly. He then hid behind some trees in a cane field.

Later he saw both luminous UFOs moving over the forest and then zoomed up into the sky and disappeared.

HC addendum.
Source: Vladimir Lebedyev, TASS, and Vladimir Yeletskih, 'Behind the brink of the miraculous,' Voronezh, 1992.   Type: C

* * * * * * *

Location: Las Vegas, Nevada.
Date: May, 1990.
Time: 4:00 a.m.

The witness was on his way back home to California and stopped off at the Tropicana Casino in Las Vegas and played black jack into the night. He went to the restroom and on his way back to the tables he stopped and watched a peculiar individual walking up the stairs. The person had a hat and sunglasses on, yet something wasn't right with the way he was walking or climbing the stairs. It looked like he was stuck in mud, his knees sort of came out to the side as he tried raising his feet to take the next step.

The witness noticed also that there were about three more that looked just like him at the top of the stairs, some taller. They were all skinny, tall and had whitish hair that seemed to shimmer as if light was bouncing off it, the witness had never seen hair like that before. His immediate reaction was "what a freak" he thought to himself.

Suddenly the one on the stairs stopped, turned, looking at the witness, the others at the top were looking down at him and at the witness who felt guilty for staring and decided to get back to his table.

HC addendum.
Source: Brian Vike new reports.   Type: E
Comments: After reading about Charles Hall, the witness made a connection between this bizarre group and the "tall whites" that Hall talked about. The witness went on to encounter several UFO's around Cactus Springs, Nevada.

Location: Baku, Azerbaijan.
Date: May, 1990.
Time: Night.

A young man named Eldar, from the village of Nachichevan, a student at the Azerbaijan Polytechnic Institute, was on his way to his aunt's house after having visited some friends. At the time the city of Baku was occupied by Soviet military troops as a result of riots and conflicts between Azerbaijani and Armenians and it was after curfew hours, everyone was locked in their homes.

Walking next to the old universal department store, Eldar noticed a faint light shining from the basement area. He suddenly noticed movement inside the basement and saw someone's head appear and call out, *"Hey boy, help me get out of here!"* the stranger spoke to Eldar in pure Azerbaijani language. When Eldar approached the stranger he noticed that the man was unusual in appearance, and appeared unnaturally "aged." The stranger was holding a strange flashlight in one hand and was desperately trying to get out of the basement. From outside the basement, a large black suitcase (like a diplomatic pouch) was visible on the ground nearby. Eldar stretched his hands and helped the "aged man" crawl out of the basement, and closed the window.

At this point Eldar realized that the man was holding a strange globe-shaped device which emanated light, which penetrated through the man's hand, lighting up his tendons, veins and muscles. The witness became numb with fear after seeing that, and almost decided to run away to his nearby home. But the elderly stranger asked Eldar to accompany him across the underground crossing located under the boulevard.

Eldar's feeling of fear increased as the stranger appeared to read his thoughts and began asking numerous questions. The stranger spoke in very pure Azerbaijani, too pure in nature sounding like the literature variant, which increased the boy's unease and suspicion. The stranger was about 180cm in height, with a normal size head and dressed in quite common clothing.

Suddenly he said unexpectedly, *"Son, come with me, you will see things you have never seen before."* With those words the strange man took a small oblong shaped device from the black "suitcase," a device which nowadays would have resembled a portable "pocket" computer. He then said to the astounded Eldar, *"If I press these two buttons, we will appear in my world, and you will not regret it. Think about my proposition. It can change your life completely."*

Confused thoughts quickly began circulating in Eldar's head and then he glanced at the computer like device that the stranger was holding and at the opened suitcase, which inside he could see a number of tubes and unknown instruments. As the stranger stared coldly at him, Eldar decided to end the episode and without saying a word he took off in a

72

sprint towards his aunt's house located only several meters away. But once he arrived at the home a suddenly sense of curiosity made him return, despite the sense of fear and worry present with him, but he somehow overcame that.

However, once back at the underground crossing the stranger had completely vanished. Back home Eldar was unable to sleep for a long time (the witness was to have a further contact with the same entity in May 1992).

HC addendum.
Source: Zaur Ismail-zade, Baku in 'Fourth Dimension and NLO' newspaper of the Yaroslavl UFO Research group #3, 1994.   Type: E

* * * * * * *

Location: Chernobayevka, Kharkov region, Ukraine.
Date: May 4, 1990.
Time: Evening.

A local tractor operator, Vladimir, was reportedly abducted onboard a UFO. After finishing his work he laid down on the grass in the forest for a respite. Soon he saw a UFO land about 50 meters from his location and several humanoid entities (not described) exited the object and walked towards the witness, the humanoids then dragged Vladimir into the object.

Next the memory of the witness was partly erased; he remembered only partial details of his abduction, such as mountains, huge green forests and what was apparently, a UFO base (possibly on another planet). He was returned one day later. No other information.

HC addendum.
Source: Vladimir S. Mantulin, Kharkov Anomalous Phenomena Research Group, Ukraine.   Type: G

Location: Sungla, Saaremaa Island, Estonia.
Date: May 14, 1990.
Time: 11:45 p.m.

Local resident Mrs. Vinbe Hari was at home when suddenly the door of her house opened. However she did not pay much attention to it, expecting her husband to return from the fields. Her 15-year old son Unar was already asleep. The witness turned around and was stunned to see a very tall man, completely unfamiliar to her and immediately after that three more similar appearing men entered her house directly through the wall. The strangers were more than two meters in height.

The alien that she first saw then asked her in perfect Estonian, *"Where is your husband?"* Regaining her composure the woman answered that he was at work. *"Let's go with us,"* continued the stranger, *"You will see how we live and what places we visit. We will show you our planet."* Confused, the witness said that she was only wearing her nightgown and that she was supposed to milk the cattle in the morning. But her alien guest insisted, *"We will return you in the morning."* And noticing that the witness had then walked to her bedroom to dress, the humanoid said, *"You won't be able to move out of this room."* The stunned woman attempted to walk into her bedroom but an invisible obstacle hindered her. After several furtive attempts she looked at the alien who was smiling and said, *"You don't need to dress, you won't feel the cold. Don't be afraid, we will not harm you."* Becoming afraid she asked the aliens why they had chosen her, she was 51 years of age. She offered her son in her place telling the aliens that he was very smart. "No we don't want your son," answered the alien guest and approached the bed where Unar was sleeping, and then alien stretched his hand over the boy and this one seemed to go into a deeper sleep.

The stranger then spoke with the other humanoids in a strange metallic-sounding voice in a totally unknown non-terrestrial language.

74

Soon after that the other three humanoids walked out of the house, again through the walls at the same time the witness heard a deafening clapping noise. Afraid, the witness decided to run immediately to the other room, but again was unsuccessful. The alien stretched his hand towards her and she touched the hand, which felt very soft. Then both walked straight through the wall and the loud clapping sound was heard again.

The alien vehicle was located nearby and both levitated in the air towards it. The alien held her by the hands floating together. When the aliens took the woman inside the craft, she saw the three other humanoids sitting around in the cabin on soft chairs, in front of what appeared to be control panels. The door to the UFO closed and it then zoomed up, leaving Earth's atmosphere and entering deep space.

Finally after an undetermined length of time, the object landed on an unknown planet. There she was taken into a building or structure where she was interrogated by the aliens for about 1 ½ hours in the presence of five additional aliens. After the interrogation she was brought back to earth and to her home.

The aliens visited her exactly one month later and again took her onboard the alien craft where possibly genetic experiments or "manipulations" were conducted on her. Despite the persistent attempts of researchers to obtain additional information, Vinbe Hari refused to divulge all the details, she remained evasive and silent.

It was evident that something more profound had occurred to the witness onboard the alien spacecraft.

HC addendum.
Source: Hans Hansovich Raucik, All-Union Ufological Conference, October, 1991.
K. Vitalyev, UFONIKS "Fourth Dimension and the UFO" Newspaper of the Yaroslavl UFO Center, #1, 1998.   Type: G

* * * * * * *

Location: Skalitsa, Bourgas Province, Bulgaria.
Date: May 19, 1990.
Time: Night.

Three women, aged 45 were walking along a street when they caught sight of three dark silhouettes standing about four meters in front of them. The creatures, which appeared to be made out of a thick black substance, walked quickly away from the women and disappeared into the moonless darkness.

After a while a pulsating spherical object, spinning counter clockwise, popped up in front of the villagers who quickly ran away from the area without looking back.

HC addendum.
Source: Miroslav Minchev, Bulgaria.   Type: C?

* * * * * * *

Location: Sharkhinau, Gissar Region, Tajikistan.
Date: May 23, 1990.
Time: 11:00 a.m.

A girl named Dina Shakirova had arrived home from school when it suddenly became very hot and she experienced a terrific headache. She approached the window and something suddenly blinded her. She managed to open the eyes slightly and saw a luminous sphere hovering outside the window. The sphere was about the size of the living room. A hatchway opened and he saw light inside the sphere. Sitting with their backs to her were two robot-like figures wearing metallic clothing.

Next to them sat a woman wearing a black & white dress that stared at the witness. She had "unpleasant" facial features. There was some type of instrument apparently attached to her head. The woman seemed to speak as the witness heard a clicking noise and then a mechanical voice that told her that she must go with them. Afraid, she refused the invitation.

The aliens then made a strange request, they asked the witness to bring them water. But then she suddenly lost consciousness. When she came to, she felt pain in her right foot. She was then taken to the local hospital where her blood pressure was measured at 140 over 90. Her hands were very cold and her pupils seemingly dilated. On her right foot an orange burn mark was found, shaped like the rays of the sun and a humanoid figure.

HC addendum.
Source: X-Libri UFO, Russia, Vadim Orlov 'Anomaliya,' newspaper, St Petersburg #27-28.   Type: A or G?

Location: Obilnoye, Tselinskiy area, Rostov region, Russia.
Date: May 28, 1990.
Time: 9:30 p.m.

Tractor operator Vladimir Prokofiev, a local resident, was out in the fields cutting grass to take it to his property, when he suddenly felt his body getting heavy, like being filled with lead, his hands and legs were growing numb. Afraid he looked around and was stunned to see three human-like figures standing at about ten meters from him.

Visible under the moonlight, they were tall, over two meters; the one standing in the center of the trio was obviously a woman. The woman was probably their leader and all three were dressed in shiny, tight-fitting gray overalls without seams. Moments later Vladimir heard the woman talking in a bizarre "mechanical" voice resembling that of a robot;

"Calm down," she said. *"We want to invite you to travel with us to our planet. The trip will not take more than 15 minutes and then we will return you back to Earth."* After hearing such an unbelievable proposition, the witness became confused, not knowing what to say. Prokofiev then bluntly asked, *"How would you return to Earth?"* *"Here is our craft,"* responded the alien woman who at the same time turned around, the witness also turned around and saw a landed disc-shaped craft, encircled by a large metallic flange, emitting light and standing near the edge of the forest. It had a flashing rotating light on top, similar to those of a police vehicle. The light emitted yellow, then red, and then blue on the stepped flat terrain. *"So, do you agree?"* asked the alien woman in flat emotionless monotone. The witness answered, *"No, I feel good here and besides I have four kids which I have to raise. Do I have the right to risk my life? What if something happened during to space flight which would cause me never to return to my home?"* The alien woman became silent, as if thinking his words over.

Then she said, *"You have no reason to be afraid, this will be completely safe for you. However you have time to think over our proposition. A catastrophe will soon be upon the Earth. We can save you from it. Return to this place. Your presence here would mean that you have agreed to go with us. Do we have a deal? We will return here in one month. Please don't worry but now we must move you to another location. Have you been over there?"* With these words the woman pointed her hand to the nearby hamlet of Revvoensovet. Prokofiev answered, *"I have recently visited that hamlet during a business trip."* The woman then said, *"So in this case no need for us to go in that direction. And there to the left, when was the last time you went in that direction?"* *"Very long ago, about ten or twelve years ago,"* said Prokofiev. After hearing his answer, the alien woman smiled slightly and said, *"Very well. You will fly there; sit comfortably on your machine."*

Obeying her request, Vladimir sat on his three-wheeled scooter, sidecar. He then attempted to start the engine, but it didn't work. Watching him the alien woman told him, *"Don't bother to start the engine it is useless. The engine would start on its own accord only after three hours after we deliver you to your destination."* At this moment the alien craft with a multicolored flashing light on top illuminated the witness in a bright powerful beam of light, surprised Prokofiev closed his eyes.

Seconds later a powerful force lifted his scooter into the air and began flying him to the location previously mentioned. The beam of light had by now died out but the witness still flew through the air just like having a pair of wings. The stunned Vladimir felt the air whistling in his ears, he was now terrified, seeing forests, gullies, and dirt roads flashing beneath him. The scooter was flying at about twenty meters above the ground. Vladimir held on to the handlebars while his heart raced. He was almost ready to jump as complete horror had by now seized him. After about 10minutes the scooter suddenly inclined to one side and began to sharply descend. Soon it landed smoothly and after touching the earth it rolled for several meters on the ground, just like an airplane. Prokofiev was numb and looking around realized that he was at a location not familiar to him. By instinct he glanced at the speedometer and it was the same before the amazing ride, so was the fuel level. Vladimir attempted to start the engine but soon remembered the alien woman's word. So Vladimir sat on the ground and waited, thinking about what had occurred. He was finally able to start the engine (exactly after three hours) and raced home.

In the morning a co-worker at his job told him that others in the village had seen a UFO with three flashing colored lights over the area. Prokofiev interrupted him and told his amazed co-worker what he had experienced the day before. His story caused a sensation in the village. Soon a crowd of people rushed to the location where Prokofiev had landed on with his scooter, searching for any suspicious traces. They found peculiar tire traces which indicated seemed to indicate that they had started suddenly out of nowhere as if landing from the sky, which seemed to confirm Prokofiev's tale.

Indeed on June 28, remembering what the alien woman had told him about returning for him, Prokofiev went to bed feeling a bit nervous. After falling asleep a mysterious force aroused him from bed, almost pushing him off. Afraid he walked to the threshold and stared at the sky. There he saw the UFO which looked like a very elongated ellipse and was flying towards the northwest and continuously changed colors almost through the whole range of the spectrum. According to Prokofiev he then heard a voice directly inside his head, saying, *"We can't enter in contact with you. There are too many people around you."* After that the UFO vanished in the distance.

That same night resident from the nearby village of Olshanka reported seeing a UFO circling over the area. Prokofiev remained convinced that the aliens were intent on kidnapping him but were unable to carry out their plan because there were too many other people around.

HC Addendum.
Source: Alexey K. Priyma, 'The 20th Century Chronicles of the Unexplained,' Moscow, 1998.   Type: C

* * * * * * *

Location: Kemerovo, West Siberia, Russia.
Date: May 28, 1990.
Time: Various.

Reportedly, Contactee A.I. Ananyev, entered into telepathic communication with an alien civilization. He heard a voice in his head that told him that they have specially selected him for the contact and data transmission because his "brain frequencies" and other parameters are what they needed for such contacts.

The aliens informed him that they were from the planet "OMA" in the constellation of Libra. As they related to him, their planet is five times older than the Earth, and is quite cold and getting colder. Life on their planet had appeared when it was still warm. Now the cold planet "has difficult horizontal multi-level streams of mass," yet the planet has biological life (probably now dwelling in underground cities and complexes).

The aliens there can easily enter into the so-called "information field" and communicate through mental impulses or telepathy. They also informed him that they are connected with Earth for scientific research purposes and can easily travel between various star systems many light years distant. The aliens also confessed to A.I. Ananyev that they "recruit" and take some people, (humans) from Earth to their planet (apparently to work for them) as well as residents of other planets in our part of the galaxy.

Reportedly the civilization on Planet OMA has connections with numerous extraterrestrial civilizations. A.I. Ananyev had not only telepathic, but also "out of body" astral contacts with this civilization. No other information.

HC addendum.
Source: Pavel Khailov, Bezhetsk, Tver region, Russia.   Type: F

79

Location: Near Zagorsk, Moscow region, Russia.
Date: May 29, 1990.
Time: 2:00 a.m.

Soldier Anatoly I, stationed at an undisclosed military installation, was relaxing on his bunk, listening to his recorder, when suddenly two red colored humanoids appeared at his bedside. The strange intruders were only one meter in height, with huge dragonfly like eyes. The humanoids examined the tape recorder, lifted it and overturned it. Then one of them looked at Anatoly and he seemed to lose consciousness.

He regained consciousness at daybreak in a glade in the woods close to the barracks. He was suffering from an unaccountable fear. He was found by other soldiers and quickly taken to infirmary, there he was tested for drugs and other narcotics and was found to be clean.

HC addendum.
Source: Victor Sytenkov, UFO Navigator Digest #57.　　Type: E or G?

* * * * * * *

Location: Moscow region, Russia.
Date: Summer, 1990.
Time: Daytime.

Vyacheslav X. a research member of a technical department of a local Military Industrial Enterprise was spending the weekend at a resort complex located several dozen kilometers from the city, enjoying nature and the calmness. On this day he was resting in a clearing near the forest on the banks of a small river. As he sat on the ground he was suddenly confronted by several humanoid figures standing in the clearing. They were dressed in metallic silver like suits, tight fitting to their bodies; all the humanoids had slender proportional figures, with legs and arms, and all about 1.5-1.8 meters in height. They wore helmets joined with the suits without any visible seams. Their faces were hidden behind darkened visors. One of the humanoids then entered into telepathic communication with the witness, who heard the alien's voice straight inside his head, while the others stood and observed the scene. They were positioned in a semicircle.

After a short conversation, the humanoid showed the witness what was apparently weaponry, they had narrow pipe-like devices in their hands, and one alien projected one end of the device to the ground and in a moment the grass caught on fire and burned out, there was no visible beam or laser from the device. Despite the obvious alien behavior and appearance of the intruders, Vyacheslav at first thought that he was part of some kind of "experiment" being conducted on him by the Soviet

80

Military Industrial Complex that were testing some type of ultra-modern military technology, connected to mind control and light beam or heat weaponry, and he was just a guinea pig chosen for the test. However the aliens told him that he had been chosen by them for this contact and promised that he would soon go in a journey with them. Being seized with curiosity, he agreed to go, he felt no fear. The next moment he lost consciousness. After that he remembers flying over the surface of a strange rocky desert, covered with rocks, ravines and deep canyons; he could see everything on the screen or a window.

They soon landed and a door opened and they left the craft. The aliens soon drew his attention to several flying insects in the air and asked the witness, *"Do you have such insects in your world?"* this made him realized that he was indeed in contact with extraterrestrial entities and he was in their world. Stunned he looked around his environs and saw unearthly vegetation, trees which remotely resembled palms but different, small bushes with leafs like that of a ficus. They soon approached some kind of lake. Vyacheslav saw that the water was of an unearthly color, very blue, an extremely deep azure. The aliens allowed Vyacheslav to examine his surroundings; he took his shoes off and put one leg into the water, probing the water by touch. He did not see anyone swimming in the lake. The place was very different from middle Russia; it was more tropical with a very high humidity. The moment he had walked outside the spacecraft he had been covered with sweat, his face turned red in color.

The next moment the aliens took off their helmets and all the humanoids were indeed very beautiful females, about 1.5 meters in height, with light brown hair, and very correct features. All the female humanoids emanated heat (possibly indicating a heightened biofield or biological energy). All the alien females looked extremely attractive, amazingly beautiful; he had never seen such beauty on Earth. He felt their extreme unearthly attractiveness irradiating a hot energy from their bodies. Apparently they were able to function very well in such a hot environment. The witness was puzzled, not understanding why the aliens had exactly chosen him for the contact and visitation to their planet. He was indeed told that very few earthlings are chose for such a unique contact. Later the witness was returned back to Earth. He couldn't remember the return flight a well, and returned to his senses lying on the same meadow that he had been taken from.

HC addendum.
Source: 'UFOs Chronicles of Secret Cases,' TV Program aired by
Ren-TV channel, Moscow, 2004.   Type: G

Location: Agryzskiy area, Tatarstan, Russia.
Date: Summer, 1990.
Time: Evening.

Several members of the UFO research group "Okno" (Window) had arrived in the area from the city of Kazan and had camped out at about three km from the nearest village among a pine forest. As they were returning to their camp one evening several members of the expedition felt a strange influence emanating from an unknown source of energy.

Quite unexpectedly a strange humanoid creature appeared at the edge of a meadow in the pine forest. The entity was not very tall, probably about 1.5m in height, but very muscular and of strong build, with huge front extremities and unpleasant, clearly inhuman features on his face, which resembled that of a "fish." The entity emanated a faint light from its entire body.

Several of the UFO researchers approached to within five meters of the entity and at that same moment the body of the humanoid appeared to dim and darkened, like a dying electrical light. Then the group of Ufologists was seized by an immense feeling of horror and quickly walked away from the area.

While walking back to the campfire the men noticed that clouds in the evening sky began to assumed symmetrical straight line shapes, until they transformed to even arrow-like shapes, pointing in one direction. Later the men visited the location where they had seen the strange humanoid figure and found a broken pine tree.

HC addendum.
Source: Dina Kuntseva in: 'Mir Zazerkalya' (World beyond the Mirror) Newspaper.
Moscow, #22, October, 2005.   Type: E

* * * * * * *

Location: Erzovka, Volgograd region, Russia.
Date: Summer, 1990.
Time: 3:00 p.m.

55-year old Valeriy Vasilevich Krasnov, was returning from the city of Volgograd in his car. Tired, he had pulled over to the side of the road to obtain some rest and a meal. He was suddenly seized by a sense of fear. He felt like he was going to die of a heart attack, but suddenly a thought appeared in his head: *"No, this is not your heart. Don't be afraid, we will not harm you, only will ask you some questions and will answer your questions if you have any."*

The witness looked around and could not see anyone. *"Who are you and what do you want from me?" "Be calm, first of all. We are friends, and will not do you any harm."* Krasnov replied, *"So why are you not visible?" "If you relax and become ready for communication, we will appear now."*

Suddenly two figures started materializing, like a photograph being developed. It was an incredible sight. The outlines of the figures appeared, and then everything became clear and the entities became visible, a man and a woman. They were very much human like. Dressed in light silver overalls, with a wide white belt with strange devices hanging from them and multicolored blinking lights. Their faces and hands were bare and their skin was blindingly white. Their hair was gold and they had amazing eyes of an ultramarine color that radiated amazing light. Both were very tall about 1.9 to 2 meters in height and stood smiling at the witness.

The woman was stunningly beautiful and shapely. Both looked to be about 20-25 years old. Their eyes were slightly slanted, had a small nose, clearly visible mouth, but immovable, as well as their faces. They had very proportional figures with long thin fingers. When they moved they did so slowly and gradually. All communication was telepathic.

The aliens approached the witness and began asking mundane and private questions. It felt like a police interrogation and the witness felt uncomfortable. He felt as his brain was being scanned. After answering their questions, Krasnov was allowed to ask questions himself.

The aliens said that they hailed from the Canis Venatici constellation, more specifically from a planet called "TATS." They had been on earth for two years already and that their previous visit had been one hundred years ago and had lasted for about ten years. They traveled in a star ship shaped like a disc, with six crewmembers.

They also said that they traveled between dimensions. That is a very responsible and dangerous process that must be carefully controlled. They also said that every dimension has intelligent life and that there are some aggressive civilizations that are striving to conquer the Universe and that there were "backward" civilizations, like Earth. They said that they had a base on the moon and were concerned about constant monitoring by earthlings.

The ETs were governed by what they called a "council." They did not conduct negative experiments over people (humans), did not abduct humans by force that it was strictly forbidden by the "council." They did not recognize the human civilization because of its aggressive tendencies and behavior. They also said that humans were out of control of their "Council" and that it was now too late to do anything. This "Council" consisted of different civilizations that regulate many interstellar laws.

Suddenly the belts of both aliens began radiating a bluish light and they said: *"The time of contact is now over. We must return to our ship."*

They said that they would be back in August, 1990. Both figures then disappeared.

HC addendum.
Source: Gennadiy S Belimov, Anton Anfalov.
Comments: https://en.wikipedia.org/wiki/Canes_Venatici

* * * * * * *

Location: Near Salsk, Rostov region, Russia.
Date: Summer, 1990.
Time: Afternoon.

    16-year old Yuri Churikov accompanied by his mother Tatyana, were walking along a local ravine, when Yuri suddenly stopped and stared at a certain direction, Tatyana also looked and noticed what appeared to be a ball flying over the nearby reeds, resembling a soap bubble. The 'bubble' quickly approached, shimmering like a rainbow. Both stared in disbelief as the ball began to grow in size until it was a huge sphere. The color resembled that of a 'watermelon' with alternative dark green and light green bands.

    Mother and son both saw one of the 'slices' slowly move forward and move away from the 'watermelon' on its side. In the opening, a soft pink light streamed out. Suddenly some unknown force picked up Yuri and floated him in midair face up, slowly, head first the young man entered the hovering sphere through the opening. At the sight of this incredible spectacle, Tatyana's legs buckled and she fell unconscious on the ground.

    Meanwhile, inside the 'watermelon' Yuri found himself in a sort of hollow pink space. Incredibly, his fear was now completely gone, he felt very calm. He suddenly heard a voice that was somehow 'mechanical' in nature and sounded as if from all sides. The voice then asked the young man,

"How do you live?"

Yuri answered best he could, *"I am sixteen years old,"* confused.

"What is sixteen years?"

"That is the calculation of my life," answered Yuri.

"And what does 'years' mean?" asked the voice.

Yuri said, *"A year is one turn of the Earth around the sun."*

"Orbit around the sun?" asked the voice and then added, *"Draw it please as it happens."*

    And then in a pink space, a blue screen like square appeared. According to Yuri, no sooner had he thought something, as he knew he could not draw, this scheme suddenly appeared in the blue square in front of him. He immediately understood that everything he thought would appear on the screen, and he didn't have to draw anything. He

84

mentally pictured a variety of clarifying details and these all appeared on the blue screen.

Then the voice asked again, *"How do you live?"*

Yuri detailed a report on the peculiarities of Earth life in his mind. Mentioned, in particular was war.

"What is war?" followed immediately, a new question.

Yuri mentally described a country trying to conquer another. After a brief pause the voice said, *"Do you mind if we display now a 'map' of your life?"*

Hearing that, Yuri became nervous and asked, *"Will this hurt my health?"*

"No," was the response, *"We do it with only one purpose, to help you and all earthlings. We can change the map of your life by inserting different 'cassettes or tapes,' we do so only with good intentions."*

"Okay, I agree," answered Yuri.

As soon as Yuri spoke these words, before him appeared in a pink haze, a black dot. It quickly grew in size until it became a brown colored 'hat.' The helmet or hat floated in mid-air very close to Yuri who was able to see an emblem on it resembling a full-blown white rose. For a while the helmet hovered motionless in the air, and then it dropped on his head, covering Yuri's face with some type of transparent film.

Then from somewhere on his right, there appeared a light and within the light, he saw three humanoid figures, wearing green coveralls. They had two five-fingered hands and (incredibly) only one leg. This last detail Yuri insisted on categorically. Figures then perform a smooth motion, as if in a slow dance. Their faces were impossible to discern, since they were hidden behind mirrored reflective shields.

After a few seconds Yuri went to sleep. While asleep Yuri saw images of his life, on a sort of silver screen. He saw his life as an outsider looking in. Finally at the end of the last flashback, Yuri opened his eyes and the helmet floated away somewhere to his side. The voice then said, *"Thank you."*

Yuri was then floated out of the opening of the object and landed on the ground on his feet. Then in an instance the giant watermelon then transformed into a tiny rainbow ball, which promptly sped off into the heavens. Tatyana, who had been lying on the ground in a swoon, woke up, hearing her son calling her. The next day they reported the incident to a local newspaper.

HC addendum.
Source: Alexey Priyma, Russia.   Type: G

Location: Valle, Riba, Cantabria, Spain.
Date: Summer, 1990.
Time: Late evening.

Artura Abascal Otero was standing with her husband, Santiago Saiz, at the entrance to their home, when a very nervous neighbor yelled at them that he was watching something in a field next to their homes.

All three witnesses then saw a strange humanoid figure, about 1.5m in height, wearing a sort of blue robe and a "sparkling crown" around its head that floated just above the ground encased in a sort of luminous cloud. The humanoid had its back turned to them so they were not able to see its face, and quickly floated away disappearing behind some nearby trees.

HC addendum.
Source: http://alaluzdelasvelas.iespana.es/ovnisenespana/   Type: E

* * * * * * *

Location: Zolotoye, Leninskiy area, Crimea, Ukraine.
Date: Summer, 1990.
Time: Late evening.

After a UFO landed on the border of the village, close to a large military aerodrome and reservation at Bagerovo near the Sea of Azov, local residents encountered three short humanoids walking on the street near their houses.

The aliens were dwarf-like, about 1.2m in height, dressed in shiny coats of silver color, which covered their short bodies completely. One male witness was able to see the face of one of the aliens, which he described as having a sallow complexion, with green-brown-gray skin, flat protrusions in the place of noses, and slanted eyes. Their heads were most probably hairless but were covered in tight-fitting cowls. Frightened, the witnesses hid in their homes.

The aliens moved quickly away and vanished behind some houses. What attracted the aliens to the area was the apparent concentration of important locations and bases, such as the construction of nuclear and solar electric power plants in the nearby hamlet of Szhelkino (which were later halted due to public outcry). Also the huge Bagerovo airbase previously used for storage of nuclear bombs, which is now abandoned, the area apparently has some residual radioactive pollution, which also attracted the aliens.

HC addendum.
Source: Alexander Pismennyi, Anton Anfalov.   Type: D

86

Location: Remedios, Las Villas, Cuba.
Date: Summer, 1990.
Time: Night.

Anisia Arias stepped out into the patio area of her house, and noticed a small bright light flying high over the area. At first she thought it was a satellite, which they frequently saw in the area. The bright light was moving in a north-bound direction towards the Polar Star. She remained watching the light until it suddenly retreated and began descending at high speed, remaining hovering at about 500 meters from Anisia at about 100 meters from the ground. She could see the object better now and described it as a semi-oval disc-shaped craft, with a dome-shaped protrusion on top made of a material resembling aluminum, very bright. The craft was encircled in a bright halo of light.

According to Anisia it was 'a beautiful sight.' Suddenly without warning, the object flew towards the witness at an incredible speed, stopping only about five meters from her. She was now within the bright halo of light, which according to Anisia, resembled a bright fog. She could see something inside the dome but was unable to see any details. At this point she suddenly lost consciousness. Not knowing what had happened, Anisia became conscious now inside her home. She felt as if she had been 'dropped' from a height, her knees buckled but she was able to maintain her balance. She could see the light from the object shining outside her home and could hear a strong buzzing sound. She knew the object was hovering outside but she was very afraid.

Anisia then ran outside to the patio again, to see if her roof had caught on fire, but her legs felt very heavy and tingly, she also felt very exhausted. She was able to see the bright object as it ascended rapidly out of sight, leaving in the same direction it had come from. She remained standing on the patio and found it difficult to walk. Her mother kept asking her what had happened, but she was unable to answer her since she felt very tired. The next day, her eyes felt very sensitive to light and some trees that had been directly under the hovering object began to wither and die.

In May of 1997, Anisia was hypnotically regressed and was able to remember being transported onboard the hovering craft by several blond haired normal looking 'men' that were extremely thin, one of the aliens had a mustache. She described the interior of the craft as white and round on top. She was then made to sit on a white chair. She remembered that the men touched her skin and squeezed her cheeks. The entities later introduced several needle-like implements on her right arm.

HC addendum.
Source: Hugo Francos Parrado.   Type: G

Location: Playita de San Juanito, Tenerife, Canary Islands, Spain.
Date: June, 1990.
Time: Daytime.

A bicyclist named Carmelo, was cycling near some rocks on the beach when he suddenly spotted an entity coming out from behind the rocks, which he described as totally white in color almost shiny, it was tall and was walking sort of crouched over. It's very long arms almost touched the knees.

As the stunned witness watched, he was surprised to see two other identical humanoids come out from behind the rocks. He was watching from about 400 meters away but was convinced that the strange entities were not human. Concerned he pedaled quickly away. According to the witness, he later found out that others in the area have encountered similar entities.

HC addendum.
Source: http://www.angulo13.com/ovnicanarias.htm   Type: E
Comments: Translated by Albert S Rosales.

* * * * * * *

Location: Near Odessa, Ukraine.
Date: June 4, 1990.
Time: Evening.

Two young pioneers, Andrey A, and Maxim where at a summer camp near the Black Sea and where exploring the area near the water shore when they suddenly came upon a landed UFO, a hatchway opened and a figure jumped out to the ground.

The figure was about one meter in height wearing a tight-fitting silvery suit. On a thickset head it had only one large eye and had long dangling arms with four fingers. The figure moved about like a robot. On the object a slot-like door opened. From inside it something looked at the two witnesses who were now unable to move. Soon the short one-eyed figure returned to the object.

Immediately the craft became bright orange in color and took off, disappearing over sea into the distance. An interesting detail was noted, the children thought that they had only seen the UFO and alien for about five minutes, but when they returned to their camp, the teachers were concerned since apparently they had really been gone for more than an hour.

HC addendum.
Source: Yaroslavl UFO Study Group #12, 1992.   Type: B or G?

Location: Near Yelverton, Devon, England.
Date: June 12, 1990.
Time: 10:50 p.m.

A Devonport dockyard worker was driving along an unclassified road from Bere Alston towards the main A386 at Yelverton. The road was unlit and about a mile from the nearest buildings. As the witness approached the A386 from Crapstone (known locally as the Rock) he noticed a six-foot tall silver suited figure with a 'bucket' on his head, walking normally *"in a determined manner"* towards him. The figure took no notice of the car and the 'bucket' appeared to have no eyeholes or openings.

The witness, who was a former policeman, thought initially that the figure might be someone dressed for a fancy dress party. However, he was intrigued enough to turn his car around at the next junction, some thirty yards away, and drove back along the road for sixty yards, before turning right onto another unclassified road, leading towards Yelverton. He drove a further fifty yards without seeing the figure again. Wondering where the figure could have gone to, the witness turned his car around so he could resume his journey to work. As he did so he saw the silver-suited figure again, this time by a large natural outcrop of granite, from which the area got its name, the Rock.

The witness stopped the car and turned his spotlight on the figure. Despite the powerful beam of light, the figure appeared completely unperturbed. The witness sat in his car for several minutes watching the strange silver-suited figure *"acting in a definite manner."* After a while, the witness became afraid, he started his car and drove past the figure to get onto the main road. The witness drove straight to work and upon arrival, at 2315 hours, reported the incident to the Devonport M.O.D. Police. The M.O.D. Police contacted Plymouth police, who sent a patrol car to the Rock to investigate, nothing was seen and the patrol car reported back at 23:45 hours.

HC addendum.
Source: Bob Boyd, Plymouth Research Group also Mike Freebury in 'Killers on the Moor,' pp. 218-219.   Type: E

Location: Moscow region, Russia.
Date: June 20, 1990.
Time: 12:20 a.m.

43-year old Zinaida Gavrilova was late to her regular bus route that took her to the local military garrison where she was a resident. When she exited the monorail she realized that the last bus had departed 30 minutes before. So she decided to walk home alone on a straight narrow road that ran through a pine forest. At night this road was lighted by lanterns, set in two rows on both sides of the road. At about 12:20 a.m. she approached a 16meter long concrete bridge which was stretched over a small river in the forest. The bridge was also lighted by lanterns.

Suddenly she saw a strange column of smoke and when she walked closer to it the column darkened, became dense and transformed into a humanoid figure. The figure was that of a very tall woman in a black dress down to her ankles. Her height was more than 2.5 meters; she had a protruding forehead, huge slanted eyes, and blue in color lacking eyebrows or eyelashes. The color of her eyes was of a pure blue, shiny, like mother of pearl. Her face was pale, triangular in shape and sharply narrowed at the bottom, ending in a small pointy chin. Zinaida could not remember the nose or lips. On her head she wore a black oval-shaped helmet, and a black pelerine (cape) fell from her helmet to her shoulders and back from. She had very long arms. On her chest area the alien woman had a circle of light, resembling a flat bulb; the light emitted from this light did not illuminate its surroundings.

The alien woman began to speak in a strange feminine but "squeaky" voice. She asked Zinaida, *"Where are you going?"* Zinaida answered, naming the small military garrison where she lived. Then the alien woman said, *"Come with me. Come with me. Come with me."* Zinaida distinctly heard the phrase repeated three times. The woman turned her back and began walking away, Zinaida following her. At this point Zinaida blacked out and later returned to her senses sitting on a bench near the control box to the military garrison. She felt light headed, and her temples ached. Very slowly Zinaida rose and walked to the control post. Surprised to find the control post empty (it was supposed to be manned 24 hours daily) she walked past it and into her five story apartment complex belonging to the officer's staff. There her son waited for her and asked where have she been, both her son and her husband were getting ready to mount a search for her. Zinaida then looked at her watch and realized that it was already 1:30 a.m. Apparently 60 minutes had slipped away from her memory. Zinaida then looked into the mirror of her anteroom and was again surprised to find her hair neatly tied up in a soft bun behind her head; she could not remember who had done that. She briefly recalled the moment when she first saw the column of smoke and then the alien woman and lastly when the woman asked her to come with her. She became hysterical and screamed in horror.

The next day Gavrilova was in a catatonic state, she would fall asleep and then wake up minutes later. In the evening she telephone a female friend and told her, *"I met a witch!"* Happily this female friend was connected with Erast Demishev who was an old friend of the main investigator: Alexey Priyma. The latter arranged a hypnotic regression session in order to reconstruct the events of that night. Zinaida agreed to the session and asked for it to be done immediately.

It appeared, according to the results gleaned from the session that immediately after the alien woman had asked Zinaida to "come with me" Zinaida found herself inside the military stadium which was part of the military garrison. The distance from the stadium to the stone bridge was only about 1km. The football field was lit up by a bright white light.

Gavrilova could not explained where had the alien woman gone to, instead she could see a huge silver-colored globe or sphere, about 6-7 meters in diameter, slightly tapered on the bottom. From a hatch on the globe a ladder reached the ground. The ladder was angular consisting of links, zigzagged in shape. Near the globe the witness saw two very tall "men" in light gray tight-fitting overalls. The height of each entity was more than 2.5meters. One of them approached Zinaida, took her by the hand and led her to the globe. His touch was icy. Inside the globe the witness saw numerous round and rectangular shaped lights on the walls. When some of the entities touched Zinaida she felt a piercing cold, not painful, but very cold. Besides the tall humanoids, Zinaida saw a small humanoid sitting on an armchair inside the cabin. This other creature had a small body, thin legs and arms, and a large round head. Its eyes were shiny "mother of pearl" color. It did not move while it sat on the armchair. The two very tall humanoid males had broad shoulders, long arms and legs, and slanted eyes.

The humanoids began to tell her, *"You should come with us."* They didn't say anything else. Moments later one of the tall humanoids began to twirl Zinaida's hair into a tight bun on her back. He then sat her on a tall armchair. At this point Zinaida suffered a blackout.

Her next memory was of a tall alien man in the light gray coveralls taking her by her hand, like a child, and leading her outside of the sphere through the opened hatch. At this moment she saw "another world" before her: the sky there was slightly greenish. Later after analyzing her memoirs, obtained during the regression, Gavrilova concluded that she had visited an "artificial planet," or an artificially created world encased in a huge glassy "sky dome." Zinaida then saw a long street, on which the globe had landed. At the far end of the street she saw another sphere, of a much larger size than the sphere which had delivered her to this world.

The houses that stood along the street were white, low and long. On top of the roofs and in between the houses the witness saw white rods, a very large number of rods, different in size, some very high others short. The rods which were between the houses were taller than the ones on top of the houses, most of the rods were straight but a few were curved or spirals, everywhere there was white wet sand. At first Zinaida thought that she was walking alone in the street, but to be more exact, not "walking" in the literal meaning of the world, but floating. But soon she realized that one of the tall male aliens was holding her hand, and he was the one that was walking. The alien man emanated an icy "wave." He was dressed in gray slippery clothing. Like the tricot of the circus artists, tight fitting. She could not remember his nose and lips. But his eyes were large, with deep eye sockets. He had no eyebrows or eyelashes and his eyes were light "mother of pearl" color. No one else was in the street with them.

The alien man slowly walked on the deserted street from one sphere to the other and took Zinaida into the second sphere. While walking he spoke telepathically to Zinaida asking her, *"Would you like to say here? You will feel good. You can live here."* But she didn't agree and said, *"I don't want to live here. I have a family. I can't leave my husband and son forever. Take me back to the stadium!"* The alien man answered, *"Ok, we will take you back. But you must stay for a short time in this city. Somebody you are familiar with wants to see you."* Zinaida then asked, *"What is the name of this city?"* The humanoid answered, *"Kuili"* They didn't speak anymore after this. Inside the other sphere Gavrilova saw several long tables. In between the tables there were armchairs. A very bright light emanated from everywhere in the object. The walls were smooth and bare. Several tall alien women in tight fitting light gray suits were moving around the room. The humanoid then carefully placed Zinaida on the floor. Zinaida then seemed to "freeze" in place unable to move, a sickening, nauseating feeling of complete paralysis seized her entire body.

Then one of the alien females, without moving her lips, attempted to convince Zinaida to stay in the city of "Kuili" forever. *"You will feel very good in Kuili,"* she persisted. Translating her thoughts directly into Zinaida's brain she said, *"Why do you want to return. Why that desire? Stay with us!"* But Gavrilova categorically refused to cooperate. Then two of the females grabbed her like "a log" and placed her on one of the shiny white tables. On the place where Zinaida had a scar on her chest area, the aliens pressed a small rectangular shaped plate. A large blue screen then appeared near the table after emerging from somewhere below. On the screen a lighted pulsating dot immediately became visible. Then the alien female took her body from the table.

The tall alien man again grabbed her by her hands and took her out of the sphere. While leaving, the alien woman who had been trying to convince Zinaida to stay in Kuili forever said, *"If you like we will again come and get you and take you ourselves."* *"I agree to visit Kuili one*

92

more time," said Zinaida. *But you again would have to return me back to the stadium." "The next time you would not want to return to Earth. We will meet again for sure!"* said the alien woman. The aliens then took Zinaida back into the sphere and apparently returned to Earth.

Researcher Alexey Priyma, together with Zinaida and his colleagues Erast Demishev and Vitaliy Shishenko visited the place of the UFO landing and examined it. They used instruments to study the alleged place of contact. Indeed, a magnetic detector detected an anomalous strip there, where according to the witness the alien woman in black was standing. It was about five meters in length, staring about a meter from the stone bridge. At the stadium the researchers found the evident place of the UFO landing. It was a clearly defined round trace on the grass that was seven meters 18 cm in diameter.

HC addendum.
Source: Alexey K. Priyma 'XX Century, Chronicle of the Unexplained. From Prophecy to Prophecy, Moscow, 1998.   Type: G
Comments: One of the most vivid otherworldly journeys I have read.

* * * * * * *

Location: Carboneras, near Viator, Almeria, Spain.
Date: June 22, 1990.
Time: Between 2:00 a.m. & 6:00 a.m.

Four soldiers from the nearby military base of Alvarez de Sotomayor were standing guard duty close to the local power plant. It was the night of the full moon with a beautiful view of the beach area. At one point one of the men noticed that the moon had changed position and was now brighter, now appearing as a large bright white light hovering just above the shores of the beach. One of the men suggested that it could be a reflection from an aircraft, and two of the men decided to continue their round which took them around the power plant, as they turned the corner a large bright glow surprised them, and it was originating from the beach area.

As they watched in horror, the bright light vanished and now they could see two very tall 'individuals,' taller than any normal humans standing within the waters, just by the shore. The figures were totally static, and appeared to be staring intently towards the power plant at Carboneras.

The soldiers attempted to approach the strangers but were soon overcome with fear as they noticed that the two figures appeared to be hovering and balancing themselves just above the ground.

As they ran away they noticed another bright glow behind them, looking back they noticed that the two strange figures had now disappeared.

HC addendum.
Source: Alberto Cerezuela, La Cara Oculta de Almeria.   Type: C?
Comments: Translated by Albert S. Rosales.

* * * * * * *

Location: Zvarykino, Alekseevskiy area, Belgorod region, Russia.
Date: July 6, 1990.
Time: 5:00 p.m.

An elderly local woman, Anna Dmitrievna Yerygina was taking her goats to pasture at a new location and was walking them on a lonely road when suddenly a strange woman stepped from somewhere to the right of the road. She seemed to be about fifty years of age, but also somewhat youthful in appearance. She was dressed in a light-gray loose fitting overall that covered her all the way down to her heels, she had long sleeves, and she wore something on her head resembling a cap that covered the top of her head completely. The strange woman was thin, tall, with normal human facial features. She approached Anna and greeted her, Anna responded in kind and the strange woman than asked her if her goat milk was tasty. She said yes, but frankly liked cow milk much better.

The stranger was silent for a moment and then invited Anna to go with her, to a location. She added that the trip would only take two to

94

three hours, and that she would return back safely. Hearing the strange proposition, Anna was frightened and at first refused, thinking about her family and her sick husband, she also worried about the goats, since they could not be left alone. The strange woman then put her hand on Anna's shoulder and a strange calm came over her. *"Don't be afraid"* said the woman. She told Anna that the goats will be fine and would remain on the track.

Anna then silently followed the stranger. She had a strange feeling that the woman wanted to take her "forever" not for a short trip, like she had stated. She also wonder why they "needed" her, together with the strange woman, Anna approached an object, oval in shape that had suddenly appeared on the meadow. It was not there before; it had suddenly materialized there.

A man stood near the object and invited Anna onboard. A door opened on the object, resembling two leaf folds. Anna entered the object and saw several seats inside. She sat on one of them, and the alien woman on the other. She could now hear a humming sound and Anna saw the man sitting on what appeared to be a control console. It was neither dark nor light inside, but some kind of middle state. The walls were matte, apparently made out of non-transparent glass.

Her next memory was of appearing in a strange location, and understood right away that it was a foreign world. Anna accompanied by the woman in loose fitting overalls remembered walking on something "soft." Soon she found herself fin a room with several other people inside. One of them stood by the wall, like a guard, and the others sat around a large oval-shaped table. Someone had dressed Anna in the same type of loose fitting coverall that the woman wore. She then heard a loud male voice, *"Do you feel good here?"* She agreed, and said that it was like "heaven." She felt very cheerful and her mood was excellent (mind control?).

One of the men sitting on the oval table then said, *"How is your life on Earth?"* Anna answered that it wasn't bad, but had not much joy. One of the aliens suddenly interrupted her and told her that they knew everything about her and told her not to be afraid, that many humans had visited them.

Then she was treated to something resembling bread on a porcelain plate and a drinking bowl with a woodened spoon protruding from it. Anna tasted the dish twice and drank the pink-colored liquid. It was all very tasty. She later recalled that the aliens emanated "spiritual warmth." The woman accompanied her everywhere. Except for the woman, no one else in the room approached her. After she ate, her memory became blank and she found herself standing in the same meadow where she had been originally taken from. The woman in the white loose fitting overall stood nearby smiling. She told Anna that she wishes her well and that they would meet again.

Several days later Anna went outdoors to her yard as her husband stood on the porch smoking. Suddenly he heard his wife's voice speaking to somebody, but he could not hear the other voice. According to Anna, she suddenly heard from behind her *"So we meet again."* She turned around and saw the same strange woman, however this time wearing a tight-fitting overall and a helmet on her head. She invited Anna to come in a journey with her, adding that this time it would take three days. She was told that she had been to their planet on the previous encounter. The woman reiterated her invitation. However, Anna refused the invitation. At this point the alien woman smiled and asked for a glass of water. While Anna was pouring the water in the mug, the strange woman disappeared in plain sight.

HC addendum.
Source: 'Zarya' Local Newspaper, 'Leninskaya Smena' and Alexey K. Pryma, XX Century: Chronicles of the Unexplained, 1999.   Type: G

* * * * * * *

Location: Nar Brzozka, Lubusz, Poland.
Date: July 8 or 9, 1990.
Time: 4:00 p.m.

The witness, Richard P. was on his way to Germany when he decided to rest after an exhausting several hours trip. He stopped the car on the side of the road near a bridge under which flowed the River Bobr. The sun was in the east and a light breeze was blowing and on the ground there was a visible mist. Richard got out of the car to stretch his legs and get some fresh air and then he walked into the nearby forest.

After walking for about thirty meters through thick brushes and shrubs he heard a strange sound, far different from the sounds of forest birds. As he looked towards the source of the sound, he saw an object

96

with a rather peculiar appearance. The object (or UFO) was in the shape of an inverted bowl gray-green in color, on the lower section of the object there was a large gap from which an intense light shone. Also at the bottom of the object there was also visible light, but with a much lesser intensity.

The object seemed to rest on some type of 'pillar' which resembled legs that fastened the object to the ground. The object was on the banks of the river. Richard estimated the object to have been about twenty-five meters in diameter and five meters high. He also noticed a quite unpleasant odor resembling "burnt chocolate."

Around the object he could see several humanoid figures and also some inside the object. There was a total of about fifteen 'creatures' that resembled 'mummies.' They were about 1.3 meters tall, with 'interconnected legs' and were dressed in tight-fitting dark green uniforms. Their hands did not have the typical 'human' elbow joint, even though they were very flexible and bent freely in different directions. The hands were discernible but the witness does not remember the number of fingers which were probably connected together except for the thumb. The faces could not be seen, it was covered with a white color plate, resembling a welding mask or two-way mirror. The head and the ears were a noticeable highlight. The head was separated from the trunk, and was directly connected to the neck. The trunk or torso was relatively bulky and looked like "a stuffed bag."

According to Richard the humanoids were performing very strange acts of 'research' around their craft. They held some hand-held devices that resembled tubes and with them they seemed to probe the local vegetation apparently 'measuring it.' Richard added that the strange beings seemed to move in strange 'jumping' motions.

The witness observed the scene while hiding behind some overgrown shrubs, but according to him the humanoids seemed aware of his presence but completely ignored him and kept busy with their 'measuring instruments.' However after about a minute of observation the witness lost consciousness.

He woke up in the same place after about an hour, he was standing up. The humanoids and the object had already vanished. Quickly he walked back to his car and went on his way to get to the border crossing. After the event, Richard P. went the whole day noticing the unpleasant taste of "burnt chocolate' in his mouth. These symptoms disappeared in the evening. He also had trouble sleeping for several nights.

HC addendum.
Source: Archives of Damian Trela, Poland. dam.trela@gmail.com
Type: A & C

* * * * * * *

Location: Vistabella, Zaragoza, Spain.
Date: July 18, 1990.
Time: 3:00 a.m.

71-year old farmer Pedro Oros was working on his potato, tomato and bean fields when he noticed a "strange moon" emerge from behind a nearby hill and fly in his direction. The moon turned approached and hovered above the path about six to seven meters from the object and about two meters above the ground.

As the witness looked closely at the light he noticed that it was really what appeared to be a luminous human-shaped figure which remained still above the ground. The humanoid figure was about 1.90m in height with a large head, white skin, huge slanted black eyes and thick lips. His head was encased in what appeared to be a luminous crown. The bizarre luminous figure remained in place for at least three hours. During that whole time the witness continued to work on his fields which were now brightly illuminated by the luminous "crown" on the humanoid. At times when the light became intense Pedro felt dizzy but the light would immediately dim as if sensing his discomfort. On several occasions he shone his flashlight at the humanoid which displayed some discomfort by grimacing.

After some time Pedro went into his shack to eat. During that time he could not see the strange humanoid. Soon he heard what appeared to be knocks on the roof; he walked outside and saw that the humanoid was still there, unmoving. Around 6:00 a.m. when it began to turn light, Pedro looked in the direction of the humanoid and saw that it was gone but now could see the "luminous moon" flying towards the same hill

98

where it had originally come from. That same night other locals around Zaragoza reported seeing a mysterious light flying over the capital of Ebro. And around midnight on the same night, a man in the village of Luesma located several hundreds of meters from Vistabella was chased by a luminous sphere that seemed to have originated from the same location as the luminous humanoid that Oros had seen.

HC addendum.
Source: Bruno Cardeñosa '50 años de Ovnis' Las Mejores evidencias.
Type: E
Comments: Translated by Albert S Rosales.

* * * * * * *

Location: Lake Pairon, Western Pamirs, Tajikistan.
Date: July 23, 1990.
Time: Early morning.

Victor Novikov together with a guide had camped overnight on the shores of the lake, in the morning he got up and went to the fireplace. It was still dark. In the tranquil silence, he heard from a distance, footsteps of a creature. With his flashlight, Novikov flashed in the direction where the footsteps were coming from.

He saw a 2-2.5meter hairy human-like creature that stood at a distance from where they were camping. Novikov whistled. The creature whistled back, turned around and stood motionless. Its eyes emitted a phosphorescent light.

It stared at the witness in a "very serious, sharp and unfriendly manner." Then it uttered some groaning like screams, turned and disappeared in the mountains.

HC addendum.
Source: Victor Novikov, 'Night rendezvous in the Hissar Mountains,' 2003.   Type: E

* * * * * * *

Location: Near Shimskaya, Novgorod region, Russia.
Date: End of July, 1990.
Time: 9:00 p.m.

Two luminous "inverted saucers" flew one after the other at a height of 15-20 meters above the ground and in the direction of the observers. Under the "plates" were two humanoid figures suspended on two 'seats' that were noticeable not attached to the main flying machines by any visible devices. These figures were apparently flying on their own accord without any visible means of propulsion, but in sync with the larger saucers. On their heads were glowing helmets similar to motorcycle helmets, which were opened, however the frightened observers were not able to see any facial features.

The observers had been in a vehicle, they were L. N. Krotov, his parents, and a niece. Behind the wheel of the car had been the father of Krotov, N. I. Mikhailov. As the object flew close to the car it shook but stopped shaking when the objects turned away.

HC addendum.
Source: http://zhurnal.lib.ru/kizilow_g_i/ufo23072007.shtml
Type: A? or E?

* * * * * * *

Location: Bryansk, Russia.
Date: August, 1990.
Time: Daytime.

A young female student, Darya, was standing at a bus stop when suddenly she felt something approaching her from behind. She turned her head and saw a small yellow globe, the size of a tangerine, hovering at a close proximity from her. The globe emitted numerous yellowish beams of light from its circumference. To Darya, the sight was extremely beautiful. She took the globe in her hands and then opened her palm and the small globe continued to hover in mid-air. Darya felt a burning

100

sensation on her palm, like millions of needles piercing her skin, however she felt no pain. Amazingly no one else paid attention to Darya, and there were several other people at the bus stop. Darya then waved her hand and the small globe vanished.

Soon after this encounter Darya saw the same yellow globe in her backyard but this time she was also confronted by two humanoids of general human shape, a man and a woman, which fed her some yellowish quite tasty food. Strangely Darya felt neither fear nor awe at the sight of the strange visitors, and took everything in stride.

As it was later established, these humanoids came from a star system about 72 light years from Earth. She was to have a further contact in which the aliens took Darya to their planet.

HC addendum.
Source: Guram Tsushbaya (Odessa UFO Center) 'The Mysterious World,' Odessa, 1994.   Type: E or F?

* * * * * * *

Location: Astrakhan, Russia.
Date: August, 1990.
Time: Evening.

A local metal worker was resting on a street bench after having worked all day. He suddenly looked up and saw an object hovering over him, resembling a large star. On the edges of the star he saw bright flashes of light. Then the "star" descended and he was able to see the borders on the metallic surface of a strange craft, consisting of several segmented metal structures, joined by some type of rivet-like objects. Moments later a grayish cloud enveloped him. The fog seemed to condense and assumed a white tint. The fog then became gray again and vanished.

The astounded man then found himself in a strange colored room. Next he was confronted by several humanoid entities in the room. The humanoids were human-like, very attractive looking, with beautiful features. The aliens communicated with the witness and invited him to drink some multicolored liquids, which were quite tasty, but very difficult to compare with any drink on Earth. The alien crew then gave the witness a tour of their ship, into the different compartments of the circular alien craft.

The man walked along the corridors with strangely pressed bas-reliefs or pictures on the walls. Then they showed him what appeared to be a power plant, but before doing that they put a kind of spacesuit on him. Then they entered the main engine compartment (apparently the power source emitted dangerous emissions to humans). The stunned

101

man saw lots of sophisticated equipment and then he was returned back to the Earth.

Soon after the encounter the witness began research into what he called "magnetic liquid" which was what was used to power the UFOs engine. The aliens informed the witness among other facts, that they wanted to prevent the crash on the bridge of the Russian vessel on the river Volga back in the spring of 1990, and sent their saucer in order to prevent the collision. But the alien spacecraft also experienced "technical" problems and lost power, so another alien craft had to approach the first one and "transmit" power to the first one. But it was too late to prevent the tragic accident on the Volga.

Amazingly, another resident of Astrakhan, a Mrs. Fadeeva confirmed the incident. She reported seeing two UFOs in the air before the incident with the ship and noticed the moment when something like "lightning bolts" jumped between both UFOs.

HC addendum.
Source: Major E. Suetin of the Inner Troops, director of Astrakhan UFO Center, 'Rabochaya Tribuna,' Moscow, December 2, 1990.   Type: G

* * * * * * *

Location: Wimbledon, London, England.
Date: August, 1990.
Time: Night.

The main witness and a friend were camped out in a tent in the garden of the main witness home when they began hearing buzzing sounds and a distant humming noise.

In a dream-like state the main witness saw a man of average height, with sandy brown hair and dressed in a silver-blue metallic suit with a double cross crescent logo on the chest area. Three of four other humanoids accompanied the man. The other humanoids were shorter and jaundice looking with brownish hair that looked artificial; they also had "weird" eyes.

The witness was apparently taken onboard a craft and was told by the more human looking being that their ship used crystal power as means of propulsion. He communicated by using telepathy.

HC addendum.
Source: David Birch, Steve Holt, London UFO Studies, Skylink #6 & 7.
Type: G

Location: Tamasi, Tolna County, Hungary.
Date: August 3-4, 1990.
Time: 9:30 p.m.

After working the whole day on the vineyard the foreman a man named Nagy, was sitting in his car in front of the cellar and was contemplating the surrounding landscape when he observed a large reddish sphere descending over some nearby trees.

The next moment the witness apparently blacked out and came to, surrounded by a bright light. To his horror he saw two short creatures standing in front of the cellar wall. The two creatures stood side by side on the grass. Nagy attempted to exit the vehicle, but inexplicably, the doors have been locked from the outside and the keys are lying on the dashboard. Quickly he rolls down the window and opens the car door. The area around him is now in complete darkness. The vehicle lights appear to be malfunctioning.

In the dim light he could see one of the figures about 120cm in height, with blue-green flesh, incredibly thin arms and gnarled hands that touched the ground, in between the fingers there appears to be a sort of membrane. The creature's head is large and pointed; he could also see large pointy ears, huge eyes and a narrow slit for a mouth. He attempted to drive away but the vehicle would not start. Suddenly the instrument panel in the vehicle starts to flash and Nagy again blacks out. Next he finds himself in his garage at home (apparently he lived within in the vicinity or within the vineyard). Confused, he came out of the car and told a neighbor he has no idea how he got home.

In the morning a circular area of flattened grass was found in the vineyard and that same night the witness, along with his wife and children, saw a reddish sphere flying from behind the trees. It quickly disappeared at high speed.

HC addendum.
Source: Kriston Endre RYUFOR Foundation Hungary.   Type: C or G?

103

Location: Owen Sound, Ontario, Canada.
Date: August 5, 1990.
Time: 3:45 a.m.

The Martens family woke up to see "dancing lights" that were apparently disturbing their cattle. The lights were yellow/orange in color and looked like they were connected to something very large. The lights gradually changed to a deep "crimson red" and began to revolve around each other it gathered some kind of green haze or fog and suddenly vanished.

That same night one son had a nightmare about a "shining angel" in the house. And the eldest daughter saw in the house a "person" who seemed to be quite bright, almost blinding her with light.

HC addendum.
Source: Barry Arnold   Type: C?

* * * * * * *

Location: Volgograd, Russia.
Date: August 8, 1990.
Time: Evening.

While Valeriy Vasilevich Krasnov was alone at home watching TV, the two aliens he had encountered before, materialized in his room, right in front of him. This time, the alien man, communicated with the witness, while the woman studied the apartment, took water from the sink, looked inside the refrigerator, etc. The man said that they were returning to their planet and had come to say goodbye. He switched the TV and the fan off without touching them. He told the witness that his apartment was primitive that it had nothing to make life easier, nothing for comfort and suitable rest.

After the examination of the flat, Krasnov then began asking additional questions. They told him that they knew the history of earth well and were constantly monitoring it, possessing huge number of "memory cells" and video material describing the history of the earth.

They said that they lived in a binary star system. That their planet "TATS," was beautiful, with a population of 20 billion. It contained rich flora, beautiful lakes, rivers, and seas, with a large number of animals, birds etc, including representatives of the fauna found on Earth. They lived in large, completely automatic flats, and eat exclusively food from plants.

Every year residents of their planet are medically examined. The people that are found ill are transported to their planet's moon where a huge medical complex is located. Their dead are cremated and they do not have cemeteries. There is strict discipline on their planet and violators are sent to explore and study new planets. Their industrial plants are located underground. They have no religion but believe deeply in the "Council." They will return to earth again in the year 2094. The aliens bade goodbye and vanished in plain sight.

HC addendum.
Source: Gennadiy S Belimov, Anton Anfalov.   Type: E
Comments: According to the contact data from other sources, another name for the planet "Tats" is "Tio" and it is located near the Sun-like double star of Beta Canum Venaticorum, 27 light years from Earth.

* * * * * * *

Location: Chernobyl area, Kiev region, Ukraine.
Date: August 15, 1990.
Time: Morning.

The female witness named L.O. Kozyreva, an employee of NPO "Pripyat" (a scientific production unit located inside the Chernobyl restricted area, which was radioactively polluted after the nuclear incident at the nearby atomic power station in 1986, and now cordoned off by a 30km forbidden perimeter), was walking to her job, which had to do with monitoring the environment in order to register changes in nature influenced by the radioactivity in the area.

Suddenly she saw a semi-transparent sphere descend from the sky at about 200 meters in front of her. The globe then landed on the asphalt road. A tall humanoid then exited the object, the entity was about 2.8m to three meters in height, and the top portion of his outfit was red and the lower area black. A horseshoe shaped plate was shining in his chest area. The alien man had black hair and "looked very beautiful." When he glanced towards the witness she was suddenly struck by some kind of electric charge and her legs were paralyzed.

Suddenly a red "Zhiguli" vehicle appeared on the road. When the car approached the alien the humanoid suddenly vanished and the man that was sitting behind the wheel of the car then suddenly appeared in front of the startled witness.

When this man approached Kozyreva, she was again charged by the same electrical current (apparently the alien had somehow energized the driver of the car with electrostatic current).

After the incident L.O. Kozyreva noticed a strange brown spot, the size of a five Kopek coin that appeared on her leg. Two other researchers investigated the case and confirmed the presence of an anomaly at the reported landing site.

Other workers of the Chernobyl area have reported numerous UFO observations since the 1986 incident.

HC addendum.
Source: 'Nauka, Fantastika' magazine #1-2, 1992, Ukraine, quoted by 'Stalker,' Dnepropetrovsk #1, 1992.   Type: B

* * * * * * *

Location: Near Interior, South Dakota.
Date: August 18, 1990.
Time: 8:30 p.m.

Several witnesses saw a low flying object with what appeared to be lighted windows and two rooms with lights on the inside. They could see two gray colored figures with large teardrop shaped heads inside the object. One of the figures appeared to be sitting down and the other standing up.

The craft continued on a northbound course and then there was a very loud boom like sound, and an emerald green light was seen. The craft was reported as cigar shaped. After the craft disappeared, several jets and helicopters were seen in the area.

HC addendum.
Source: Franklin Carter.   Type: A

* * * * * * *

Location: Dubna Region, Russia.
Date: August 19, 1990.
Time: Evening.

Cyril Timofeyevich had gone to a familiar field where had had his previous encounter six years before. As he sat in the field he shouted, *"Where are you my friend?"* Later as he sat in the clearing, he heard noises from behind him. Turning around, he saw the familiar helmeted robot-like figure standing a few feet away. In the same robotic voice he instructed the witness not to approach, and that he just wanted to talk to him.

The witness asked about his flying sphere and if he was alone. The alien confirmed that he was alone. And then the robot began telling Cyril many curious things. He mentioned that earthlings still did not know how valuable the earth was. He also predicted that soon humanity would be able to eradicate a very terrible disease (AIDS?). Cyril asked if there were other planets in our solar system with earth like life. The answer

106

was no, only on Mars where there any small biological forms and on the moons of Jupiter. He also mentioned a planet possibly located in our solar system, unknown to humans.

Cyril then asked when they would meet again. It answered that they "are always with us." The robot then said that in 12-15 years, men would be able to prolong life.

When the conversation ended, a cloud formed around the robot and it then rose up into the air about a meter and then dissipated. After the encounter, Cyril slept for 24 hours straight. When he woke up his eyes were red and itchy.

HC addendum.
Source: Anomalia website, Russia.   Type: E

* * * * * * *

Location: Outside Shapsugskaya, Krasnodar region, Russia.
Date: August 24, 1990.
Time: Evening.

Three witnesses, Dorofey Vladimirovich Dubanos, Sergey Lymar and another man called Sasha, were having a picnic in an exotic place near a local ancient dolmen when suddenly they saw a light cross the sky disappearing behind the clouds. Soon at about thirty meters from them a strange dark object appeared, shaped like a vertical capsule, crossed in the middle by a square plate.

The three stunned witnesses watched as three human looking figures stepped out of the "capsule" and approached. The witnesses could not tell much about their appearance because it was dark. *"Who are you?"* asked Dubanos. The response was, *"We flew down here to talk to you, but we don't have much time."* The answer was received telepathically inside of the witnesses' heads. The three men were somehow attracted to the aliens and approached them, and stood facing them. "Where are you from?" asked Lymar. Again the telepathic answer was, *"Constellation of Orion, that's where our motherland is."* And then Sasha, asked the third question, *"How many years has your civilization lasted for?"* the answer was an astounding 12 million years.

All three witnesses exchanged glances, glad that they were able to freely communicate. Lymar asked the aliens what their purpose was here on earth and the answer was that, they had come to warn humanity about a terrific catastrophe that threatens our planet. *"What kind of catastrophe?"* asked Dubanos. The cryptic answer was, *"Soon, the polarity of the magnetic field of Earth will change. Global climate changes will appear, caused by the slowing rotation of the Earth."* Lymar then asked, *"Are you capable of preventing this?"* The answer was

107

somewhat reassuring, *"We will do everything to prevent this mortal danger to occur."*

There was additional conversation, mostly about inhabited planets in the universe, but the witnesses only vaguely remembered this portion of the conversation. Soon the object behind the aliens changed shape to resemble the front of a rocket or missile, the aliens then entered the craft, which then zoomed up and disappeared in a couple of seconds. The bright light again crossed the sky and a terrific storm soon followed.

HC addendum.
Source: Aleksey K. Priyma, 'UFOs Witnesses to the Unknown,' Anton Anfalov.   Type: B
Comments: Sadly, the alien's predictions appear to be coming true. Our global climate is drastically changing, and the future appears bleak if something is not done.

* * * * * * *

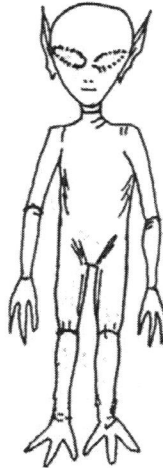

Location: Near Laguna Cartagena, Cabo Rojo, Puerto Rico.
Date: August 31, 1990.
Time: 3:00 a.m.

Mr. Miguel Figueroa was going to his place of business, and arriving there, found that there were about a dozen cars parked there. Given the early hour he was astonished, and he asked what was going on. The entire group of people seemed to be highly excited, especially one woman who was screaming that she had just seen some children or strange little men, passing by, who had huge heads and huge eyes. They had passed in front

108

of the cars, and the people were still parked there and talking about it, "because the things were still there."

Mr. Figueroa replied that no doubt somebody had wanted to play a trick on them by dressing up, or something of the sort. But his curiosity aroused he drove on in the direction of the road towards Boqueron which was whither the little men had gone. And to his immense surprise, he saw, beside the highway, five most strange little beings, two of them taller than the rest, about four foot, while the others were about three feet. He said, "Their clothing or something, I don't know whether it was clothing or their own skin, because they were all gray from head to feet. But at the knees and elbows they had what looked like sections that passed one into the other." Their heads were big and egg-shaped. Compared to their bodies, the heads were large, and their eyes were big and shining. He noticed also that their ears were long and pointed, just as the people at his place of work had said. He said that on their feet they had only three large toes, and on their hands only three large fingers.

As he drew closer to them, his headlights lit them up. Then one of them, turned around towards him, and he noticed that it had large slanted eyes emitting a very brilliant white light. He could also see that for noses they had merely tiny holes, almost no noses at all, and their mouths were extremely thin and tiny, as though with no lips at all. Their chins were very small and very pointed. And then the rest of them all turned around and became enveloped in a very bright light. It was a very powerful light, like a welder's torch, that blotted out the headlights of the car.

Figueroa became frightened, and seeking to cover himself, reversed the car and backed away from them a bit. And when he pulled off to a distance, they turned away again and continued walking on again along the road just as though nothing had happened. However, Figueroa still followed them at a distance. A bit further on, he saw that when on the road they came to a little bridge over a ravine, they jumped down, one after the other, and went off towards the left along the edge of the ravine and vanished there, while Figueroa remained sitting in his car petrified with fear.

HC addendum.
Source: Magdalena Del Amo Freixedo, FSR Vol. 36, #4.   Type: E

Location: Fili Park, Moscow, Russia.
Date: Autumn, 1990.
Time: About 7:00 p.m.

A witness, a man named I.G. was walking his dog in Fili Park located about 100 meters from the Rublyeskoye Highway. His dog suddenly ran away, and the man felt an irresistible force carry him to the middle of the park. He walked about fifteen meters and saw his dog jumping between trees. Looking up to the sky he saw something fly very fast above him.

He then felt a tremor and thoughts mixed in his head, as if under some kind of influence. He then saw a huge arc or horseshoe shaped object, about 25-30 meters in size, quickly move over the trees at a very low altitude. He followed it and saw the object slow down and descend into the forest. His dog began running towards the object, attracted by the light. The man also ran at top speed towards the landing site.

He found his dog near a stump sniffing at something. Simultaneously he saw two humanoids. They were taller than the witness, about 1.8 to 2 meters, and dressed in dark blue overalls. Both aliens stood facing each other, half turned towards the witness. Aliens had openings instead of ears, and their fingers were long and bony, their skin was matte and smooth, and their hair short and evenly cut.

I.G. succeeded in having a conversation with the humanoids, which spoke without moving their lips, apparently using telepathy. The humanoids told him, *"We landed in your forest. We need to find out what type of force field influences our craft from under the ground in this area."* *"We will not hurt you; we are just checking the presence of powerful forces in these fields."* They added that they had arrived there from, 'the other side of the world.' *"Today we will work some and then fly northward."* I.G. then asked, *"Are you from an extraterrestrial civilization?"* The telepathic answer was the following, *"Our civilization is similar to yours. We are very close but we cannot tell you anything more. The time of contact is not now. We enter into frequent contacts with different people of your planet and 'system' that do not bring us future complications."*

The alien promised the witness that he would cure his sick sister and told him that they would meet again. The witness answered that he was ready but was still apprehensive of them. The alien answered, *"No need to be afraid, we don't use any weapons in such situations."* The witness then said that he wanted to go home, that his wife was probably waiting for him. The aliens stood still for a while and then walked towards the bright light visible behind the trees.

The witness glanced at his electronic watch but it was not working, then at a very quick pace without looking at his feet the witness walked directly to his house as if being guided by an invisible force. He remembered that during the walk he never looked back and ignored everyone else in the street. He found his dog near the porch. He never visited the park again and was reportedly ready to submit to a hypnotic regression to confirm the encounter.

HC addendum.
Source: Vladimir G. Azazha, PhD, 'The Other Life,' Moscow, 1998.
Type: C

* * * * * * *

Location: San Diego, California.
Date: Fall, 1990.
Time: Late night.

The witness, who at the time was suffering from an incurable cancer, was just about to go to sleep with her husband when they were suddenly startled by a noise. She opened her eyes and saw four humanoid figures, about 3 ½ foot tall standing beside her bed. She screamed and her husband attempted to rise but one of the beings waved his hand at him and he fell backwards unconscious.

The woman was then levitated out of the house and down into a nearby schoolyard where a round craft with a blue beam of light touching the pavement hovered. She was then floated up the beam and into the object. They sat her on a chair and a taller alien entered the room, communicating with her telepathically.

The tall alien then used an instrument with a roller at the end of it and rolled it over the witness arms and shoulder area. She remembers nothing else and woke up the next morning apparently cured of her cancer. She remembered seeing strange symbols on the walls of the craft.

HC addendum.
Source: Linda Biafore, Alternate Perceptions #28, fall 1994.   Type: G

* * * * * * *

Location: St Thomas, U. S. Virgin Islands.
Date: Fall, 1990.
Time: Daytime.

A group of friends had gathered in one of their apartments after a public rally for the re-election of Governor Alexander A. Farrelly for food and drinks. It was a clear sunny day without a cloud in the sky. They were all about to sit down to eat when one of them looked out of a large picture window and noticed a massive cloud formation in the sky. They all saw helicopters, marked and unmarked approaching the cloud formation. The rest of the sky was clear and blue.

Suddenly a yellow golden, pinkish light beamed from the clouds at one of the helicopters. The helicopters immediately withdrew. For a brief time they all witnessed a huge massive ship just hovering in the sky, over portions of land and water. There appeared to be smaller metallic objects moving things surrounding the ship. One of the witnesses looked down on the ground directly below the massive object and noticed a copper colored, robotic figure moving back and forth.

They all stared in shock wondering what was happening. However before they could reach for a camera it was all over. They remember looking back into the sky and everything was gone, they had apparently lost track of time.

Two of the witnesses still refuse to talk about it today. The next day reports came in of a similar event from neighboring islands, however the National Guard and news media claimed it had all been a passing storm.

HC addendum.
Source: http://mufoncms.com   Type: C?

* * * * * * *

Location: Togliatti, Samara region, Russia.
Date: Autumn, 1990.
Time: Late night.

Watchmen at one of Togliatti's automobile plants began noticing strange things. There would be powerful 'knocks' on the walls of the one story building they were guarding. The knocks varied in intensity and the men could not explain their origin. The building was positioned in the northern part of a large 'Lada' car building complex and was very much isolated from the other buildings in the complex. Immediately after the knocks, the guards would rush to inspect the area of the sounds and would not find anything, and then they began to hear footsteps on the roof of the building. It sounded as if several men were walking on the roof at the same time. Examination of the roof did not yield any clues.

This went one for about one year, and the watchmen gradually became accustomed to the strange occurrences. But one night a watchman on duty noticed that someone had somehow activated the ventilation system in the workshop and that the headlights of a tractor in the garage were also lit up, amazingly the TV-set was also on, despite the fact that it was disconnected from the electrical outlet.

Concerned, the watchman armed himself with a rifle and entered the large hall in the workshop where the mysterious phenomena was happening in a regular basis. Once inside the hall he saw two strange humanoid entities. Basically they were human in appearance, but were gray in color. Their height was only about 1.2 to 1.3 meters, dwarf like. The witness did not see any additional details since it was dark in the hall.

Suddenly a crater-like opening appeared over him in the air, the 'crater' was positioned downward, curving, seemingly going somewhere into space. His hair stood up on his head and his shirt began to float up, he felt as if he were inside an aero-dynamic tube or vacuum, exposed to a powerful stream of air. Instinctively the watchman fired his rifle several times into the hovering crater. He saw the sparkles from the bullets appear on the ceiling. After this the crater disappeared. The two humanoid figures had also vanished.

Later upon investigating, the watchman found all his cartridges on the floor, but the bullets were never found, they had seemingly disappeared into some kind of parallel universe. After the events that night everything returned to normal and the mysterious phenomena did not reoccur.

HC addendum.
Source: Tatyana Makarova, Togliatti UFO-logical commission, 'Cross of Centaurs' Newspaper, #4, 1999.   Type: E or F?

* * * * * * *

Location: Near Kremenchug, Poltava region, Ukraine.
Date: September, 1990.
Time: Evening.

On the southeaster outskirts of Kremenchug a group of teenagers, among whom was a girl named Lena Barhotina had gone for an evening swim in the Dnieper River. The place selected for the swim was a sandy beach covered with willow thickets. Not far from the shore it was all scrub.

When all the teenagers went into the water, Lena remained on the shore to watch over things. She was standing at the water's edge facing the river, watching the bathers when suddenly she heard a strange sound from somewhere behind her, it sounded like the lament of 'a small child.'

Turning her head she saw standing about ten meters away a strange creature. She described the creature as about three feet tall, slightly resembling a 'kangaroo' with small front limbs and a small tail. Lena was able to clearly see the creature; it had large red eyes, a small nose however she could not see any ears. The being suddenly made a short clumsy leap in the direction of Lena.

Terrified and crying Lena immediately ran into the waters yelling at her startled friends. They could not comprehend her great fear, because

113

they didn't see anything. When Lena told them what she had seen, they searched the brush and Willow Grove and found on the sand clear three-toed prints bout 23cm in diameter, similar to a bird.

That same summer similar tracks had been found on the sandy shore of the river which gradually disappeared into the water.

HC addendum.
Source: Archives of Transcarpathian UFO Club, 'UFODOS.'   Type: E
Comments: An early Chupacabra hybrid in Ukraine?

* * * * * * *

Location: Villa Devoto, Buenos Aires, Argentina.
Date: September, 1990.
Time: Night.

Maria T. (involved in a previous encounter) suddenly woke up after feeling someone touching her neck. Upon opening her eyes she soon realized that she is unable to move her body. At the same time she heard an unintelligible voice emitting guttural sounds. Next to her stood a greenish phosphorescent figure that seemed to gesticulate and emit the guttural sounds.

The figure seemed to be totally comprised of light and she could see two huge black eyes, emitting a reddish glow, and a slit-like unmoving mouth that crossed the face from one side to the other. Upon being touched by the creature, she felt that its skin was rough & hot, which burned her on the neck and arm.

Seconds later she was able to move again, and the creature next to her bed glided over the floor and disappeared through the closed window. Maria was terrified and unable to go to sleep again and went to check on the window; there she found an area about 80cm in diameter, which appeared to be totally burned, leaving behind a brown stain on the center of the window.

Days later she found a strange mark behind her right ear about 1cm in length. Also a plant that she kept on top of the television set dried up and died without any apparent reason.

HC addendum.
Source: Liliana Flotta, Eduardo Grosso, 'Terror Nocturno, Historias reales de visitantes Extraterrestres.'   Type: E

Location: Goryachiy Kluch, Krasnodar region, Russia.
Date: September, 1990.
Time: Night.

Feeling a strange compulsion, local resident Ivan Martynovich awoke and walked outside his house. Suddenly he saw a stranger walking towards him. Ivan could see the figure clearly since there was a light pole nearby. The stranger was tall, wearing a tight-fitting cloth. He had a totally hairless head, with beautiful ashen colored skin, and light, clear blue eyes.

The strange man took Ivan by the elbow and in a moment Ivan felt himself ascending into the air and floating towards a hovering object in the sky. The object was cylinder-shaped, with both ends sharpened and pointed, like a pencil. In a strange and hardly noticeable way, both Ivan and the humanoid suddenly appeared inside the object. Ivan did not see any control panels or chairs. Several similarly appearing humanoids were standing in the room and talking to each other. Their strange language consisted of sharp words, "each word not longer than a syllable."

Suddenly one of the tall aliens said imperiously, *"I am!"* and all became silent. The alien leader then addressed Ivan and Ivan somehow saw the words appear in front of his eyes and he was able to understand. They proposed that Ivan review his life and amazingly he was able to see the basic events of his past in what appeared to be a TV-set (holographic image?).

They invited Ivan to visit their planet and he immediately agreed. One of the aliens then said something and the craft began to move. Not the slightest movement or sound was felt by Ivan. The aliens did not mention the name of their planet. In a matter of moments they had arrived at the alien "planet." The craft landed, and a platform jutted out from it. They walked outside and Ivan felt the soil under his feet. With an alien guide, they walked to a location filled many numerous small flying machines standing up with opened upper sections that Ivan could only compare to bicycles. They sat him on one of the objects and Ivan asked the alien if it belong to him, the alien then explained that in their planet they had no notion of "yours" and "my" they never hurried anywhere or worried about if they "could go or not."

Somehow Ivan was able to understand everything that was being said to him. Then they zoomed over the treetops and Ivan saw warm and uncommonly clear environs. The Sun-like star was warm and moving in a straight line Ivan saw green flora, gardens, forests and blue lakes. The alien dwellings were not big, and each house was different, not higher than three floors. *"Why don't you have any tall buildings?"* asked Ivan. The answer was, *"We use the same energy source, our Sun, and it must be distributed evenly."*

Ivan was most amazed by the alien animals. He had never seen such a variety of types, but most amazingly he learned that they were all domestic pets. Only the larger animals, remotely resembling mammoths, walked free and were of some danger to the alien species.

The aliens he saw in the planet were tall, slender; smooth, with unbelievable blue eyes and blue skin, the emanated inner harmony. Their movements were graceful and quick, as their speech. And their reflexes and speed exceeded those of humans many times over.

The alien food consisted of fruits and berries from the forests, but they apparently did not cultivate anything, it just grew by itself. (?) They told Ivan that they did not kill to eat, that the animals gave them milk and the forests their vegetable dishes. Ivan wanted to taste their food and drink but the aliens told him that if he did, if would "influenced him" in a way that he would have to stay in their planet.

The aliens took Ivan into one of their houses. A pet animal, remotely resembling a dog met him. The animal sniffed the air around him and then lay down by his feet. An alien woman then came out and she was introduced as *"Ri,"* which was the name they used for any "mother" of their species. She was beautiful and young in appearance. The alien woman (Ri) told Ivan that she had lost her son while he was studying the earth, killed in an accident on a space flight. She further stated that their average lifespan was 500 terrestrial years.

'Ri' claimed that they had been observing the Earth for 11,444 years. They did not want to see humanity destroy itself. They further warned that humanity was at the edge of destroying itself in two ways, *"Humanity will die out as a result of a global brain disease."* And also that, *"the Earth will move out of its present orbit and will be destroyed."*

They told him about the destruction of a similar planet (to earth) in our solar system that moved out of its orbit and became the present day "asteroid belt." One of the asteroids had struck the earth once, but the earth was not destroyed, it only reversed its poles. From time to time they studied humans more closely, studying the birth and death of people that had agreed to stay on their planet, they had come to the conclusion that the human brain was similar to theirs but humans were incapable of utilizing all of the brain's capacity.

They also added that if Earth humanoids would stop the use of atomic, chemical and other weapons, the air would became purified and we would be able to use solar energy more efficiently. They said that they could help Earth humanoids in achieving that goal. The sun for them was life; they did not have any prisons or places of worship in their planet. *"The temple of worship was in each living being's soul."* They indeed had their own equivalent of the Ten Commandments, and lived according to them. Their birth is joyful, without pain or fear. And in the same way they pass on (most in a natural way).

116

When Ivan returned to the craft, he saw a large number of aliens that had gathered to see his departure, running towards the craft from different locations. He felt numerous telepathic impulses. In one massive united thought they all told Ivan, *"God help you,"* to which Ivan, replied, *"Not me but us,"* meaning the dwellers of the planet Earth.

Ivan was returned home on the same night. He found that he had been absent for four hours. His wife, Lubov Vasilievna, met him and confirmed the incident to the source. It is reported that Ivan's health suffered after the encounter.

The aliens had told him that the visit to their planet had cut Ivan's life expectancy by ten years. Back on Earth, Ivan realized that most of the information given to him, most earthlings did not want to hear.

HC addendum.
Source: A. Gorbanyeva, 'Komsomolets Kubani,' August, 1991.   Type: G

* * * * * * *

Location: Lamia, Peloponnese, Greece.
Date: September 2, 1990.
Time: 9:30 p.m.

A group of twelve to thirteen UFOs, crossed Greek airspace approaching from the north. At the end of the Peloponnese they made a half turn and followed the opposite trajectory. Numerous eyewitnesses confirmed this fact. As the formation neared Lamia, three of these objects separated and one of them appear to ignite. After apparently scanning the area the three objects landed, quickly extinguishing any flames or lights.

According to the Karatrantou family who lived nearby, the objects apparently remained all night on the ground performing repairs. According to some of the family members they watched the objects fly over them and later they heard three loud and successive explosions resembling what they thought was dynamite. Then a large red object appeared in the sky, much larger than the others and seemed to be engulfed in flames. As the stunned family watched, the object seemed to fall to the ground. They could see flames and black smoke rising into the sky. It had fallen on a hill located opposite from their position.

A few moments later several smaller objects now approached and surrounded the apparently stricken craft, these moved very quickly and resembled bright stars. The smaller objects descended and appear to form a circle around the larger burning craft; the witnesses thought it was an attempt to prevent the flames from spreading. Mr. Karatrantou took out his rifle and pointed in the direction of the objects. Through the telescope sight he could see small shapes or figures passing in front of

117

the burning object, he could not tell if they were men or animals. These moved feverishly around the craft, always within the luminous circle now formed around the craft. There they remained for about ten hours.

In the morning there was very little smoke left. Upon investigating the site a strange spongy substance was found, and the trunks of several pine trees had been severely scorched. When one of the men touched the pine trees, blisters appeared in his hands. On the area where the larger object had fallen, there were circular holes on the ground each surrounded by mounds of earth.

It is reported that a strange piece of equipment was found that had what appeared to be two interlocking antennas and a lightning bolt engraved on the side. This item was given to the local authorities. Mr. Karatrantou added that as he watched the small shapes move about, he saw them pouring some type of liquid on the fire, which transformed the smoke into a red-black color.

HC addendum.
Source: IPANI France, 'Modern UFOs in Greece.'   Type: C

* * * * * * *

Location: Tahkunas, Hiiumaa Island, Estonia.
Date: September 11-13, 1990.
Time: Late evening.

Anatoly Snetkov, a soldier at a local barracks, had gone outside to use the latrine. Near the latrine area; he spotted a strange creature approaching from the nearby forest. The creature was about 1.7m to 1.9m in height. He stopped and saw that the creature was moving very slowly taking short steps. It seemed to have huge dark eyes, with a narrow face and large nose. Its arms hung down and it appeared to have a luminous area in the center of the body. Anatoly became frightened but suddenly the strange figure disappeared into the woods. At the site, Anatoly discovered strange prints showing two large toes about 35-40 cm in size.

The next night September 12, around 9:30 p.m, three boys, Ilham Ergashev, Hassan Halmatovi, and Rassul Askeroviga were walking their dog near the forest close to the Army barracks when suddenly the dog became agitated and began growling and howling uncontrollably. The boys then spotted a strange creature standing at the edge of the woods about six meters away. The creature was tall, with broad shoulders, and large black eyes, it appeared to be hairy. The boys experienced a strange feeling and became frightened of the dog that now seemed ready to pounce on them, however the dog then hid its tail between it legs and ran away, the boys also ran away terrified.

The following day, in the evening, another soldier, A. Snetkov was on his way to the barrack's canteen using the perimeter road of the base, when he was suddenly overwhelmed by a strong sensation of fear that he could not control. Looking outside the fence he saw a strange creature staring at him. He described the creature as short with wide shoulders, the legs appeared to be unusually top heavy and the bottom too thin, and it appeared to be furry. Terrified Snetkov's hands began to tremble and he had difficulty in walking. He managed to walk slowly back to the barracks still trembling.

Upon arriving he told the other soldiers who armed themselves and went out to look for the creature, however they could not find it but they all heard a terrible inhuman scream coming from the forest. That same evening Vjatsheslav Gorelikov watched a strange creature in the woods that screamed frightfully on four occasions, "the voice resembled that of an amplified megaphone." Also later that evening, Bahrom Abubakirov was walking through the edge of the forest when he heard a sound and noticed the creature standing nearby, the witness eyes suddenly began to burn and tear.

As he tried to leave he realized that he couldn't move either, after what seemed to have been an eternity, he was suddenly able to run away in a panic. He described the creature as having a dark upper section, the center chest area giving off light (!) with a small face, big nose, large teeth, and long clawed hands.

HC addendum.
Source: Leonid Spassov, September 18, 1990.   Type: E

* * * * * * *

Location: Mahachkala, Dagestan, Russia.
Date: September 13, 1990.
Time: 8:00 p.m.

A local woman named Irina M. was returning home from work when she looked at the sky and saw a quickly moving light, yellow in color, which was flying from the southwest to the east. It was moving faster than a normal aircraft and she immediately thought it could have been a UFO. The object began descending at high speed, increasing its dimensions noticeably. The object was round and silvery and hovered in midair not too far from the witness. Astounded the witness saw floating next to the object, a humanoid figure.

The figure was human-like, tall, and slender, with a pale young face without wrinkles. He had very kind blue eyes. The alien was dressed in a loose-fitting tunic, silver-white in color. The alien stood in mid-air gazing at the witness intently. The alien seemed to be encased in a bright halo of light.

The witness became concerned, fearing that she would be abducted by the alien, leaving her children alone and rushed home as fast as she could. Near her front door she looked back and saw the UFO departing, decreasing in size and vanishing in a few seconds. Apparently the only other witness to this event was a stray dog that frequented the area.

HC addendum.
Source: 'Iks,' UFO Newspaper, Mahachkala Dagestan #4, and Anton Anfalov.   Type: C

* * * * * * *

Location: Cuautitlan, Mexico.
Date: October, 1990.
Time: 6:30 a.m.

The 16-year old witness and a friend were playing "pelota" outside an automobile factory (where he worked) when, surprised by a vivid light, they turned around and saw a craft about five meters wide hanging nearby, a few inches off the ground, near the object stood two short entities. These little men were about 1.2 meters in height, with oblique blue eyes, a penetrating gaze, and wearing gray clothing with a sort of emblem on the chest area. The heads were totally bald, but of what would be a normal size on a larger being.

They then heard a voice addressing them, in perfect Spanish, though no lip movement was detectable on the entities, and the voice sounded rather "like coming from some apparatus." Among the things he was told was that these beings were from another world and were here, "to prepare people for a new cosmic race." The voice also foretold certain events that the young man said had indeed since come about.

After about twenty minutes the entities moved toward the craft and vanished into thin air. The main witness suffered from seizures soon after the incident.

HC addendum.
Source: Luis Ramirez Reyes, FSR Vol. 42 #1.   Type: C

Location: Port Bourgeney, near Talmont-Saint-Hilaire, Vendee, France.
Date: November 5, 1990.
Time: Late evening.

The witness was jogging in a park and as it grew dark he noticed three short figures looking at him standing about 30 to 50 meters from him. The three figures had child-like bodies and had thick beards and what appeared to be large helmets.

Terrified, the witness watched as the figures rose up about ten meters into the air and suddenly became luminous forming a sort of triangle, which rose up into the sky and quickly disappeared from sight.

HC addendum.
Source: Jean Sider, M. Claude Bertin & Joel Mesnard.   Type: E?

* * * * * * *

Location: Minas Gerais, Brazil (exact location not given).
Date: November 15, 1990.
Time: Night.

A man and his vehicle were taking inside a hovering disc shaped craft. Inside he was met by tall human like beings that identified themselves as visitors from Alpha Centauri. There was much communication. No other information.

HC addendum.
Source: GEPUC Brazil.   Type: G

* * * * * * *

Location: Alexandrovka, Kyrgyzstan.
Date: December, 1990.
Time: Evening.

Three girls going for a walk after school, encountered a man over 2.5 meters in height wearing a shiny gray suit. Suddenly the figure transformed itself into the likeness of one of the girl's grandfather whose name was Nicolas. He invited the girls inside the house he was standing in front of and offered them cake.

Suddenly the door creaked open and the grandfather figure along with the refreshments disappeared and instead of a cake on a table there was a strange device with a red light and a button. The "house" then went up in the air. Undeterred, one of the girls pressed the button on the

121

unknown device and they all three suddenly found themselves on the street and it was already dark.

HC addendum.

Source: http://vzglyadzagran.ru/news/belye-preshelcy-2.html#more-52998
Type: G?

1991

Location: Jacuba, Itauna, Minas Gerais, Brazil.
Date: 1991.
Time: 8:00 a.m.

While working in a barn at the Hacienda Capon Oscuro, Ze Melado looked outside to see a small humanoid figure, green in color, with large ears, and large dark slanted eyes. A stunned Melado fainted. Another farm hand saw the being with a flashing red light on the forehead area. The goats in a nearby corral stampeded and ran away from the area.

Melado later woke up and did not see the short green humanoid again. Later a strange tumor-like protrusion emerged on Melado's neck. Doctors removed the growth but Melado lost movement to his arms, but he later made a complete recovery. Investigators also found a forty meter in diameter circle on the ground of decayed grass.

HC addendum.
Source: Joao Gabriel UFOVIA Brazil.   Type: E

* * * * * * *

Location: Moncayo, Zaragoza, Spain.
Date: 1991.
Time: 8:00 a.m.

Three soldiers, among them radio operator Juan Lopez, were deployed in maneuvers in an isolated area when one night, the men saw a bright red light surrounded by a bluish ring of light, flying over the wooded area. After a while it seemed to disappear behind some trees. After this the soldiers went to sleep.

123

The next morning, while the men tested the radio equipment, the three soldiers came upon a landed oval-shaped craft on a field. The object was silvery in color and reflected the sun's light. On its surface, it had a row of circular windows which seemed to have a sort of design on the top resembling a "sea wave." Behind the windows the men could see some movement and they could also see a door or hatch on the object. The craft was about seventy meters in diameter and was resting on four metallic leg-like protrusions that were partially interred on the ground, possibly as a result of the object's weight.

After several minutes of watching the object, the door or hatch opened and a ramp was lowered to the ground. The men then heard voices of what appeared to be "children," and immediately after some twenty short humanoids with large heads exited the object. Their heads were hairless and each wore a tight-fitting blue coverall. The beings walked around the object as if inspecting it and then divided themselves into three groups.

Eventually they returned to the object and the ramp was retracted and the door closed. Emitting a low humming sound, the craft lifted up and disappeared at high speed towards the nearby mountains.

HC addendum.
Source: http://alaluzdelasvelas.iespana.es/ovnisenespana/   Type: B
Comments: Translated by Albert S Rosales.

* * * * * * *

Location: Southeast of Kadima, Israel.
Date: 1991.
Time: Afternoon.

According to sources an eleven year old boy of Yemenite origin disappeared for half a day while walking home from school. When he finally returned to his hysterical parents late at night, he was unable to remember why he was late and had no recollection of the previous hours.

Two weeks later, he remembered that he had been abducted by "giants" and taken into their lair. There he was medically examined and a small device was surgically inserted into his left arm near the wrist. He was later taken to a clinic where a small device was removed from his arm.

HC addendum.
Source: Barry Chamish, Return of the Giants.   Type: G
Comments: It appears that the witness was initially implanted with some kind of tracking device that was removed by earth doctors. So what happened to the implant?

124

Location: London, England.
Date: 1991.
Time: Evening.

The witness had decided to attempt a telepathic contact experience at the Charing Cross railway station. Once there, he asked in his mind, *"If there are any beings from elsewhere, within the vicinity of Charing Cross station could you please come and prove it?"*

After concentrating for about half an hour he boarded a train and thought nothing more about it. He noticed that the carriage was full being the height of rush hour. He felt that it was strange that no one standing was interested in sitting down in the available seat directly opposite the witness by the window. Just before the train departed a man entered the train from the left side and immediately sat in the seat in front of the witness. The witness noticed that the man was dressed in a tan colored suit and tie with a matching attaché case. He was around six foot three, had short blond hair brushed back, blue eyes and had a Swedish appearance. Although the witness had made no connection that the stranger was one of those beings at the time, he noticed that the man was acting strangely by observing the other people on the train. He even at times turned around to look at the other people seated behind. He then leant forward and began to observe his own hands, which the witness also felt was unusual.

It was at this point that it occurred to the witness that the stranger might be one of those "beings." So he asked the question telepathically, *"If you are a being from elsewhere, please place your right index finger on the right side of your nose?"* As soon as the witness had telepathically asked the question, the stranger responded by doing just that, very slowly and carefully placing his finger on his nose, holding it there for some time, before lowering it. The witness asked if he could do various other

125

gestures to confirm if he was from elsewhere, but he did not respond to this. The only other time that the stranger responded in exactly the same way, was when the witness asked if he *"Was one of the beings responsible for the crop circle phenomenon?"*

As the journey approached its end, the witness was thinking, *"I am not convinced that you are from elsewhere as you could have been placing your finger on your nose by coincidence."* The stranger immediately responded to this with apparent frustration. The witness then asked the question again in his mind, *"If you are from elsewhere then please tap on your attaché case three times?"* With both hands on his attaché case, he slightly shook his head, and then started to tap with both hands firmly a total of three times. He did this three times in a row, (three sets of three) and then stared directly at the witness.

Up until this point the witness had not established direct eye contact with the stranger, but had little choice to stare back at this point. As he did so he noticed that the man's face was asymmetrically perfect, his eyes slightly slanted and pale blue with flecks of violet in the irises. His cheekbones were high set. Feeling somewhat overwhelmed the witness was thinking in communicating verbally with the stranger, but then after about twenty seconds the train arrived at the destination.

Being somewhat stunned by the experienced the witness broke the stare and continued to gather his portfolio and depart from the train. After arriving home the witness wrote on a piece of paper many details of his experienced and drew a portrait of the stranger. But a few minutes later the paper completely disappeared from the room and was never found.

A few months later the witness spotted an oval-shaped craft, around 100 feet across. It seemed to move around the sky like an "insect." The object had an upper section in blue with a row of circular windows across the middle. It had a pulsating light on its underside and appeared to be translucent in nature; it disappeared at high speed from the area.

HC addendum.
Source: FSR Forum, Harry Challenger.   Type: E

Location: Cape Canaveral, Florida.
Date: 1991.
Time: Evening?

While monitoring a space shuttle mission, in the secret Mission Control Center at the Kennedy Space Center, Clark McClelland was flabbergasted to observe an entity that was eight to nine feet in height in the open Space Shuttle pay load area while it was in earth orbit. The entity was very tall, much taller than the two NASA astronauts floating near it. He could estimate the height due to being familiar with the sizes of the interior of the Pay Load Bay of the shuttle. He was not able to view all facial features, other than thinking he recognize two eyes, a nose and since it had a large helmet on, nothing else was evident. It was in a body tight type uniform space suit. He saw it at a distance on a 27 inch TV monitor.

It appeared that the NASA astronauts were familiar with the entity. The entity appeared to be communicating with the two NASA astronauts. There was some NASA commentary, from the Houston Space Center, but there was no mention of the entity. Following a few statements, the audio discontinued, and he could not recall if he heard any other comments. McClelland was in a secret monitoring office, and it may have been their mistake in Houston Mission Control to allow his monitor to view the incident. He could not say anything else other than that. It suddenly was on one of his several monitors. He had several opportunities to observe various shuttle operations while in progress. He also observed many UFOs flying near the shuttle on many missions. The STS-48, the famous shuttle mission when they took several 'shots' at escaping UFOs, he was on duty for that amazing incident, NASA said it was ice crystals.

A large single, unknown spacecraft was safely in orbit behind the shuttle. It appeared as a somewhat short-winged object and did not appear to have been used as a spacecraft for traveling stellar distances. It appeared to be too small for that and probably would not be capable of deep space flight other than on board another more sophisticated carrier craft designed to be used for deep space flight. He witnessed this astounding event for a total of one minute and seven seconds by keeping the lapsed time on his astronaut watch. He wrote a detailed report, the report was not forwarded to the NASA mission launch director. He had no witnesses and had he made an official report, which he did not, it may have caused him job difficulties.

About two months following the incident, he was informed of another report by another aerospace engineer. This person was also involved in the launching of space shuttles. This shuttle engineer observed a similar entity, eight to nine feet tall, inside the space shuttle crew compartment as it orbited earth. It was slouched over to protect its head from hitting the shuttle overhead structure. Again, it was communicating with two much smaller NASA astronauts. Neither the United States Space Program nor any other foreign Space Program known on earth, constructs their spacecrafts to accommodate such physically large entities.

HC addendum.
Source: Clark McClelland, http://www.stargate-chronicles.com Type: X

* * * * * * *

Location: Manuel Urbano, Acre, Brazil.
Date: 1991.
Time: Night.

Local Indians reported being attacked by a huge hairy humanoid with sharp claws and fangs, which they called the 'Mapinguary.'
Several men were reportedly killed and eaten by the beast. A scientist, Alceu Ranzi from the Federal University of Acre organized a search expedition but was unable to find anything.

HC addendum.
Source: Pablo Villarrubia Mauso.   Type: E

* * * * * * *

Location: Near Wausau, Wisconsin.
Date: 1991.
Time: Night.

A Wausau man who wishes to remain anonymous was driving near Lake Du Bay and the Little Eau Pleine River just north of the Marathon County line when he spotted a bizarre creature at about 15ft in front of his vehicle.

It had a human-like body and no fur and it was grayish tan in color. The creature was very thin with outlined well defined muscles. The witness could see the ribs on its side and it glistened a little as if were wet or it had oily skin. It had not tail and it was hunched over, so the witness saw the whole left side.

It then turned its head straight and shot off into the woods. According to the witness he had never seen anything move at that speed before. There were other reports of a same or similar creature plus reports of UFO like lights also in the same area. Other witnesses said the creature had large yellow cat-like eyes and a triangular shaped head.

HC addendum.
Source: Linda Godfrey.   Type: E or D?
Comments: Date is approximate. Witness sketch sent to Linda Godfrey. Used with permission.

* * * * * * *

Location: Perm Region, Russia.
Date: 1991.
Time: Late night.

Hunter, A. I. Kurentsev was sitting by a bonfire in the taiga when he suddenly felt an uncommon fear. Looking up, he saw flying over a nearby boulder, an enormous dark humanoid figure, which resembled a man. In an apparent attempt to avoid a collision with the boulder the creature flew over the hunter totally ignoring his presence. The witness noticed that it had membranous wings, similar to a bat.

The same or similar creature was again seen in the area in 1992, it reportedly had a human face with enormous bright eyes, underdeveloped feet and wings more than two meters in width.

HC addendum.
Source: SKYZONE Russia.   Type: E

* * * * * * *

Location: England (exact location not given).
Date: 1991.
Time: Late night.

The witness (involved in other encounters) was sleeping in his car as he was involved in crop circle and UFO monitoring at the time. He awoke to see a pair of eight-foot tall figures standing facing him in the area directly in front of his car. He could see the silvery sheen of moon glint on their hooded helmets and the shining textile covering of their heavy 'diving suits.'

A similar figure appeared inside his house late one night in 2001.

HC addendum.
Source: East to West UFO Society Group Newsletter #44.   Type: E

*   *   *   *   *   *   *

Location: Orizaba, Veracruz, Mexico.
Date: 1991.
Time: 11:00 p.m.

A well-known and respected local doctor (wishing to remain anonymous) was alone in his office late in the evening when he suddenly heard loud banging at the now locked front door. Rushing out to open the door and see who it was, he was surprised to see a very tall, Nordic-appearing man with otherwise normal features who asked for his help, since he had been injured.

The doctor admitted the stranger and tended to his wound. The stranger had a very large wound on his leg which he claimed was caused by metal rod that had been embedded in his leg as a result of some sort of accident. The doctor dressed the wound and bandaged it as best he could but warned the stranger that this sort of wound could bring forth the onset of tetanus.

The stranger agreed to remain overnight in the doctor's office. The doctor told him that if the wound was infected in the morning he would have to be transferred to a hospital. The doctor went home, leaving the stranger in the office.

In the morning the strange man had disappeared but had left behind a strange note (message), he told the doctor that he was from another dimension, unknown to humans, that his ship had suffered an accident thus the injury. He thanked the doctor but left no other details.

HC addendum.
Source: Rossana Tejeda Lopez, 2006, 'El Durmiente de Orizaba.' Type: E

Location: South of Moscow, Russia.
Date: 1991.
Time: After midnight.

The witness was driving from Kursk to Moscow and after a long drive he pulled over to the side of the road to get some rest. Finally he dozed off but was suddenly awaken with an unusual feeling. He was not able to move his body and something evidently was vibrating inside his head. He heard a voice of an invisible entity telling him not to be afraid, that he was being constantly watched (monitored?), *"We order you not to resist. Are you friendly?"* added the voice. The witness replied, *"yes, I am friendly."*

At this point the witness noticed a strange luminous cloud hovering above the road, near his car. The witness felt that this cloud was apparently "guiding or controlling him." Suddenly it seemed to him that an entity materialized next to him on the passenger seat. It was a strange humanoid entity (no additional details). The strange creature then told the witness *"I am going to regenerate you."* A beam of light then caused the witness to lose consciousness. He remembered only much later, that after he was struck by the ray of light, he found himself sitting inside an alien craft wearing a helmet on his head. The room was full of unfamiliar equipment and he was surrounded by several "creatures of unearthly outlook." On control panels and screens the witness saw what appeared to be bizarre symbols and signs that were unfamiliar to him.

Apparently using a device connected to his helmet the alien leader told the witness that they had good, benevolent intentions and telepathically informed the witness, *"You have been chosen for contact. You are under control of our powers."* Then the aliens provided him with some information about their aims, they added that they were able to communicate telepathically with all human beings and could understand all the languages on Earth. They claimed that they used a "form of universal language" a language that was used by all the creatures in the universe. They also informed the witness that they could influence human thoughts and change behavior.

The witness then saw mental images, like a video recording, of alien life in their planet. They gave a detailed description of existence on their planet, which was mostly covered with water. After all the information was given to him, the witness was returned to the same location he had been in his vehicle. At this point the witness felt immense joy and tranquility; he felt pure love and "being one with the Universe." The witness apparently has further ongoing contacts but no details are given.

HC addendum.
Source: Georgiy M. Naumenko, 'Extraterrestrials & Earthlings, testimonies of contact,' Moscow, 2007.   Type: G

Location: Gorodischenskiy area, Penza region, Russia.
Date: 1991.
Time: Unknown.

A group of researchers of anomalous phenomena from the city of Penza, led by L. Polyakov were exploring a so-called anomalous area outside the hamlet of Gorodische in order to conduct an in depth study of its surroundings. From the beginning of their research the group felt the presence of someone invisible among them and also of a strange "electrical current" running through their bodies. They also located an area of a possible UFO landing where the trees were crushed down and some of the other trees their tops were cut off.

During one of his expeditions Polyakov heard the following telepathic information in his mind, "You should gather the most ill and bring them to a definite location." He did exactly what he was told. At the location a very powerful energy or influence overwhelmed the group and at least one very ill man was completely cured. Some other members of the group experienced other "contacts" in the area and were shown how the aliens moved through space, "jumps" to parallel worlds, and other incredible things.

On his next visit, Polyakov's group separated into three separate groups, consisting of two, three and four men. They then saw a white circle of light and perceived the following telepathic message, *"Your leader, please make twenty steps ahead!"* When he did that, three dark humanoid forms appeared before them. Above the humanoids, Polyakov and the others saw a "module" or some kind of object, hovering in the air. From the rear of the object a black spot "opened," then the men saw everything being "sucked" into the "black hole." The men then heard a telepathic voice explaining to them that they had just seen the transition into a parallel world. After that, the men heard, *"Well you have seen enough. We have a very small amount of time, bring the next group here."* The next group of men saw the same thing that Polyakov's group had seen.

The aliens further explained that they were representatives of the so-called "Pink planet" from the constellation of Libra. They are also humanoid in shape, but their life has a phosphoric foundation, not albumen, like the humans on Earth. Their height was about 1.8m, and they wore silvery clothing. The star (or sun) of their planet is a red dwarf, special M class and the atmosphere in their planet dissolves the colors of pink-red, hence the name of their planet (We humans call our planet the blue planet). The aliens also showed the men holographic images of their landscape, cities, transport and roads.

They also showed the men how planet Earth looked from outer space. Their civilization has conquered the secrets of teleportation and telepathy and long ago had freed themselves from their bodily "husks"

132

and can easily transfer their "bodies" (or soul?) to energetic states in a multi-dimensional space.

HC addendum.
Source: Interview with L. Polyakov in, 'The Working Tribune' Newspaper, Moscow. September 5, 1991.   Type: G or F?

* * * * * * *

Location: Donetsk, Ukraine.
Date: January 14, 1991.
Time: 11:00 p.m.

After her second contact in July, 1990, Irina Vladimirovna M. began to receive telepathic messages from the aliens. The alien in contact with her gave his name as "Rtsah" and informed her that the earth was being visited by 45 of their smaller craft, which had left a much larger mothership. There were about 4000 humanoids in the mothership. Their task was to look for signs and contact persons on Earth with specific features that only they knew. A crew of 7-8 humanoids traveled to earth in a globe-shaped spacecraft. The crew consisted of different specialists, a contact specialist, which was in charge of the earth "contactees." A specialist in architecture, climate researchers, fauna, a crew specialist and a cook. Their food is soft and needs special preparation.

On the above date they proposed that Irina visited their mothership in an "astral" flight. At 23:00 hrs she entered in contact and received the order to lie down, prepare and to cover her body. As soon as she did that she was momentarily "switched off." The first thing she saw was a huge disc-shaped object of a blinding color, with an uneven surface, having some geometrical protrusions. About fifteen humanoid figures were walking on the surface, dressed in special spacesuits. They were holding some long sticks and probing the geometrical forms from time to time on the surface of the spacecraft. All fifteen figures then turned around and accompanied her astral body to the entryway of the disk. When she was entering the spacecraft she said, *"You did not come so I came to you."* She then blacked out.

When she came to she was inside the spacecraft. She was walking along a corridor 4 meters in diameter. Rtsah and many other humanoids accompanied her. Like everyone present, she was dressed in a long cloth that fell to her heels. The alien men wore their flowing robe more loosely fitting while the females more tightly fitting, with a large number of pleats, crossing the garment in unbelievable combinations. Some of the alien women had hair, but most of them were hairless. They entered a huge hall, where a crowd of humanoids waited. All of them then began to approach Irina, and became ill, exactly like the first time she was

133

contacted by Rtsah. Her heart began to beat irregularly. In a moment Rtsah moved behind her put his hands forward and all the aliens stopped. No more approached her further except for a small entity that had very long arms, a round head, lipless mouth, small teeth, and huge eyes. Most of the representatives of the crowd had green skin, but there were some with totally white skin.

While everyone looked, Rtsah accompanied Irina to another room and sat her on a fleecy constantly moving surface. He told her that the surface was used to purify and massage the body. When Irina and Rtsah were alone, she was able to notice additional details about the alien's anatomy. He had round shoulders. His ear hollow was located approximately near the corner of the eye, and it was covered with something, when she touched it, it opened like a shell. The alien had neither nipples nor a navel. She then asked him to show her the anatomy of his brain and through a holographic screen she learned that their brains consisted of three sections, the biggest was in the back of the head. The brain was like a cap, which covered the back of the head and the frontal bone area. It was powerful by volume, very folded and had no such chaotic curves as the humans have. More geometrically correct. Its cervical part narrowed as it went into the spine and spinal cord. The spine bone was spiral. There were large and opened rings and within those rings she was able to see esophagus and trachea. The alien's thorax was larger in comparison to his abdominal cavity. His lungs resembled that of a human, narrow on top and broad on the bottom. There were what appeared to be "hearts" (heart muscle?) inside each lung. Two hearts that worked in unison. The blood was yellow. Rtsah said they did not have much blood, and it served a number of functions, similar to humans. The alien's bowels were shorter, with only one exit opening. Procreating organs were on the same place as of humans, but in a special socket. In the necessary moment the pocket opened.

Their lifespan was more than approximate 1300 to 1500 terrestrial years. Their year is longer than that on earth, 450 days and consisted of ten months. The name of their civilization was "Mlonzels" and their planet's name is "Basurgana" located near the star "Prigesh" in the Orion constellation.

The commander of the alien ship was the oldest alien, more than 900 earth years. After her visit to the alien mother ship, other shorter contacts occurred while Irina was at her job. The image of an alien woman appeared. She said, her name was Reya and her function was to patrol the earth. They told Irina that they had been very active during the Persian Gulf War (first one) in January 1991. At one time while busy at her job the aliens attempted to contact Irina and she resisted, they reprimanded her and reminded her that she must always be ready to enter into contact. During the last contact Rtsah told her he had transferred her to another humanoid by the name of "Kinzul," who will continue her training and education.

HC addendum.
Source: Gennadiy Ya. Leszshenko, 'Edge of the Unknown or What is Behind the Curtain,' Donetsk, 1994.   Type: G or F?

* * * * * * *

Location: Ronneburg, Germany.
Date: January 19, 1991.
Time: 9:00 p.m.

A 38-year old woman was walking along the main street that was totally deserted, when she saw an approaching light overhead, as it got closer she could see that it was a large disc-shaped object with a transparent dome on top. The object emitted a loud humming sound as it briefly hovered over the road.

She could see three very tall human-like figures apparently operating some controls inside the dome. She waved at the figures and they waved back. They seemed to be wearing scaly silvery metallic uniforms with belts that had a peculiar insignia on the buckles, resembling three overlapping leaves. The object soon shot away at incredible speed.

HC addendum.
Source: Michael Hesemann, Etcon Intl. Ulrich Magin.   Type: A

* * * * * * *

Location: Charleston, South Carolina.
Date: January 28, 1991.
Time: Evening.

Elizabeth Baron was in her home, in her art studio doing a commissioned painting of the Blessed Virgin Mary. All of a sudden, she saw three extremely elderly little men in the corner of her studio. They were wrinkled and she knew they must have been at least 90 years of age. They looked at her with deep compassion in their eyes as if they were anxious to see how she would react to their appearance.

They immediately began talking to her through mental telepathy. At the time she had been teaching meditation to about 75 persons at a fitness center. These were the stranger's words, *"The most important thing your world can learn is meditation because it will lift your vibrations to a higher consciousness. Thank you for teaching this to your people."* She cried and thanked them for thanking her and then

135

before she could look up and wipe the tears from her eyes, there was a sort of flashing light and they were gone.

HC addendum.
Source: http://mufoncms.com and www.elizabethbaron.com   Type: E
Comments: Were these humanoids some sort of 'ascended masters' much talked about by mediums and other New Age gurus?

* * * * * * *

Location: Volzhskiy, Volgograd region, Russia.
Date: February, 1991.
Time: 3:00 a.m.

66-year old WWII veteran Nikolay Fyedorovich Pahomov began experiencing strange phenomena in his house for example, light switches would switch on by itself and the TV-set would turn on by itself, one time when it was disconnected from the wall socket.

Five days later the witness woke up in the middle of the night jolted out of his bed by a strong electrical current. He opened his eyes and saw a very tall woman, standing within a halo of luminescent light near the foot of his bed. She was about two meters in height, dressed in a shiny smooth silvery overall, which tightly fitted her figure. She had long light-colored shoulder length hair. But the woman's face was not human, it resembled that of a bird.

The witness became concerned about the visitor's appearance and suddenly heard a telepathic voice telling him not to be afraid that he would not be hurt. *"Why have you come?"* asked Pahomov. The woman reminded him that once a while back he had asked for help because of a painful stomach illness and they were here to help him. Pahomov then told the stranger that he had heard that extraterrestrials were able to perform intricate surgical procedures and requested that she perform one in his stomach. However the alien woman refused, saying that they did not have the "power" to do that but were able to help otherwise.

He asked when she would return and was told, *"On the second day after the New Moon,"* and the woman added that he should warn his family not to approach or enter the room during the encounter, because it was dangerous to cross the "biofield." And then the strange woman disappeared, walking backwards into the wall and melting into it.

HC addendum.
Source: Gennadiy S. Belimov, 'The Other Worlds, On Line,' 1997, Alexey K. Priyma, 'UFOs Witnesses of the Unknown,' 1997.   Type: E
Comments: This was to be Pahomov's first contact of a total of four.

Location: Patagonia, Argentina.
Date: February, 1991.
Time: 3:40 a.m.

Looking for the fabled underground city of "Iberah," the main witness, Miguel Villegas (involved in other contacts), was camping on the shores of a local lake with some friends when suddenly in the early morning all the animals in the area became disturbed, including horses, deer, dogs, etc. Also the surface of the lake became also disturbed as huge waves became apparent, as if in anticipation of 'something' to come.

Villegas stood up and looked around and saw at about 30 meters away a very tall human-like figure about 2.5m in height, wearing a shimmering white gold coverall. The figure had long shoulder length blond hair and large slanted eyes. He smiled at Villegas emitting an aura of love and tranquility.

The entity communicated telepathically with Villegas and welcomed him to the 'city.' He told Villegas that one day when the time came and he was ready he among others will enter the underground realm of Iberah.

After that brief communication the entity vanished in plain sight.

HC addendum.
Source: http://www.astroufo.com/entervistamv.htm   Type: E

Location: Sornay, Saone et Loire, France.
Date: February, 1991.
Time: 3:00 p.m.

The witness was attracted to bright lights in a meadow opposite to his house, about 100 or 150 meters away. He called his daughter and wife who brought over a pair of binoculars. With the help of the binoculars they saw five small beings dressed in metallic gray suits with boots of the same color. Their heads were covered in a sort of helmet with a rectangular clear window in the middle. They seemed to be engage in the collection of grass and dirt. On the center of their chests they have a bright white light.

According to the witnesses they somewhat resembled the famed "Michelin man" of the tire commercial. Some are seen to bend down to pick up plants. A few meters behind them is a dome-shaped bright orange object. During the observation a car is seen to drive by the area and stop, apparently to observe.

Later an anonymous witness comes forward to report that while driving through the area his car suddenly stopped dead and he was then surrounded by several small "men." He was able to see a dull dome shaped object in the field.

HC addendum.
Source: Lumieres Dans La Nuit.   Type: C

* * * * * * *

Location: Tbilisi, Georgia.
Date: February 3, 1991.
Time: 10:20 a.m.

A local female journalist, Irina Adamashvili saw on the slopes of one the mountains that surround Tbilisi a gigantic anthropoid figure which appeared suddenly out of nowhere. It was a massive dazzling white humanoid silhouette that appeared on the gray-brown slope. She watched riveted to the scene the figure which resembled that of a man wearing shiny coveralls. The figure glided rapidly above the ground in a straight line along the slope as it reached a bitumen road it then moved in a strange gait, taking large steps and somewhat bent at the knees. The stunned witness thought that the height of the entity was at least 3-4 meters. The figure was then lost from sight behind a mountain slope.

HC addendum.
Source: 'The Georgia Herald,' February 6, 1991, Mikhail Gershtein, 'Russian Ufological Digest,' January 28, 2002.   Type: E

Location: Near Tucson, Arizona.
Date: February 16, 1991.
Time: 2:00 a.m.

The witness suddenly awoke and went outside her home to see a huge metallic cylinder-shaped craft hovering over the area. It had a pink pulsating light on its front and a blue light at the rear. She could also see a large door. She suddenly found herself inside the object where she saw different types of equipment illuminated by a brilliant blue glow.

Inside the craft she encountered three types of humanoids, one was human-like that appeared to be in charge, several small gray humanoids with pear-shaped heads and huge black oval-shaped eyes, and a third type of being described as tall and reptilian in appearance, with green scaly skin and huge golden-colored eyes.

HC addendum.
Source: Gem G. Cox, Enigma #57.   Type: G

* * * * * * *

Location: Volzhskiy, Volgograd region, Russia.
Date: February 18, 1991.
Time: Night.

A 23-year old local woman named Larissa S. was abducted onboard of a disk or saucer-shaped object in the middle of the night. Onboard she was exposed to an unceremonious and very unpleasant medical examination by several gray skinned entities with large heads and small thin bodies.

As the final verdict, she heard a voice inside her head that told her that she was not fit for the alien's plans (whatever they could have been). In forty minutes she was returned to her bed, she remained in a state of complete shock until the morning.

HC addendum.
Source: 'Mir Nepoznannogo' World of the Unknown, Moscow, #19-20,
October, 1995.   Type: G
Comments: Rare abduction report from Russia describing the stereotype gray alien.

Location: El Yunque, Puerto Rico.
Date: Late February, 1991.
Time: 2:00 a.m.

Three couples, including two current police officers had driven up to the mountain and had parked at a rest stop. They were standing next to their cars talking when they noticed two little men coming down the road ahead of them. The beings were about four-foot tall, very thin, with long thin arms and legs, they had large heads and large black protruding eyes and their skin was light gray in color. They wore dark green outfits that covered everything except their faces and hands.

The beings walked past the witnesses speaking among themselves in a peculiar language. They suddenly stopped, did an about face and walked back the same way they had come. At this point two of the men, who were armed, took out their weapons and attempted to follow the beings, but these seem to notice, stopped looked at the witnesses and then shuffled into the brush at a brisk pace, soon disappearing from sight.

HC addendum.
Source: Jorge Martin, Enigma, #46.   Type: E

* * * * * * *

Location: El Yunque, Puerto Rico.
Date: Late February, 1991.
Time: 7:30 p.m.

Freddie Gonzalez, his wife and their young child, were taking a drive around the rainforest area on Route 191. After cruising the area, the road took a turn and the pair inadvertently took a detour deep into the forest.

After a while they came up to a camouflage gate deeper into the forest and after inspecting it they decided to drive through it. As they drove on the path in the woods they noticed that it was well lit by blue light bulbs on each side of the road, they drove through some hills for about two miles when the road abruptly ended. At its end there was a large metal gate and a building like structure on the other side of it.

At that moment two six-foot tall man-like figures appeared and ordered the pair to stop and asked who they were. The men wore tight-fitting black one-piece suits, resembling diver's outfits, a wide black belt, black gloves, and large black boots with gold-colored metallic straps. They also wore large dark oval shaped helmets with dark visors. Their faces were not visible.

In eerie metallic-electronic sounding voices the strangers ordered the witnesses to step out of the car. The child remained sleeping in the back seat. One of the men took a long thin metallic tube with a mirror like tip and seemed to examine the vehicle. The figures asked the witnesses how they got there and then looked at the sleeping child inside.

They then held a short conversation in a grave guttural language resembling German. One of the "men" then left the area and a blue pickup truck now arrived at the scene. Two men wearing blue coveralls were in the vehicle and spoke in Spanish to the witnesses, again asking them how they got there. The men then looked at the child and commented something in a low tone of voice to the strange figure in black that remained on the scene.

At that moment Freddie noticed a glint of light coming from what appeared to be a rectangular shaped hollowed out area in the nearby wooded slope of a hill. There appeared to be several huge glass-like doors and inside there was a disc shaped object that was encircled in rectangular shaped windows and was 30 ft in diameter, it appeared metallic & aluminum in color.

Thinking that he was seeing something he was not supposed to see, he quickly averted his gaze. The men did not appear to notice that Freddie had seen anything. The men in the blue pickup then ordered the couple and their child to follow them out of the area in their vehicle. They were quickly escorted out onto the main road.

HC addendum.
Source: Jorge Martin, Vieques Poligono Del Tercer Tipo.   Type: E or C?
Comments: Translated by Albert S Rosales.

* * * * * * *

Location: Tenay, France.
Date: End of February, 1991.
Time: 5:45 a.m.

Nadia, a 21-year old student was walking on a path next to the local cemetery when she saw standing about 100 meters away a humanoid figure about 1.6 m in height.

The figure had a large head and what appeared to be a bizarre beak-like protrusion on its face and its body appeared to be covered in bristle like hair, it also had large black eyes and long thin arms. The figure noticed the witness and appeared surprised; it then scampered into the woods and was lost from sight.

HC addendum.
Source: Denys Breysse, Project Becassine.   Type: E

Location: Near Ulan Bator, Mongolia.
Date: Spring, 1991.
Time: Unknown.

While local nomads reported seeing flights of disc-shaped objects over the region, a woman near the capital reportedly encountered a landed disc, along with several human-like beings that emerged from the craft, communicating with her by using telepathy. She was then given a ride in the object and flown over the capital. No other information.

HC addendum.
Source: Fortean Times, #61.   Type: G

* * * * * * *

Location: Near Nerekhta, Kostroma region, Russia.
Date: March 8, 1991.
Time: Night.

Filaret Yakolevich (involved in previous encounters) was sitting on his sofa when he heard a strange bell-like sound at the front door, he approached the door and opened it and encountered two humanoids standing on the threshold. One was about two meters in height, the second approximately 1.8 m in height, possibly a female but at this point the witness could not tell. Both humanoids were dressed in bright green suits. On their heads they wore transparent helmets. He could see very large wide eyes behind the helmet.

He felt no fear as the strangers invited Filaret to go with them. They walked out of the court and the witness mentioned that he was not dressed properly for the cold weather. They told him not to worry, that they would create a comfort zone around him. The humanoids then stood one on each side of the witness and he began to feel very comfortable warmth.

Then in very rapid movements, as if flying, they reached the edge of the woods. There he saw a UFO resembling a flattened sphere of light gray color with a violet sheen. There were no windows or hatchways visible. From below a semitransparent pipe went into the earth. But it was not a support, since the craft appeared to hover about 15 cm from the snowy ground. In some manner all three entered this pipe and were instantly pulled inside the UFO. Inside he found himself in a room 10 x 12 meters in diameter, and about 4.5 meters in height. All angles were rounded. Two doors were seen, and an escalator leading upwards apparently into another room.

He was surprised that the inside the UFO was considerably larger than it appeared to be from outside. Aboard the ship he saw eight

142

additional extraterrestrials. Outwardly they appeared practically equal. Their eyes were golden in color. All wore transparent mask-like helmets. Their hair was short & dark in some of them and light brown in others. He could hear the conversation between the aliens even though their lips remained tightly closed.

The aliens answered some of the questions posed to them by the witness. They explained to the witness that their biological structure was completely different from humans. They did not have heart or lungs, or a digestive system. Their basic organ was some kind of "energy," based organ located where humans had their liver. It resembled a mineral grainy mass. They told the witness that they had visited other areas on earth, including Argentina and the Russian town of Nalchik. Furthermore Filaret learned that the UFO did not require fuel. They somehow were able to dominate gravity and use null space and zero channels to travel.

At this point Filaret expressed his desired to visit their planet and he was told to sit down on a chair very close to a screen. On the screen, which was about 50 x 80 cm in size he saw surprising pictures, he saw other planets and constellations. He then saw what he was told was their planet of origin. He saw beautiful scenes containing enormous trees, without leaves. On the branches were located beautiful houses, multicolored and cube-shaped. Below this huge "trees" grew normal earth sized trees. The air inside the craft smelled like sweet mint, which made him feel very comfortable.

HC addendum.
Source: X-Libri UFO, Russia.   Type: G

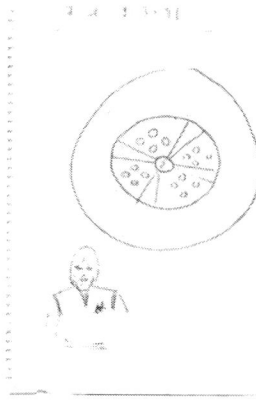

Location: Near Lugo, La Coruna, Spain.
Date: March 8, 1991.
Time: Night.

The witness, Ismael R. (involved in other incidents, some quite controversial) was returning at night to his home, when suddenly a bright light descended over his vehicle and began to follow him closely. Following a strange impulse he took out a small handheld recorder and began filming the light, he was even able to record what appeared to be the sound of the object when it flew over the vehicle.

Soon a beam of light from the object enveloped Ismael and he suddenly found himself inside a large disc-shaped room. There a tall blond haired humanoid wearing a tight-fitting silvery-white diver's suit compelled Ismael to lie on a sort of cot-like bed where he was medically examined. He was then released back into his vehicle.

HC addendum.
Source: Lo Oculto, 'Ovnis en España.'   Type: G

* * * * * * *

Location: Ixtapan, Cuernavaca, Mexico.
Date: March 14, 1991.
Time: 2:00 p.m.

14-year old Ivan Morales was celebrating his birthday, when he stepped out of his house to see a bright green glowing figure on a field about fifteen feet away.

Terrified he called out for other family members and many came out, upon seeing the figure, his brother reportedly collapsed, others were too

144

scared to come out. After about one minute the green glowing figure disappeared.

HC addendum.
Source: http://www.etcontact.net/newsite   Type: E

* * * * * * *

Location: Volzhskiy, Volgograd region, Russia.
Date: March 15, 1991.
Time: Night.

66-year old WW II veteran, Nikolay Fyedorovich Pahomov, suddenly awoke in the middle of the night and saw a pale red-orange circle of light floating about one meter from his bed. Within the circle, stood an alien woman, unlike the previous visitor (February) this woman had a normal human face. He saw her as if through a transparent slightly matt glass. She was dressed in a shiny overall with a rolled up collar, without zippers or fastenings. She was tall, but not taller than 1.8m. Her outer appearance was that of a woman of about 25-30 years old. Her face was kind, attractive, with gray-blue eyes. They spoke for about 7-8 minutes, the woman spoke via telepathy while Nikolay answered in a loud voice.

The voice of her husband awoke Nikolay's wife, Nina Iljinichna, in the neighboring room, but an unknown wave of fear came over her, which forced her to cover her head with the blanket remaining very still, hardly breathing.

Nikolay then asked the alien, *"Why have you come to visit me?"* The woman words appeared in Nikolay's head, *"Do the following. Place the palm of your right hand on the solar plexus and wave your left hand closely, not touching the stomach, over your bowels, strongly straining the fingers of that hand. Do this for a period of 1-2 minutes for several days and all will be gone."* Nikolay again remembered when he had prayed for divine or "alien" help for his chronic stomach problems. He then asked the woman if they could give him the ability to cure people. He was told that he did not need it.

He then asked, *"Will I die soon?"* He was told he would live for some time still. He then asked if the soul survived death. The alien woman answered, *"Your biological mass will die but the soul will remain and may then enter another person in time."* He then asked about religion and the alien woman explained to him that their civilization first visited Earth about 4 million years ago and that religion had been "implanted" to keep people in tightly control with fear and discipline. He then asked how long would the difficulties in Russia would last and was told until 2000, that everything would stable after that (not true). *"Is it true that extraterrestrials abduct people?"* The witness asked, the woman

145

answered that the Earth was most frequently visited by three extraterrestrial civilizations, one, which was aggressive in nature.

He then asked, *"Where are you from?"* The answer was, *"Our base is in Sirius, and the distance to earth is overcome in 15 seconds."* (!) Pahomov then asked what kind of "fuel" did they use and was told that none, that they used the earth magnetic field and of the "cosmic magnetic field." He then asked how often did robots visit the earth, and was told quite frequently. Pahomov then asked the woman directly, *"Are you real, do you have a soul?" "I am a real woman,"* smiled the alien stranger for the first time.

Pahomov then asked, *"What do you need from me?"* The woman then told him to build an antenna and to place it in the window facing the southwest. That it must consist of eight rings of copper wire from 50cm to 2cm in diameter. The antenna would protect him from harmful influences of "space rays" and would help in their communication process. Nikolay was also led to understand that the aliens track, and even numbered people. *"Would you return?"* He asked. The woman said that not immediately and then her image began to disappear and the light began to dim, finally vanishing completely. After this visit, all the family members including Nikolay felt ill for three days.

HC addendum.
Source: Gennadiy S. Belimov, 'The Other Worlds, On Line,' Volgograd, 1997, Alexey K. Priyma, 'UFOs: Witnesses of the Unknown,' Moscow, 1997.   Type: E

* * * * * * *

Location: Near Serra de Maresias, Sao Paolo, Brazil.
Date: March 16, 1991.
Time: 2:00 a.m.

Trucker Carlos Alberto de Jesus, 38, was traveling on Route BR101 one night when he came upon a landed luminous oval shaped craft on the side of the road. Moments later the truck engine stalled, and another car, a sports vehicle also stopped behind the truck.

Seconds' later two humanoid figures, small in size about 1.2 m in height emerged from the object. They wore a one-piece light colored outfit, with a diver's helmet with transparent visors. They had what appeared to be tubes connecting from their backs to the helmet. Behind the visors, De Jesus could see shiny cat-like eyes.

The humanoids stared at the trucker and then turned around and "floated" towards the landed object. The object then projected a cone of brilliant light that enveloped the two humanoids, and they then disappeared. The object then rose up, rotated and shot away at incredible speed. At this time, the truck engine re-started and the witness drove away into the night.

HC addendum.
Source: Fabio Avolio, Grupo Vega, Brazil.   Type: B

* * * * * * *

Location: Edwards Air Force Base, California.
Date: April, 1991,
Time: Unknown.

A construction contractor working at an underground installation thirty stories deep, was walking down a hall with another man when some doors opened unexpectedly.

They then caught sight of a figure at least nine-feet tall, wearing a lab jacket and talking to two human engineers. The figure was humanoid with long arms almost down to his knees, a large head with huge black slanted eyes and greenish skin. Security personnel then ushered both witnesses out.

HC addendum.
Source: Elaine Douglass, Right to Know Forum, Sep/Oct 92.   Type: E

* * * * * * *

Location: Tenjo, Colombia.
Date: April 2, 1991.
Time: 4:00 a.m.

A local peasant saw a large metallic cylinder shaped craft land nearby as he rode his donkey on his way to work. A blinding light enveloped him and he felt being lifted and taken onboard the object. Inside his head he heard assuring words telling him that he was not going to be hurt.

He then met four, four-foot tall humanoids that appeared to be covered in a perpetual mist. The object then entered a huge "mother-ship" type craft. He was then examined on a table and cured of kidney stones. Also a small microchip was surgically placed in his left shoulder.

He was later deposited back on earth at a place almost 600 miles from his home.

HC addendum.
Source: Louis E. Mejia, Earth Station Foundation.   Type: G

Location: Cogullos, Burgos, Spain.
Date: April 28-29, 1991.
Time: Various.

A couple, Nectali Saiz, and his wife Ermitas Rodriguez, were working in a field collecting firewood, when they first spotted bright, multicolored lights resembling that of ambulance. Soon after, the lights disappeared and they spotted a metallic, cigar shaped craft resting on the field.

Suddenly the craft vertically positioned itself and descended onto the field (locally known as "La Mata"), about 1,500 meters from the astounded couple. When all the lights on the object dimmed, a 'door' on the object became visible, and eight humanoid like creatures emerged from the object.

The witnesses described the figures as human-like with long dangling arms, with bodies covered in blondish hair and reddish faces. The bizarre humanoids seemed to move around in strange hops and jumps. According to the witnesses the humanoids apparently communicated with them using hand gestures, which they responded in turn. They additionally described the creatures as about two meters in height, having very large pointy ears, with claw-like feet. According to the witnesses, despite the distance, once the door on the craft opened, they were able to clearly see details due to a very bright light that emanated from inside the object.

Mr. Saiz reported that one of the creatures approached him and grabbed his right wrist, causing him severe pain that remained for several days after the encounter. His wife, Ermitas, reported suffering from nightmares after the encounters in which she saw herself onboard the UFO. Both also suffered from some sight loss during the whole month of May.

Ermitas Rodriguez, reported seeing a bright light on the same field again the following day and woke up her sleeping her husband again. They watched the metallic, cigar-shaped craft descend on to the field. This time seven humanoid occupants emerged from the craft, the humanoids were of the same exact description as before, and remained moving back and forth on the field for some time, according to the investigators, small 'footprints' were found on the field, which appeared to have deep heel-like impressions.

HC addendum.
Source: Javier Sierra, 'Mas Alla,' 1991 and 1992.   Type: B

Location: Olivares, Puerto Rico.
Date: May, 1991.
Time: Unknown.

Eunice Acosta, a local resident, who has also witnessed many UFOs near the radar blimp and is the sister of another witness (Dolin Acosta), claims to have fought off and prevented an apparent attempt at abduction by these creatures.

Another local resident, Eleuterio Acosta, a very serious eighty-year old man who lives just in front of the radar blimp facility. He says that he was once surrounded by five of these small grey creatures as he entered his home. He managed to confront them with a stick and yelled at them, at which point a sixth, taller creature of the same type communicated with the other five, and they all jumped out through a window and fled quickly, heading towards the Sierra Bermeja.

There is also a claim by some of the policemen who stand guard at the radar facility, who say they encountered several of the creatures when the facility was being built in 1989.

HC addendum.
Source: Jorge Martin, 'Alien Update,' p. 27.   Type: E

* * * * * * *

Location: Lancaster, California.
Date: May 14, 1991.
Time: 11:00 p.m.

Pam (involved in other sightings) reports that three "grays" appeared by her bedside and started to lift her off the bed. She lives in a large, custom built pentagonal desert home that has one large room without partitions. The kitchen, bedroom and living room are open to one another. She started to struggle with the grays, the four foot and a half foot category, when she spotted a human in the living room area. A man dressed all in black, was holding a device that resembled a small TV and dangling a cord. Pam heard the man say, *"You have no electricity."*

At this point she somehow freed herself from the entities and went to grab a light cord that would switch on a light from her twelve-volt system. The light would not come on. She then yelled for her husband to awaken. Events then took a bizarre turn.

Hearing her 100-pound Labrador barking in the yard, she and her husband went to the north facing kitchen window.

Her attention was draw to another man who lay prone on a projecting part of the roof near a ladder. The man was dressed in full-dress Air Force blues. The three grays were now on the ground below the

149

man as well as a K-9 sentry dog that was poised to attack Pam's dog, Casey. In the sky over the yard there were a number of red lights. The man yelled to the grays, "get her out of the house," while Pam yelled back "don't kill my dog."

In the wake of this panic, Pam next remembers sanding alone outside and behind their generator shack. The man, the dog, the grays and her husband were no longer in sight. Red lights were revolving above her and a thick fog was emanating from ports set around the large craft hovering above.

Her next memory was that of awakening, seated on her bed at 3:50 a.m. Pam believes that she may have been taken to a base inside the Tehachapi Mountains and that she was cautioned not to reveal what she knows. She felt very threatened by this incident.

HC addendum.
Source: Bill Hamilton, Mufon Ufo Journal #286.   Type: G?

* * * * * * *

Location: Mini Mini, Puerto Rico.
Date: May 14, 1991.
Time: Various.

Two teenagers were playing in an isolated field and encountered a small circular silvery metallic object on the ground. It was very shiny and had a small dome-like sphere on its top. The boys approached the object and began touching it.

Suddenly a small hatch opened on the bottom of the craft and a long thin green arm came out grabbing one of the boys by his leg. As the boy struggled to get away a second thin arm emerged and grabbed him by his arm. The boy grabbed a piece of wood and began striking one of the creature's arms. He managed to cut off one of the fingers and the creature let go. The finger fell to the ground oozing a green liquid. The witnesses attempted to retrieve the severed finger but dropped it during the panic. They both fled but later returned to find both the object and its occupant gone.

The evening of the same day, an adult witness was looking out his bedroom window when he briefly saw a short green skinned figure with large pointy ears, a pear-shaped head, and large red oval shaped eyes. The figure quickly scurried away into the brush.

The following day, May 15, on the grounds of the local elementary school, a short green humanoid with red oval-shaped eyes, and huge pointy ears, apparently approached and attempted to communicate with one of the kindergarten class children. It spoke to the child in a strange

150

"chatter-type" language and it ran quickly into the brush when some of the other children approached.

Near the same spot of the previous encounter, two boys were playing near the woods when they heard a noise and saw a strange being emerge from the woods. The being was described as short and bright green in color, with an oval shaped head, large almond shaped eyes and huge pointed ears. It was thin with very long arms with three digit hands, the being stood looking at the witnesses emitting a strange "chatter" like noise. The witnesses threw fruits at it then chased it, but it ran quickly and disappeared down a drain aqueduct. At one point the being grabbed one of the boys by the foot making him fall.

HC addendum.
Source: Jorge Martin, Enigma #42.   Type: A? & E

* * * * * * *

Location: Bukit Tunggal, Terengganu, Malaysia.
Date: Middle of May, 1991.
Time: Daytime.

Around the same time as there were a series of micro-terrestrial encounters involving children at a school in Terengganu, at another location several kilometers away, an unidentified man caught a tiny entity measuring only two inches tall. The entity, seen by a schoolteacher, was described as human-like. It was kept in a bottle. When the teacher saw it, she said it was still alive. However, she does not want to disclose the identity of the person who caught it for some unknown reason.

HC addendum.
Source: Ahmad Jamaluddin.   Type: H?

* * * * * * *

Location: Barrio Las 700, Arecibo, Puerto Rico.
Date: Last week of May, 1991.
Time: Night.

The witness had gone to the seashore to inspect some fish traps and was approaching the water when he noticed three short figures bending over the water's edge, apparently inspecting something on the ground.

Suddenly the three beings turned and looked at the witness emitting a bright red light from their eyes. The beings had thin bodies; large round heads and appeared identical to each other.

151

The witness who had been walking with his bicycle then attempted to flee the area, falling several times as he attempted to mount his bicycle. He felt some type of mental communication from the beings, who urged him to stay. He was finally able to peddle away from the area.

HC addendum.
Source: Jorge Martin, Evidencia OVNI #1.   Type: E

* * * * * * *

Location: Rural Maine (exact location not given).
Date: Summer, 1991.
Time: 2:00 a.m.

The witness had gone to bed late at night when he suddenly heard what could best be described as "tones" in his head. It was as if he was wearing headphones, the notes seemed to move from ear to ear. As the tempo of the sounds increased, they were joined by, not so much a voice, but a feeling that said, *"Relax, Don't be afraid."*

Suddenly it felt as he had stuck his head out a car window that was accelerating from 0–300 in just a few seconds. Then everything stopped. He floated in total silence, looking through what seemed like a filter at the Earth many miles below. Next, he was in a very old place. In design, much like a university or cathedral. There were "monks" there, tall beings in long hooded cloaks whose faces were hidden from the witness. He followed one of them outside where he sat beside a small river surrounded by very fine sand. The tall humanoid showed him a book with pages that moved. As he sat there he was overcome with the most amazing sense of awe. It was as though everything suddenly became clear, and he knew what life was really about.

Suddenly things shifted once again. He was standing on top of cliff. The cliff was a dusty yellow/orange color. The ground below was torn up, dead trees pushed up from broken dirt and rocks. He then looked down at himself, wearing what appeared to be very primitive armor. Standing beside him was an old man in similar garb. There were some horse-like animals with them. When he mounted one, it flew.

All of this ended with a loud rushing sound. He was once again in his bedroom. He was not able to speak about the incident for a long time afterwards.

HC addendum.
Source: UFO Casebook, Forums.   Type: G?

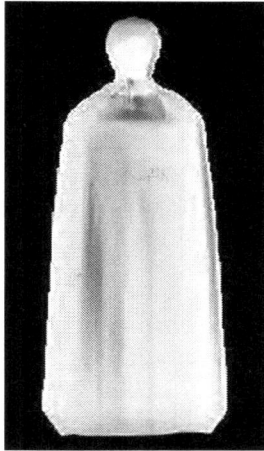

Location: Vicuna, Chile.
Date: Summer, 1991.
Time: 5:00 a.m.

Two men were sleeping on an isolated hillside, when C. J. suddenly woke up, feeling a presence around him. He looked up and saw a tall luminous figure approaching their position. The figure was about 1.9 meters in height, thin, with wide shoulders and completely hairless. It was coming directly at the witness, quickly gliding just above the ground. C.J. woke up his friend M.C. that also saw the luminous figure. The figure suddenly stopped two meters from the witnesses, turned in a 45 degree angle, then glided up to the mountain at very high speed, quickly disappearing from sight.

The next day both men observed a silvery sphere hovering above the mountain, the sphere emitted a bright intermittent flash of light. It suddenly rose up and disappeared from sight.

HC addendum.
Source: Proyecto Orion, 2000.   Type: D

Location: Near Foros, Crimea, Ukraine.
Date: Summer, 1991.
Time: Daytime.

The witness, Stanislav K., at the time a doctor's assistant in one of the medical hospitals in Simferopol was traveling with a small group of colleagues in the mountains to the north of the hamlet of Foros. Walking near a very deep ravine the group suddenly felt a strong unexplained fear, without any obvious visible motives.

Terrified, the group stood in place and looked down the ravine and saw a humanoid entity walking or moving down the mountain slope. The creature was tall, about two meters in height; its body was entirely covered with dense fur. The entity emitted a very unpleasant odor that reminded the witnesses of a decaying corpse. At that moment the group could no longer stand in place and ran quickly away from the area.

HC addendum.
Source: Dmitriy Sinitsa, 'Snowman in the Crimean Mountains?' Pervaya Krymskaya" newspaper #3, January 26-February 1, 2007.   Type: E
Comments: I believe the sudden aura of fear experienced by the group is some type of defense mechanism used by different types of anomalous entities.

* * * * * * *

Location: Near Alekseevskiy, Rostov-on-Don region, Russia.
Date: Summer, 1991.
Time: Evening.

Three men were transporting apiary (beehives) in a KAMAZ truck when they suddenly spotted three humanoid figures which crossed the road quickly ahead of them. The humanoids could be clearly seen, lighted by the truck's headlights.

The stunned beekeepers and the truck's driver noticed that the humanoids were dressed in tight-fitting silvery suits and quickly disappeared into the darkness as they moved hastily across the road. They were definitely not human beings, their silvery clothing and their manner of walking was very strange. Others in the region were regularly observing UFOs.

HC addendum.
Source: 'NLO-Liaisons of the Universe?' almanac, Lugansk, Ukraine #4 August, 1993.   Type: D

Location: Mramornoye (Marble village) Zarechnoye, Crimea, Ukraine.
Date: May or June 1991.
Time: Early morning.

A local woman (involved in a previous encounter with a low hovering disc-shaped object which scanned her with a beam of light) was on her way to work in the village of Alushta. On this day she was walking on highway towards the bus/trolley stop in the village of Zarechnoye. But before she reached the stop she noticed a "Zhiguli" type vehicle parked on the side of the road as if waiting for her, on the driver side there was the unmoving figure of a man, the car appeared to be a typical "Zhiguli" model made in Togliatti model after the Italian Fiat-124. She came up to the car, opened the door and offered the driver some money for a ride, but the rider brushed the money off, indicating that he will give her the ride for free. So she sat on the front passenger seat and the car began to move.

After moving some distance she began to pay attention to the driver, that in all aspects was bizarre in appearance, there was something "frightening" about him. The driver was very tall, about 1.8 to 185m in height, looked to be about 40 years of age, and heavy set, with dark eyes and hair. She then noticed a strange thing, the driver's eyes did not move or blink, and he had an inhuman stare, always looking straight ahead. In general the driver behaved like some type of android or cyborg, not a living human being and definitely not your common Russian or Ukrainian man. On the road they did not speak to each other and then something amazing occurred, the driver switched on something in the car's control panel and let go of the steering wheel, in amazement the witness watched the steering wheel moving by itself as if in automatic pilot, while the driver seemed to have been "switched off."

She then noticed that the car's interior included several strange control panels and instruments not even remotely resembling a typical Russian made vehicle. From the outside the vehicle looked normal, but inside it was totally "alien" in appearance. They "drove" about 20km to Alushta (located on the banks of the Black Sea) and the stunned woman walked out of the car and saw it driving away. The strange driver did not bid farewell, she never saw the stranger car or driver again.

HC addendum.
Source: Vladimir P. Boyko, Simferopol UFO Research Group, Dr. Anton A. Anfalov, Simferopol, Crimea Ukraine.   Type: E?
Comments: Another case describing a sort of "pseudo-car" with a bizarre occupant. Similar cases are apparently frequent in the areas of the former Soviet Union, but there has been cases reported in the USA, United Kingdom, Sweden, etc.

Location: Caucasus Region, Russia.
Date: June, 1991.
Time: Daytime.

A local shepherd boy, Farhat, was looking for stray cows outside his village when he heard some strange noises or "signals." He slowly approached a nearby glade and saw something that terrified him. He saw several small robotic-looking beings and a landed disc-shaped object. The disk had three rectangular landing props under its belly and a rectangular opening in the middle and a huge dome on top. The dome was segmented on two parts with a band crossing the dome on the middle on top of the disk, and both visible parts were transparent. The disk also had a cubic-shaped device that stretched to the right on a tube-like extension. This device moved in and out of the hull.

The witness hid behind some bushes and watched. The robotic beings were about 190-200cm in height, with rectangular angular bodies and rectangular heads, with straight antennas and blinking lights on top. Their "legs" were straight and were hovering in the air about 15cm from the ground. Instead of hands they had some objects resembling manipulators, shaped like springs. The aliens held a device resembling a pump and began absorbing or pumping soil and grass samples into it. After they finished their job the floated into the opening on the disk, the opening closed and the disk zoomed up and disappeared from sight.

HC addendum.
Source: 'Fourth Dimension,' News bulletin of Yaroslavl UFO Research Group, #5, 1992.   Type: B

* * * * * * *

Location: Near Queretaro, Mexico.
Date: June, 1991.
Time: Night.

Eduardo Martinez was driving not far from the city of Queretaro, when his vehicle engine and headlights suddenly quit. He stepped out of his car and was approached by two men, wearing dark blue coveralls that had dark eyes, black hair, and wrinkled skin.

The humanoids communicated via telepathy and told Martinez they were a peaceful race and did not wish to interfere with things on earth. Among other things the humanoids said to Martinez was, that they have been visiting the earth since 1971 and had at different times taken earthlings up into their spaceships. No other information.

HC addendum. Source: Contacto Ovni.   Type: C?

Location: Near La Parguera, Puerto Rico.
Date: June, 1991.
Time: 10:30 p.m.

A family of five was driving slowly along a rural road, when suddenly they experienced vehicle trouble. They were unable to re-start the car. They then decided to stay in the car overnight. Moments later they saw numerous military jeeps heading at high speed to a nearby remote radar station. Twenty minutes later they all saw a huge multi-colored light hovering next to the radar aerial. The light suddenly descended over their vehicle and they could now see it was a huge disc-shaped craft.

The frightened witnesses then saw a little humanoid jump on top of the hood of the car, it was short and thin with a large egg shaped head, with large bright red eyes that had a point of light in the center and had long arms with long thin fingers. It also had gray-white skin and wore a gray white skintight outfit. The witnesses suddenly heard a telepathic message telling them "to calm down and not to resist." Suddenly they all felt a sudden calm and lost all will to resist. Two more similar beings then appeared and one of them took the youngest child, telling him that it was a special baby and that it had a special task in the future.

The witnesses then got out of the car and were hit by a beam of light from the hovering disc; they all suddenly found themselves inside the object. They were all taken to a huge room resembling a laboratory and told to lie down on metallic tables. Several examinations and tests were performed on them. At one point a taller more human looking being appeared and told the witnesses of future events and coming world changes. Before releasing them, the humanoids told the witnesses that one day they were going to return and take their youngest son.

HC addendum.
Source: Jorge Martin, Enigma #58.   Type: G

*   *   *   *   *   *   *

Location: Centerville, Indiana.
Date: June 8, 1991.
Time: Night.

The 29-year old witness was standing in his backyard when suddenly he saw a bright light and was then transported into a triangular shaped object and into a triangular room.

Inside the room two 7-foot tall entities with flat features and slanted eyes apparently made contact with him via telepathy. They applied a pen-sized black object to his right arm, which left marks, visible weeks later. They then put a small silver box near the witness right temple causing him to lose consciousness. He awoke later in his bed feeling very ill. Ground traces were reportedly found.

HC addendum.
Source: Don Worley, Mufon Journal #298.   Type: G

* * * * * * *

Location: Zarechnoye, Nizhnegorskiy area, Crimea, Ukraine.
Date: June 12, 1991.
Time: Night.

According to the only witness of this supposed event, 22-year old local resident and construction worker, Fikret Seithalilov saw a disk-shaped object appear and land near the village several dozens of meters from him. A dwarf-type humanoid entity about 120 cm in height was seen standing near the landed UFO. The witness remarked that the entity seemed "almost transparent, like glass."
After no more than three or four seconds, the entity vanished, as well as the saucer-shaped object. The witness claims that he is a telepathic contactee with extraterrestrial intelligences.

HC addendum.
Source: Krymskaya Gazeta newspaper, Yalta, Crimea.
June 30, 1994.   Type: C

* * * * * * *

Location: Pilar, Paraguay.
Date: June 13, 1991.
Time: Night.

Mexico's Excelsior newspaper, the nation's newspaper of record, carried a brief and intriguing note on an "extraterrestrial entity" seen in the South American country of Paraguay. The account originally carried by the ANSA news wire service stated, "A radio station employee in the city of Pilar claims having seen a humanoid, presumably an extraterrestrial."
It went on to describe how Antonio Acuña, accompanied by a passenger, was driving to a radio station in the middle of the night when he was startled to see a figure on the road that "at first resembled a human being" but upon closer inspection proved to have a head, hands and feet of a different, darker color. Acuña described the entity as having "very slender fingers" and clad in a white outfit with "a strange source of light on its chest."

158

The radio station employee and his passenger told the media that the strange image "vanished suddenly." No follow up was provided.

HC addendum.
Source: Scott Corrales, Inexplicata, http://inexplicata.blogspot.com.ar/
Type: E

* * * * * * * *

Location: Gainesville, Florida.
Date: June 15, 1991.
Time: 6:00 p.m.

The two witnesses had gone into the woods outside the Gainesville Job Corps Center. As they were walking towards a campsite, one of the men stopped and claimed he had seen two werewolf-like beings float by, the other witness did not see this since he had been looking down at the time. They continued walking, when they spotted an object on the ground. It was roughly saucer-shaped and it was silent.

They advanced slowly towards the object when it suddenly disappeared (or became invisible). As the witnesses moved on, an uncontrollable fear suddenly took hold of them and they began running away from the area. One of the men looked over his shoulder to see a tall, dark; large headed being wearing a dark robe with its hand folded in front of it. The witnesses did not stop and never returned to the area.

HC addendum.
Source: NUFORC   Type: C

* * * * * * * *

Location: Monte Grande, Puerto Rico.
Date: End of June, 1991.
Time: 10:30 p.m.

The witness had gone outside for a moment, when she felt compelled to look behind her and up. She then saw two hovering egg-shaped objects right above the house. One was bright silvery in color and was emitting a golden light from inside. The other object was totally black.

From an opening on the bright silvery object, a short thin figure was seen to emerge and walk on a beam of gold-orange light, towards the black object. It seemed to enter the black egg-shaped craft, and then both objects abruptly vanished.

159

The being was described as about 4-foot tall, very thin with a large head. It had large black slanted eyes and pale gray skin. It wore a tight-fitting silvery outfit that covered it up to its neck.

HC addendum.
Source: Jorge Martin, Enigma #47.   Type: B

* * * * * * *

Location: Stupnikovo, Kostroma region, Russia.
Date: Mid 1991.
Time: 10:00 p.m.

A group of local fishermen saw five humanoids dressed in tight-fitting and shiny coveralls. Amazingly the humanoids appeared to be walking on the surface of the River Volga. No one noticed from where the humanoids had come from. All humanoids were of similar height, no more than 150cm, and wearing helmets. Their movement seemed monotonous and mechanical in nature, similar to a robot.

An interesting detail was noted; the water appeared not to be disturbed when the aliens walked on it. The witnesses noticed that the aliens had very large noses, disproportional to the size of their heads. The amazed witnesses began to enthusiastically call the strange entities over, to meet them on shore. The aliens ignored the witnesses and continued straight over the water.

After about 2-3 minutes the humanoids were suddenly covered by a small but dense cloud that descended from above like a bank of fog and then dissipated in a few minutes, after that happened the humanoids were nowhere to be seen.

The fishermen remembered that a UFO shaped slightly like a flattened globe was seen circling in the evenings over the nearby village of Zavrazhye, stopping in midair and hovering in place for time to time. They assumed that the bizarre humanoids were somehow related to this UFO.

HC addendum.
Source: Vitaliy Duatchkov, Kostroma based UFO Researcher and
Vladimir G. Azhazha PhD, 'Ufological Mysteria,' Moscow, 2002. Type: D

Location: Bohol, Philippines.
Date: July, 1991.
Time: 3-4:00 a.m.

The witness had gone outside early in the morning, when he saw a large disc-shaped object flying above the house slowly. It was circular with multi-colored lights. After it passed the house, it circled twice and then landed near a hill not far from the house. When he approached the craft, he realized that it was really floating just above the ground.

After a while an opening became visible, and a ramp descended to the ground. He then saw two figures come out of the object which he described as having large egg-shaped heads and "malnourished bodies." The two figures walked around the object briefly and collected something from the ground, after that they re-entered the craft which then rose and flew away at high speed.

Later around 6:00 a.m. he went to the site of the incident and discovered a large circular area of burned grass. He also noticed that some plants (baka baka plants, a round leave with a small violet flower) had been pulled from the ground and were missing.

HC addendum.
Source: warrener_07@yahoo.com   Type: B

*   *   *   *   *   *   *

Location: Sao Tome las Lestras, Minas Gerais, Brazil.
Date: July, 1991.
Time: Afternoon.

Farm laborer Julio Cesar Mendes was working on the fields on a hill known as "Cruceiros," when a sudden fog invaded the area. Looking towards the nearby valley, he noticed a bright light flying above the ground and approaching his location.

As the light approached and flew over an area known as "The Witch's Stone," Julio noticed that it was a disc-shaped craft that hovered at about twenty meters from the witness. He could see a transparent cupola on top of the craft, and inside was able to clearly see the figure of a man with tanned skin and short black hair, and refined facial features. The man wore a tight-fitting aviator suit.

At this point the witness became terrified and his heart started racing, however he calmed down when he heard the following phrase in his mind, *"Blessed are those who do not see but believe."* According to the witness, the craft emitted a violet-orange glow and emitted a soft alternating humming sound. Soon after hearing the phrase in his mind he perceived that someone was moving his head and was attempting to

161

introduce something into his right ear, at this moment he apparently lost consciousness.

Later Julio awoke in the same location feeling very confused. Days later he noticed a large unusual accumulation of wax in his left ear, he went to the ear doctor who immediately performed a deep auricular canal cleaning, However upon removing the excess wax the doctor was surprised to find a tiny metallic cylinder shaped object less than 1/2cm in diameter and black in color, unfortunately the discarded the object.

HC addendum.
Source: Anibal G. Mesquita, Brazil.   Type: A or G?
Comments: There is no mention of hypnotic regression being performed on the witness.

* * * * * * *

Location: Near Brewster, New York.
Date: July, 1991.
Time: Late evening.

The main witness had been receiving telepathic messages from an unknown source that invited him to come to a certain location. Along with two of his friends he went to the isolated wooded area for the prearranged meeting. As they walked down a dark road they began noticing peculiar cool spots and a tingling sensation in their feet.

Moments later as the main witness walked ahead he was suddenly illuminated by a six foot circular shaft of blue light from above. As the other two watched he appeared to become transparent and his skeleton became briefly visible. Then, as all three walked down the road they noticed about a dozen beings, about five-foot tall and wearing dark hooded monk-like outfits, moving towards them. The beings had glowing red eyes and were moving silently approaching.

The witnesses, then afraid, ran to their vehicle, the beings approached to within ten feet of the car and then turned sharply, walking through some brush and disappearing into a rocky outcropping. Then shortly after, the witnesses observed several red glowing eyes traveling down the other side of the road, however no forms seemed to be attached to them. At this point the witnesses decided to leave the area.

HC addendum.
Source: Anastasia Wietrzychowski, UFO Universe, Spring, 1994.
Type: C?
Comments: Similar case reported in May.

Location: Los Angeles, California.
Date: July, 1991.
Time: Night.

Melinda Leslie and two friends were driving through the Los Angeles forest when all three experienced a 2-hour long abduction into a metallic craft piloted by gray-type aliens. Once on board they were undressed, examined, separated and given separate messages. Melinda was able to recall the entire event consciously.

As she was laid out and examined, she hammered the aliens with questions, none of which they answered. She saw her friend sitting in a chair with a bizarre looking headset on him and she screamed out, *"What are you doing to him?"* One of the aliens replied, *"It's all right, we're giving him information. It's all right. We're educating him."* Melinda continued to let out a stream of questions, however she was rarely answered, and then, only in an evasive manner.

At one point the three friends were separated and placed into different rooms. Melinda found herself in a room with a dozen grays. One stepped up to her and said, *"Now, we're going to do something. Don't be afraid, but this is very important that we do this. We're going to put this over your head."* What followed was a bizarre procedure. A device placed over her head immobilized Melinda. The aliens stood in a circle around Melinda and pushed her back and forth like a punching clown. Melinda felt she was going to fall, but each time she was caught and pushed again. Finally, she relaxed. At this point, they stopped and removed the device. One of the aliens said, *"You needed to learn to trust us."*

Meanwhile, Melinda's friend, James was receiving a different message. The aliens came over to him and they showed him a device, different items. They told him how to make a UFO detector, and they gave him the information. When sightings happen, they told him he had a mission to document them.

HC addendum.
Source: Preston Dennett.   Type: G

Location: Brooklyn Heights, New York.
Date: July 3, 1991.
Time: 9:00 p.m.

The witness, Emil C. Rodriguez, was standing on a street corner waiting for the light to change when he got the sudden urge to look up to his right. A sudden bizarre stillness came over the area at the same time. He then saw a brightly lit oval shaped object descend from the sky and hover above a nearby building. There were other witnesses in the area who were seen looking up at the object.

The craft had four large rectangular-shaped openings. Several human-like figures both male and female could be seen looking out from the openings. The object was smooth with a small dome on top. There were two beings behind each glass panel, one male, and one female. All appeared to emit a certain radiance. One of the male beings seemed to be holding a round red-lighted device in his right hand. The male beings were described as taller than the females with long blond shoulder length hair. All had high cheekbones and had a light tanned complexion. All wore close-fitting emerald colored outfits with what appeared to be glittering crystals imbedded in them.

The craft tilted down as the beings looked down at the witness, then drifted slowly away disappearing behind some trees. The witness apparently perceived some type of mental communication from the beings.

HC addendum.
Source: Emil C. Rodriguez, Unsolved UFO Sightings, Summer 1994.
Type: A

* * * * * * *

Location: Near Uchkuduk, Kyzylkumy desert, Uzbekistan.
Date: July 5, 1991.
Time: 5:00 p.m.

The UFO research group headed by eminent Russian researcher Mark Milkhiker was expecting a UFO contact on this location on the above date according to information received through telepathic means. However, the whole operation was under military supervision and control. The site chosen was located inside the crater of an ancient dormant volcano.

Soon a luminous globe-shaped object appeared high in the sky. Excited, one of the researchers, Vasiliy Poverennov grabbed a camera and ran towards the object. The globe remained hovering in one place but suddenly a huge column of light descended from the globe and into the crater. The column of light was about 300 meters in diameter. It was X-shaped, oscillating continuously.

Suddenly two luminous humanoid figures separated from the column of light. They were evidently a male and a female. They appeared not to be solid but more like holograms. Milkhiker rushed towards the humanoids together with his wife, Galina Stebenyova, but immediately he perceived a message in his head that said urgently, *"Don't approach, our energy is dangerous!"* He felt a burn on his arm, and later medics found a strange shaped mark. All electronic equipment then began to malfunction.

Half an hour later the figures and the light vanished. The research group also departed in Mi-8 military helicopters. Everything was apparently photographed and filmed. Unfortunately the photos were of very bad quality (due to radiation?) but general images of the column of light and the humanoid figures could be seen.

It was later apparent that what was left of the Soviet military back then had organized a trap for the aliens. It was revealed that three divisions had been deployed in a state of full readiness. Their orders had been to seize the UFO and the extraterrestrials, but the plan obviously failed.

HC addendum.
Source: 'Zhizn,' (Life) Moscow #176, August 31, 2002, and Anton Anfalov.   Type: B & F?

* * * * * * *

Location: Mera, La Coruña, Spain.
Date: July 25, 1991.
Time: 2:00 a.m.

Around midnight on the above date, Jose Garcia, his wife and her parents watched a delta-shaped object similar to a tube made out of hundreds of lights. The object remained static in the sky over the coastal area it was eventually covered up by fog.

Later that morning a local couple watched two very tall human-like figures wearing maroon tunics and white hoods. Both were carrying what appeared to be carrying bags and were moving slowly like 'robots.' When the humanoids saw the witnesses, one of them removed its hood revealing long black hair. The couple hid behind a nearby fence and watched the two entities disappear in the direction of the beach.

HC addendum.
Source: Lo Oculto, 'Ovnis en España,'   Type: D

Location: Near Baku, Azerbaijan.
Date: Early August, 1991.
Time: Unknown.

Students from a local military academy encountered a strange creature near the city. It was described as huge, covered with black hair, and with one large red "eye" in the center of its face, just like a Cyclops. No other information.

HC addendum.
Source: Fortean Times #63.   Type: E
Comments: Similar creatures have been reported deep in the Brazilian Amazon.

* * * * * * *

Location: Krutaya Knoll, Kamchatka peninsula, Far East, Russia.
Date: August, 1991.
Time: Unknown.

Reportedly, V. Subbotin, while staying with a geological team of prospectors near Krutaya Hill, had entered in contact with an extraterrestrial civilization. The contact was in the non-verbal form (telepathy). He encountered a humanoid entity about 1.9m in height, of generally human appearance, but somewhat taller, he wore a tight-fitting spacesuit.

He approached Subbotin and began communicating telepathically. The humanoid creature had dark hair and mustache. The alien said that his name was "Anael." He informed Subbotin that they hailed from the "Triangle" Constellation. Reportedly they had both male and female species in their civilization. He also told Subbotin that they were in a

166

humanitarian mission on Earth and were involved in some kind of scientific research work.

During this contact, Subbotin did not see a UFO, and "Anael" pointed out to Subbotin that he was only a mere holographic projection or his "astral" double, which was sent to make contact with him. Subbotin felt the alien's voice straight inside his head.

This contact occurred right before or after the famous (infamous) military coup d'etat in the USSR which led to the destruction of the Soviet Union and "Anael" told the witness that the country will indeed have many changes, and they (the aliens) were interested in monitoring this specific situation in the country, which was a unique example of social changes which were of interest to them.

HC addendum.
Source: Pavel Khailov, Bezhetsk, Russia.   Type: E or F

*   *   *   *   *   *   *

Location: Springfield, Missouri.
Date: August, 1991.
Time: Night.

The witness, Linda Dusenberry, was in bed sleeping when she suddenly began floating out of her bedroom, towards a light and through the wall. She felt being pulled by a strong force with a quick movement.

She then encountered a strange reptilian being described as five-foot nine inches tall with a green body that appeared scaly and rough. He had pea-green eyes with pupils slanted like a cat, black and yellow in color. The being lacked hair, had a small mouth, thin arms, duck-like hands with brown webbing in between four long fingers with sharp nails on the ends.

The witness felt electricity going through her hands apparently after the being touched her. She was then told that they needed human beings to make their race stronger because it was dying out.

HC addendum.
Source: Linda Moulton Howe, 'Glimpses of other Realities Vol. I.'
Type: G

Location: Cala Tuent, Palma de Mallorca, Balearic Islands, Spain.
Date: August, 1991.
Time: Night.

A young couple, Anabel and Jose Maria were parked on the beach area in their vehicle when they observed a huge bluish object resembling a large two-story "cake" hovering over the waters just off the shore. Moments later a bizarre figure seemed to detach itself from the object and began to approach the couple. The figure was wearing a shiny monk-like outfit.

Terrified the couple drove away from the area at high speed but not before the same or another entity flew over their vehicles several times, this entity was described as somehow resembling a large manta ray with huge slanted eyes.

Soon after the incident the couple reported bizarre events at their home close to Barcelona. They heard strange noises in the house saw bizarre shadows and their clocks and watches were always out of sync. Once night they saw three strange, short thin beings with slanted eyes surrounding their bed. They became paralyzed and their next memory was of waking up in the morning with strange puncture marks on their bodies and with a feeling of having undertaken an extreme long 'journey.'

HC addendum.
Source: Moises Garrido.   Type: B and G?

* * * * * * *

Location: Cape York, Queensland, Australia.
Date: August, 1991.
Time: Night.

Two men and two women saw a blue, cone shaped object, the size of a car that flew overhead when they were camping. An hour later, a four foot tall entity with a bulbous nose, wearing a white uniform was found rummaging through their 4WD truck.

At first they thought it was a thief and shouted at it. It turned and babbled something incomprehensible and then dematerialized in plain sight of the witnesses. It later briefly materialized between the two women in the back seat when they were leaving the area.

HC addendum.
Source: www.ufologistmagazine.com VOL. 11 #5, Jan-Feb, 2008.
Type: D

Location: Niemojkow, Poland.
Date: August 7, 1991.
Time: 6:30 a.m.

The witness was bringing his cow to the pasture when he spotted
something 'shiny' in a field. When he approached the 'object,' it turned
out to be something resembling a large bipedal, winged 'owl' like
creature, whose body and head were covered in silvery tear-shaped 'tiles.'
The figure was in constant motion moving left to right, apparently
floating just above the ground but always remaining in front of the
witness.

It also possessed huge round eyes with round pupils which seemed
to 'rotate' clockwise. Between its eyes it had a 5-8cm protrusion
resembling a nose or 'beak.' The witness observed the strange creature
for about five minutes. It is also said that there were other witnesses. The
strange figure eventually rose up into the air and disappeared towards
Myszkowice.

HC addendum.
Source: K. Piechota & B. Rzepecki Bliskie spotkania z UFO w Polsce,
Tarnow. 1995.   Type: E
Comments: The Owlman in Poland?

                        *   *   *   *   *   *   *

Location: Between Tustin & Irvine, Orange County, California.
Date: August 11, 1991.
Time: 8:00 a.m.

Louis Turi (involved in previous encounters) and his wife, Brigitte,
were on their way to attend a function in Anaheim and had left Oceanside
traveling North on Interstate 5. After driving for about 40-45 minutes, a
very strange event took place at Jamboree Road. They suddenly felt very
disorientated, realized they were lost and pulled off the freeway at the
next exit, stopped in a parking lot and asked a stranger where they were.
He told them they were at the Los Angeles Zoo, which is located in
Glendale, 48 miles further down Interstate 5 from Jamboree Road, the
last road sign they remembered. The time was 9:00 a.m. They had
covered about 48 miles in 15 or 20 minutes. Bewildered, they retraced
their path back in the direction they had come, all the way to Oceanside.
They were both very confused and upset over what had happened.
Strangely enough, Brigitte had cried uncontrollably the night before, for
no apparent reason, and had had very little sleep that night.

On June 1992, Louis underwent hypnotic regression to find out if
anything had happened. The following story emerged. While passing the

169

Jamboree Road area, Louis and Brigitte began to see the road appear to widen, and they seemed to be driving into a white cloud. They could not feel the vibrations of the road anymore. A strange feeling enveloped them as if they were flying through clouds. Louis tried to comfort his terrified wife. The next thing they remembered was being in their car in some sort of craft, with humans approaching them. The beings were Nordic in appearance with light hair and wore close fitting, silver colored suits. The people told them not to be afraid, to not worry. Louis assured Brigitte that these people were friends, that he knew them. They were both escorted through a metallic door and kept in a room for a short period of time (this could have been a decontamination chamber for it seemed very hot).

Louis and Brigitte were then separated and she was taken to a different area. Louis had the feeling that he had been there before, that this was not the first time this had happened. He looked out a window and saw Earth, just as it would be seen from a satellite. One of the human types escorted him to another area. He passed by a section of the craft where he saw computers and screens, indicative of a main control area. They then led him through a glass door to another room, which contained large amounts of electronic equipment. He saw some containers with brains inside of them, human in appearance, which were alive. (!) They were enclosed in a clear glass-like shield on a pedestal with different colors emanating from them in their liquid-like state.

There were humanoid extraterrestrials present (not described) sitting by the machines. Louis was very concerned about Brigitte, however, when allowed to press a button, a screen showed the image of his wife, laying on a metal table, being examined by two humans, a man and a woman, and he was able to see that she was all right. He had been waiting for something, although he did not know what it was, he knew he had to await his turn. He was then taken to another area where he was seated in a very comfortable, blue chair and a helmet-like device was put over his head. There was a slight noise inside his head and the device began to have an effect on him. His consciousness began to expand, he felt wonderful. His head started to implode into millions and millions of parts. The feeling was indescribable. He felt as if he were experiencing the beginning of creation. This appeared to be a wonderful and powerful experience, perhaps a Cosmic Consciousness experience, one which made him cry. Later, Louis and Brigitte were led back to their car and, as was previously stated, ended up 48 miles down the Interstate with only a 15 to 20 minute time lapse.

HC addendum.
Source: Shawn Atlanti, San Diego.   Type: G

Location: Maguayo, Puerto Rico.
Date: August 13, 1991.
Time: 2:00 a.m.

Mrs. Marisol Camacho, a young woman who lives in the back of the Maguayo community next to the Laguna Cartagena, received an unexpected visit at her home by two strange creatures. She was asleep, when at about 2.00 a.m. she heard strange noises outside, next to her balcony. He got up and went to the balcony window. Someone was there mumbling in a strange gibberish. She opened the venetian blinds very slowly and there were two inhuman creatures standing there on the balcony. They were examining one of her plants, one they call 'Queso Suizo' (Swiss cheese, the scientific name of which is *Monsterosa deliciosa,* an ornamental tropical plant whose leaves have many holes). They were taking leaves from the plant and mumbling. They looked really interested in it.

She was surprised and, she doesn't know why, but she couldn't move. She was frozen to the spot, looking at them. They were almost four feet tall and had large egg-shaped heads, big at the top with a narrow chin. They were skinny and seemed to be grey, and were naked. They had big black elongated eyes that tapered to the sides of their heads, with no pupils and no whites in them. Their faces were flat, with a narrow slit for a mouth, no lips, and two small holes for a nose. She never felt any fear, she was fascinated by what she was seeing. They seemed like children to her.

They had arms longer than ours, and long skinny hands with four long fingers. They didn't seem to notice her at the window. They took leaves from the plant and left, talking among themselves in that fast mumbling gibberish. They walked slowly towards the Laguna Cartagena, entered the brush at the end of the street, and disappeared. After they left, she was able to move again.

On August 27, Marisol Camacho again heard the same sounds, got up and went to the same window, which was partially closed, and there they were again. They were either the same ones or identical to the others, examining the plant again and talking in that mumbled gibberish. But this time she was able to move and she tried to tell them something. She began opening the blinds, but when they heard this, they looked at her quickly then ran away at high speed down the street towards the Laguna again, and disappeared.

"I don't know what they want, but they don't seem to be dangerous. They didn't harm me, and they didn't harm my dogs, who slept all the time they were here. One thing for sure; they are already here, living among us. We should prepare to face that fact and I'm convinced they are there in the Laguna Cartagena."

171

A week after this second visit, many of Marisol's neighbors were witness to a brilliantly colored disc that hovered for about three minutes some 50 feet above her house at 9:30 p.m.

HC addendum.
Source: Jorge Martin, 'Alien Update,' p. 24-25.   Type: E

*   *   *   *   *   *   *

Location: Near Victoria, Argentina.
Date: August 13, 1991.
Time: 10:00 p.m.

Four men staying at a local guest house were alerted by two maneuvering lights, one yellow the other red that moved up and down then in a triangular pattern. One of the lights then descended on the road near the guesthouse. Two dark human-like figures then appeared and seemed to float above the ground moving around back and forth. They were human-like with slightly larger heads.

Suddenly the light shut off and a white bowl-shaped object could be seen. Some of the witnesses were not able to see the figures completely and only saw their arms and legs.

HC addendum.
Source: Dr. Roberto Banchs, Cuadernos De Ufologia Vol. 15 #2, 1993.
Type: C

*   *   *   *   *   *   *

Location: Victoria, Argentina.
Date: August 17, 1991.
Time: Night.

Several students at the local Escuela Hogar, San Martin, located in a wooded area, along with two staff members, observed a large luminous object descend on a field about 200 meters from the school. Curious the group of witnesses approached the area to within forty meters of the object and saw a large object on the ground.

They all then saw three humanoid figures descend from the object and glide around without touching the ground; they floated a few centimeters above it. It was impossible to see any features on the humanoids because of the intense light emitted by the object. The noise of a nearby approaching truck seemed to have startled the humanoids, which re-entered the object, and this one disappeared.

172

The next day upon inspecting the grounds a large ground trace resembling the imprint of a horseshoe was found on the ground; also the grass appeared to have been scorched.

HC addendum.
Source: Ramon Pereyra, Victoriense.com   Type: B
Comments: Note the proximity in time to the previous case.

* * * * * * *

Location: Barrio Quebrada De San Lorenzo, Puerto Rico.
Date: August 27, 1991.
Time: Late afternoon.

The witness was walking by himself on an isolated field when a round dark object descended over him. The witness felt being lifted up into the craft. He found himself inside a metallic room, apparently inside the object. He was then placed in a metallic chair that molded itself around his body preventing him from moving. He was then surrounded by four to five humanoids described as six-foot tall, with large heads, small noses, thin mouths and lips, long dangling arms and gray-yellow skin.

They mentally told the witness that they were here on a crossbreeding project between their race and our race and that it was vital for the survival of humanity. He was also warned of coming earth changes.

HC addendum.
Source: Jorge Martin, Enigma #46.   Type: G

* * * * * * *

Location: Flint River, Georgia.
Date: August 31, 1991.
Time: 11:30 p.m.

A family of four was camping along the Flint River in west central Georgia when at 23:30 the father was awakened by what he interpreted as "animal grunting noises." He climbed out of his sleeping bag and stepped outside the tent to investigate. He was stunned to see only four feet away from him a nine-foot tall alien clad in a "pearly white robe." The entity had no arms, and his bare feet were floating four feet above the ground.

The man's shouts awakened his wife, who stepped outside only to be frozen in place as her husband, similarly paralyzed, was "towed" away by the floating alien. He could not even move his eyes.

173

The man was brought into a silver sphere, more than one hundred feet in diameter, and floating twenty or thirty feet off the ground. A large door set in the craft slid in to admit the abductor and abductee. Alien and victim passed through a thirty five foot long hallway and entered a brightly lighted "large information center" crammed with monitor-less computers and bright flashing lights tended by up to twenty aliens.

The procession continued into an examination room, where the man was laid on a long black table. Eight to ten aliens looked him over but did not insert or remove anything. The man noted that the interior of the object was too large for the size he had seen, a claim made by abductees as far back as the fairy folk age.

When the exam concluded a few minutes later, the original alien brought the man outside and placed him beside his wife, at which point they both regained mobility. The couple watched as a "jet engine" fired up from the bottom of the sphere, and it rocketed away at great speed. The showy exit burned a two-hundred yard circle into the ground.

Four years later investigator John Thompson found many burn spots at the site, but countless people had since camped and fished there, hopelessly contaminating any remaining evidence. The couple's children slept through the episode, and the wife refuses to speak about it. The man has refused hypnotic regression, but has started seeing a psychiatrist. He claims a subsequent abduction, and the creatures have promised another visit, a prospect that frightens him.

HC addendum.
Source: John C. Thompson & Jim Miles, 'Weird Georgia.'   Type: G

* * * * * * *

Location: Kobelyaki, Poltava region, Ukraine.
Date: Autumn, 1991.
Time: Evening.

Residents living near the village of Kobelyaki watched an illuminated barrel-shaped object moving in the sky. It was slowly moving at an altitude of about 150 meters from the ground. Pupils at a local school were the first to see the UFO, and some pointed their flashlights at the craft. Despite the significant distance and faint light, the UFO noticed the light and immediately reacted; a shaft of light was then projected from the UFO. After approaching at a distance of 30-40 meters, the object began hovering low over the ground, from the location of the witnesses it appeared that the UFO landed on a ploughed field.

Three humanoid figures came out of the craft. One was about three meters in height, the other two, smaller in heights. The witnesses described the humanoids as having "small" heads, which barely jutted

174

over their powerful shoulders. The dark colored entities seemed to float in the air, barely touching the ground.

The young witnesses became frightened and fell to the ground, face down. And when they dared to raise their heads, the humanoids were returning to their craft. Soon the UFO left the area. There were a total of ten witnesses to this event from three different locations. Not only children, but also adults saw the object. UFO researchers from Poltava examined the place where the object hovered above and found noticeable magnetic and electrostatic anomalies.

HC addendum.
Source: Ivan D. Buryak 'Ukrainian Ufologist' Newspaper and 'The Fourth Dimension and UFOs,' Yaroslavl, Russia, #3 1997.   Type: B

* * * * * * *

Location: Palm Springs, California.
Date: Fall, 1991.
Time: Late night.

For three nights in a row the witness young baby daughter had woken up screaming hysterically. As him and his wife ran into the room the child would point frantically towards the window. On the fourth night the witness was ready and ran immediately into the bedroom with a loaded gun, as he looked at the window he was stunned to see a short figure with a round head and huge eyes staring at him.

The figure turned and ran. The figure hurdled over some bushes into the street at incredible speed then into a street, and under a streetlight it suddenly dematerialized in full view of the witness.

HC addendum.
Source: CAUS.   Type: E

* * * * * * *

Location: Lymington, Hampshire, England.
Date: October 24, 1991.
Time: Night.

The main witness and a friend were attracted to a field by a hypnotic whirring sound. A strange object hovered over the field. The craft had several metallic leg-like protrusions with a rim and multicolored flashing lights. It also had a dome with a light on top. The whole object seemed silvery-metallic.

175

The main witness approached the object and banged on it with his fists several times. Suddenly standing next to the object were three seven-foot tall beings that were very thin with pale complexions and normal facial features but with almond shaped cat-like eyes. All three wore tight-fitting one-piece outfits. One of the beings looked at the witness who suddenly felt light-headed and began losing his balance, he was somehow drawn inside the object.

Inside he found himself floating just above the floor. The floor of the object sloped down at an angle and was covered with symbolic tiles. In the center, there was a pole, and on the ceiling a spinning multi-colored light. The object somehow seemed larger inside than what it looked from outside, it seemed to be 'without end' inside. The witness mind was apparently probed while inside the craft and he felt unable to resist. The next thing he knew, he was at home in his bed.

HC addendum.
Source: Steve Gerrard, Southampton UFO Group.   Type: G

* * * * * * *

Location: Falmouth, Pendleton County, Kentucky.
Date: November, 1991.
Time: Afternoon.

The witness was working on a 160-acre farm at the time, and one day while eating lunch with a friend, he was told that there had been some hunters sneaking on to the property. He finished lunch, got his gun and started walking down the fence row, planning to cut into the woods and sneak up on them.

He had been out there around 45 minutes to an hour and was making his way through the woods when suddenly something stepped out from behind a tree. He yelled, 'friend or foe' and pointed his gun at it. He couldn't believe his eyes, because there standing in front of him and his gun was a 3 & ½ foot tall gray being. Suddenly the witness felt the being talking to him telepathically and he had the feeling that it was a young female and it was scared and telling him it was going to run up a little knoll, just then it took off running up that knoll. He followed it with his gun barrel as it reach the top of the hill, suddenly there was a flash of light and a sort of portal or door opened up out of nowhere. It was about four feet wide and probably eight feet tall, it was brightly lit inside and he could see the little being standing in it, now it looked like it was wearing a tight-fitting black suit of some sort.

Suddenly out of the corner of his left eye, he saw what looked like something running toward him, he wheeled around and right in front of him was a lizard-like man about five to six feet tall, and he was holding a

176

long staff like thing in one hand. According to the witness the being's face was more insect-like and it had blue eyes. Again he had the feeling that it was the little female being's 'father' or 'guardian.'

At this point, suddenly to his right a seven or eight foot tall, brown, hairy, Bigfoot type creature suddenly appeared standing there. The witness didn't hear it speak but heard in his mind, *"No, don't hurt him."* Just then the lizard-looking type being looked right at the witness and his eyes changed to a yellowish gold color.

The witness then turned to run and when he did, he suddenly found himself standing in the woods alone, and it was night time. He stood there in shock for a moment trying to collect himself, he then began to walk back home. Once he arrived at the farmhouse he found another farm hand that said that they thought that he was 'lost,' as they had been apparently looking for him. He didn't say a word about his encounter.

HC addendum.
Source: http://mufoncms.com   Type: E

* * * * * * *

Location: Sverdlovsk, Russia.
Date: November, 1991.
Time: Night.

Someone pushing down hard on him suddenly awakened 42-year old Victor K at night. After opening his eyes he was surprised to see a man dressed in white clothing standing before him. As Victor attempted to rise from the bed he found himself totally paralyzed and unable to speak. Mentally he asked the stranger the following question: *"Who are you?"*

Suddenly the stranger turned to him and Victor was stunned to see that instead of a face he had what appeared to be a "plate" or flat screen on his face. And then Victor saw unknown images and pictures running through the screen. Somehow Victor understood that this was the means to communicate with the stranger. Victor then asked, *"Where are you from?"* A reciprocal picture appeared on the facial screen of a volumetric image of our galaxy from a different point of view, in successive pulsations it presented several celestial bodies.

Victor then asked, *"What will happen to the earth?"* Reciprocal picture; A large apple tree, under it an anthill. Apple tree grows; it becomes large and moves aside the anthill. On the spot where the anthill grew now he sees hundreds of dead ants. Victor then asks, "How can we save the Earth? Interestingly, this time instead of a picture, he received a telepathic answer, *"Stop the unrestricted use of energy and the use of "atoms," energy on earth is obtained irrationally. The tenth planet of your solar system perished because of this reason."*

177

Victor then asked, *"What is the time difference between you and us?"* Reciprocal picture; a quiet calm creek and then a stormy waterfall then the numbers for one year and ten minutes. Victor then asked, *"How do you move in space?"* A voice answered, *"We do not move, we are everywhere all the time."* Victor then asked, are the UFOs your ships? He then received a curious answer, *"No those are terrestrial in nature, and we don't use them."* Victor asked, *"Why did you contact me?"* He heard a voice, *"We want to make you our representative on Earth."* Victor then added, *"Why precisely me?"* Voice answered, *"You possess sequential thinking. We need a representative since we expend too much energy during terrestrial materialization."*

Victor was then shown what he understood was a very ancient book. Some of the pages were black. And suddenly he understood that it was the bible and some of the information within was incorrect. The stranger then promised Victor that he would return in six months and then noiselessly dissolved into thin air.

Victor was then able to rise from bed and walked over to the kitchen where he felt as he was running a fever and fell exhausted to the floor and slept until the next morning. Six months later Victor suffered from unexplained seizures, headaches and strange markings were found on his body.

HC addendum.
Source: Svetlana Semenova, X-Libri UFO, Russia.   Type: E or F?

* * * * * * *

Location: Carolina, Puerto Rico.
Date: Late November, 1991.
Time: 9:00 p.m.

The witness was en route to a store on a roadway along a rural area, when he heard some noises coming from the nearby brush. He looked in the direction of the noises and saw two strange looking short creatures. They were three-foot tall and were wearing a tight fitting silvery outfit that was very shiny. Their heads were large and they had large pointed ears, they also had large bright white eyes.

The witness did not notice a mouth or a nose. Both of the creatures were encased in a mild glow. The beings were collecting plant and rock samples and putting them in a small vase-like container. The beings suddenly noticed the witness and ran through the brush, quickly disappearing from sight.

HC addendum.
Source: Jose Perez, Jorge Martin, Jorge Berrios, Enigma #49.   Type: E

Location: Valle de Santiago, Guanajato, Mexico.
Date: December, 1991.
Time: Various.

Terra Incognita, the official publication of Mexico's defunct *Centro de Estudios de Fenomenos Paranormales,* carried an interesting story about "humanoid aliens" in Valle de Santiago, where a UFO enthusiast was on the trail of a being "clad in a silver-blue one piece outfit, with glowing eyes that shine as if covered in gold." Reportedly, the entity's hair and facial hair (certainly an unusual detail in descriptions of alleged ufonauts) matched the creature's clothing, as did his footwear. In its right hand, the humanoid brandished what was described as a "triangle with a glowing" tip and was theorized by onlookers to be a weapon of some sorts.

According to the Terra Incognita feature (which in turns quotes a publication called "Cuestion Policiaca), a group of unnamed Ufologists visited the area, which includes a watering hole known as La Alberca. Visits by these researchers, from Morelia and Zamora, occurred during a period of seven months, in hopes of substantiating either the existence of the humanoid or stories about lights hovering over the watering hole or plunging into it.

During one of the groups visit to the site, Oscar Arredondo, a self-proclaimed Contactee and member of the expedition, heard a noise in the early morning hours and reached for his camera, breaking away from his slumbering companions and heading toward a small hill, where he saw a glow and a strange being that walked erect. Without hesitation, Arredondo pressed the camera's shutter, its sound prompting the entity to turn around saying a word. Unimpressed, the being resumed its walk, startling the photographer, as *"it was walking down a slope without falling or making any effort whatsoever, as though floating."*

The creature strode into the darkness, vanishing without a trace, but not before the photographer took a second photo, this time of its back. Arredondo returned to his companions and excitedly told them what had happened, waving his camera and the image it contained within. They agreed to convene at a location in the state of Michoacan to develop the film and proceed from there.

The publication shared the image with its readers in its issue #104, for the week of October 20-26 1992. The faded photocopied photo was included in Terra Incognita with the following information,

"A unique photo in the world, taken recently in Valle de Santiago, Guanajato, and showing an alleged extraterrestrial. It holds in its right hand a sophisticated device. It wear a luminous one-piece outfit. The figure looks human, but its eyes are much larger than normal, as they glow and are greenish in color. The photo was taken by an enthusiast who accompanied one of our correspondents."

Local residents were not as enthusiastic as the UFO media, as the phenomenon's presence had been nearly constant in the Valle de Santiago. A local grower, Ramiro Sanchez Esparrogoza, had an even more compelling story to tell,

"I once spoke to a very strange man who wore a silvery one-piece outfit. He spoke our language. He told me to plant a seed of the same plants I was growing (carrots and lettuce) in a single plot and then, using a technique known only to him, vanished before my eyes. I never saw him again and three months later I found that the carrots were one meter tall, and you can image my surprise five months later, when the carrots and lettuce heads were gigantic. I could barely carry one of each."

HC addendum.
Source: Scott Corrales, http://inexplicata.blogspot.com.ar/   Type: E

Location: Parma, Italy.
Date: December 16, 1991.
Time: 9:10 a.m.

University student Manuela B, was studying in her bedroom when she looked out the window and saw a bizarre figure floating outside. At first she thought it was a huge bird, but upon closer inspection she realized that it was a large humanoid figure, covered in greenish hair or wearing a greenish form-fitting suit. It had a squat head directly set on its shoulders, with two huge round staring luminous eyes.

The figure then began moving in a horizontal flight, slowly turning his head like a robot. It moved up and down, changing positions as if surveying the area.

At this point the witness looked out to see if there were other witnesses but did not see anybody around. She looked for her camera but by then the being had disappeared towards a strange gray colored oblong shaped cloud that emitted several lightning bolts as the figure disappeared into it.

HC addendum.
Source: Archivio SUF.   Type: B?

* * * * * * *

Location: Mainly Bekes, Hungary.
Date: December 26, 1991.
Time: Midnight.

The 21-year old witness had heard a very loud voice in his room on the night of 12-4-01, telling him *"You will meet us soon."* This was repeated for eleven nights in a row. He could not locate the source of the voice.

On the night of the encounter he was returning home from the movies when he caught sight of a hovering shiny gray disc-shaped object over the courtyard. He was suddenly compelled to walk under the object and a beam of light descended on him from the bottom of the craft. He then found himself inside the object looking out a window at his courtyard.

Two four and a half foot tall beings stood in the room with him. The beings were human-like except that they had large heads and eyes. They had long arms ending in three-fingered hands. One of the beings communicated with the witness, telling him that they had been watching him for three years and that they travel via inter-dimensional portals.

A beam of green light hit the witness on his forehead and after that he only had vague memories of traveling to a moon-like planet and of

181

seeing pyramids from above. He later found himself in his courtyard suffering from a terrible headache and feeling dizzy.

HC addendum.
Source: Gabor Tarcali, Hungarian UFO Network.   Type: G

* * * * * * *

Location: Near Longwy, Meurthe-et-Moselle, France.
Date: December 27, 1991.
Time: Evening.

Five young witnesses watched a large silvery sphere land on a field very close to their location. Two human-like figures with blue eyes wearing gray combination coveralls emerged from the object. One figure was carrying something resembling a transparent cylindrical canister.

The humanoids proceeded to walk around the object and collect various plant and soil samples and placing them inside the canister. After a while, the humanoids re-entered the sphere, which then rose up silently and shoot away at high speed. Ground traces were found.

HC addendum.
Source: Ecol #91, Denys Breysse Project Becassine.   Type: B

1992

Location: Montana Santa, Puerto Rico.
Date: 1992.
Time: Various.

At the same time of the miraculous apparition of the Blessed Virgin in this hilltop, a number of unidentified artifacts were reported in the hill's vicinity and even captured on film. Other witnesses reported brilliant, disk-like objects flying overhead.

One of the witnesses, Delia Flores, reported that she and other worshippers were surprised to see a beige van parked in the area of the religious sanctuary on the hill. Its occupants wore orange fatigues with NASA insignia, and the vehicle's Spanish speaking driver told them that the van contained a most unusual cargo, a simian creature captured in the Caribe State Forest (El Yunque). According to Flores, she and the others saw a covered cage that contained something "struggling to get out." The driver added that the creature was being taken to a secret primate research laboratory located somewhere in the island, where investigation on this sort of being was being conducted.

A local farmer discovered one morning that a number of plantain plants on his property had been destroyed by an unknown creature that left a number of deep footprints, attesting to its massive size and weight. Other residents indicated that they had seen a "hairy figure" that ran away from the area in the darkness, but they could not described it in detail.

HC addendum.
Source: Scott Corrales, Chupacabras and Other Mysteries. Type: E or H?
Comments: Did the Government or more specific NASA really involved in a retrieval operation of some type of hairy humanoid? There have been other documented incidents in which supposed NASA personnel have been reported at the site of humanoid retrievals, like Chupacabra type creatures or hybrids.

Location: Kavgolovo, St Petersburg region, Russia.
Date: 1992.
Time: Afternoon.

D. Povaliyayev was hang-gliding over some lakes over the area. In one of them he noticed what appeared to be "giant" fish. Curious, he descended, and was able to see that the "fish" were really man-shaped swimmers in silvery outfits.

HC addendum.
Source: Paul Stonehill.   Type: E

* * * * * * *

Location: Khmelnitskiy, Ukraine.
Date: 1992.
Time: 2:00 p.m.

Mrs. Movchan mother of a woman named Olga Movchan was standing in his kitchen near a window when she saw a saucer-shaped object hovering nearby. The witness "greeted" the aliens with her thoughts and wished them all the best. At this moment her legs seemed to give way and she became very weak in her knees. She thought she would lose consciousness and fall. The UFO who had been moving had now stopped.

That same day other witnesses saw the same UFO over the town. After that initial contact, the witness entered into periodical contacts with aliens. Home visitations began to occur on a regular basis. Her pets, a dog and a cat, seemed to sense when the aliens appeared. The humanoids behave very secretive, hiding from sight of the other relatives of the witness. At the time the witness was very ill, stricken with cancer and was becoming worse and worse. In despair, she asked the aliens for help.

Incredibly, the aliens did help the stricken witness. The woman confessed to her daughter that one night she was taken by an extraterrestrial that she called "Vadim." In a dark location she felt warm and understood that the alien were conducting healing sessions on her. This usually occurred between 2-3:00 a.m. She could not move as a result of the terrible pain and felt as if her veins were popping out of her body. The woman had a tumor in one of her veins, like a globule.

After the aliens cured her, the tumor began to sharply decrease in size, becoming pea-size, almost three times smaller. But being very curious the woman decided to find out what the aliens were really doing with her at night. For that purpose she met with psychic Boris Benit and conducted a séance involving regressive hypnosis on her. Suddenly during the procedure, both received a telepathic impulse which basically told them to stop the process. That the mystery was not theirs to know and that there would be dire consequences if they continued. *"You will deform the program,"* the message added. Mrs. Movchan took this advice and never attempted another "experiment." Sometime after that she noticed some strange marks on her wrist. The same thing happened to Boris. These marks remained for a long time, like brands and then vanished.

According to the witness' daughter, the aliens completely cured the woman. Then the aliens established periodical telepathic communication with the witness. The aliens also gave the witness advice on how to cure different illnesses. Accordingly she eventually became a psychic and began curing and helping other people. The very same day of her original UFO observation, many town people also saw the disc-shaped object and two workers at a local industrial enterprise disappeared without a trace and were never found.

HC addendum.
Source: Lubov Kolosyuk, 'New Aquarius,' newspaper, Samara, Russia #5, 1994.   Type: G
Comments: Unfortunately there is no description of the aliens but these appeared to have been of the human-type. There also appears to have been a permanent abduction of two humans.

* * * * * * *

Location: Aran Island, County Donegal, Ireland.
Date: 1992.
Time: Afternoon.

Brian Collins, age fifteen, was vacationing on Aran Island when he saw two men about three feet six inches tall, talking in Irish and dressed in green with brown boots. They were sitting on a bank, fishing in the ocean, but suddenly they jumped away and disappeared. Collins retrieved a pipe one had been smoking, but it later disappeared from a locked drawer.

HC addendum.
Source: George Eberhart, 'Mysterious Creatures.'   Type: E

Location: Connecticut (exact location not given).
Date: 1992.
Time: Afternoon.

A woman said that a black helicopter landed in her yard and a Bigfoot type creature jumped out, messed up the yard, and stole her clothes hanging on a line to dry. The creature then quickly climbed back into the helicopter and took off. (!)

HC addendum.
Source: Phillip J. Imbrogno, Files from the Edge, p. 168.   Type: X

* * * * * * *

Location: Guadalajara, Spain.
Date: 1992.
Time: Evening.

Researcher Angel Jimenez, was in a local village investigating reports of apparent balls of fire, which were said to rise up from a nearby mountain. While inside a wooded area, he heard strange noises which he thought were from an animal. Suddenly he saw a humanoid almost two meters in height, wearing a one-piece silvery outfit that covered him from head to toe.

The strange being took one step forward into the woods and suddenly disappeared in plain sight, as if stepping into 'another dimension.' Jimenez searched around for the silver-suited humanoid but did not find anything.

Around the same time locals reported seeing the fiery balls of light coming out of the mountain.

HC addendum.
Source:http://www.looculto.260mb.com/ovnisenespana/ovnisenespan
a.htm   Type: D?

* * * * * * *

Location: Oahu, Hawaii (exact location not given).
Date: 1992.
Time: Night.

Doug and his wife Sandy were vacationing on the big island, and were taking a drive somewhere on a remote road. There they experienced a missing time event. Later Doug was able to remember much, if not all, of what took place. He said he saw a white owl fly in front of his car, almost grazing the windshield. He stopped the car and got out. But instead of a white owl, he saw some sort of luminous human being standing alongside the road.

As he gazed at this individual, messages began to be communicated directly into his mind in the form of images. They warned of a coming global catastrophe. The images included war, disease, environmental upheavals, and starvation. He also saw scenes of people being herded into concentration like camps. Doug thought he was looking back in time of the 40's. But then he realized the people were wearing contemporary clothing.

There were many other images, but the one thing that really struck him was that he was told that the 'grays' would make their presence known to all the earth. This would be at a time when the planet was teetering on global destruction. They would present themselves as saviors of the planet and be welcomed by most on Earth, but this would be a lie.

At first they would assist the Earth's governments, including the U.S., to bring peace and order to the planet. Their ultimate goal, however, would be to eventually replace humans with a human/alien hybrid race with minds that were to be locked into a hive-like mentality. If they succeeded, freedom of thought and the spiritual evolution of the human race would be terminated.

HC addendum.
Source: http://www.unknowncountry.com   Type: E or G?
Comments: Scary, since it appears that a lot of those predictions are indeed coming true.

* * * * * * *

Location: Artyemovskiy, Sverdlovsk region, Urals, Russia.
Date: 1992.
Time: Night.

A local man named Ivan C. awoke suddenly, feeling that someone is in his bedroom. He was then amazed to see three unknown entities standing in the bedroom. All three were of very small height, about 120 cm to 150 cm in height. They wore overalls or spacesuit-like outfits. Each one carried something like an instrument panel in the chest area, resembling a round plaque. They wore helmets with two small antennas on their heads, resembling horns. Ivan was able to recall that the alien's faces were human-like but with noses without partitions.

The beings moved about in the bedroom, illuminating the area with flashlight-like instruments, which emanated a bright yellow light. They spoke among themselves in a language resembling the chirping of birds.

187

When the aliens noticed that Ivan was awake, they apparently became concerned and immediately shone a bright light on him. The witness became terrified but the aliens soon disappeared. He was not able to move as he felt completely paralyzed, but soon he was able to regain his movement. His body felt numb for a while after the encounter.

HC addendum.
Source: A. Alekseev in 'Fourth Dimension,' Yaroslavl, UFO Research Group #7 1992.   Type: E

* * * * * * *

Location: Ushtagan, Guryev (Atyrau), Kazakhstan.
Date: 1992.
Time: Unknown.

As a result of a carefully planned operation, according to a super-secret Russian military program to shoot down UFOs, a craft was shot down by an electromagnetic pulse weapon and possibly by additional surface to air missiles fired from the Ashuluk air defense range in the Astrakhan region. As a result of the directed EM impulse, the object went out of control, gradually losing altitude into the Kazakh desert about 90 kilometers from the Russian border east of the Ashuluk range.

A retrieval team that arrived in a Mi-8 Hip helicopter from Ashuluk, soon discovered a UFO partially embedded in the sand. The object was a disk about 5-6 meters in diameter, lenticular or convex lens-shaped, matt gray in color, with a broad and slight, not jutting, gradual dome on top connected with the rest of the hull and a broad and low cylindrical base. The bottom section of the object was substantially damaged with numerous dents and a narrow curved crack was found on its side. The object was then covered by anti-radiation foil & tarpaulin and transported to the Kapustin Yar State central range #4 and placed inside an underground bunker. A research team was puzzled as to how to penetrate the craft. They attempted using strong drills, including diamond tipped ones, etc. Nothing worked, the hull seemed indestructible. Finally they concentrated on the crack at the object's side and expanded it by using lasers. The hull appeared to consist of four layers. In twenty days the team made a hole big enough enabling them to penetrate inside, all wearing protective suits and masks.

The object consisted of three levels inside. The engine compartment was located on the lower level, the main power plant with reactor had apparently self-destructed automatically and premeditated. The main control room was located on the second level, it had a screen with a main control panel positioned in a semi-circle with multicolored rectangular key-shaped buttons 2 x 5 cm in size, resembling the keys of a piano, it was positioned in three rows and four small round chairs at the front. The identity of a dome-shaped cylinder in the center of the cabin's floor was later determined to have been a holographic projector. The top level appeared to have been an air locked chamber or garret which docked with the "mothership."

Four alien bodies were found on level 2, all dead. The aliens were about 1.3-1.4m in height, two were the same height, and a third was slightly taller, about 1.5-1.6m. They had large hairless heads and helmets, six finger extremities, gray-white skin, huge round eyes covered by black eye lenses, and small ears set very close to their heads. They were dressed in tight-fitting and apparently very durable suits of a metallic silver color with a violet tint, with belts and round circles on the chest area. They also wore elbow high gloves. The suits were eventually removed with extreme difficulty; silver-greenish boots were also removed.

One of the bodies was substantially damaged as a result of the impact. In extreme secrecy all the bodies were moved to the top-secret alien biological research laboratory northeast of Solnechnogorsk in the Moscow region in an underground bunker. The alien blood appeared to be a thick black liquid. The object was later transported inside a mountain behind the Polar Circle on Novaya Zemlya Island at the most secure ex-nuclear test range #6 in the Artic, together with other crashed alien disks hidden in the same bunker at Kapustin Yar. The alien bodies were eventually taken to the same location.

HC addendum.
Source: Anton Anfalov.   Type: H

*   *   *   *   *   *   *

Location: Beltyrskiy mires, Khakassiya Republic, East Siberia, Russia.
Date: 1992.
Time: Unknown.

This tragic case occurred to a 27 year old hunting inspector (game warden?), in one of the mountainous areas of the Khakassiya Federal Republic located on the extreme southern end of the Krasnoyarskiy region of Eastern Siberia about 105km southwest of the city of Abakan, the capital. The young man who had been recently appointed to the position was inspecting the territory within his jurisdiction and was in the area of the Beltyrskiye mires, who had a bad reputation and local residents spoke of it as being an ominous and evil place, the area was called "The Dead Mires."

The man, armed with a carbine, suddenly saw a huge sparkling globe-shaped object on a meadow within the mire. The globe was the size of a one storied building and was hovering about half a meter from the grass. The hunting inspector took several steps towards the object apparently causing the sphere to react to his intrusion; the object suddenly began to menacingly increase in size changing its color from pink to bright crimson. Then two semi-transparent humanoid figures separated from the sphere.

The witness became frightened and aimed his carbine at the figures. Following this aggressive act on the part of the witness, one of the humanoids took out an object which resembled a luminous net and flung it towards the witness. This luminous net completely covered the unfortunate witness, who felt like a trapped animal. Simultaneously the young man felt unbearable pain, as if his body was being squeezed by a metallic vice.

The witness then lost consciousness and when he returned back to his senses, the humanoids and the globe had already vanished. Only a circle of burned grass reminded the witness of the recent presence of the mysterious object and its occupants. The next day the man's entire body was covered by pink spots which caused unbearable itching.

When the suffering man was taken by car to the city of Abakan, he visited a dermatologist who then referred him to the regional diagnostic center. There the doctors made an unfavorable diagnosis: he was now suffering from a rare and aggressive form of cancer. Despite immediate medical treatment, the 27 year old man was dead in two months. Apparently he had been exposed to a very high radiation level caused emitted by the net-like apparatus.

HC addendum.
Source: Sergey Kozhushko, Siberian Contactees, 'Tay'ny XX Veka,' (Mysteries of the 20th Century) St. Petersburg, Russia #35, September 2007.   Type: G

* * * * * * *

Location: Normangee, Texas.
Date: January, 1992.
Time: Late night.

The witness was awakened by her dogs barking fiercely outside her bedroom window. She sat up in bed and looked out the window where the outside light was sufficient for her viewing. She was then shocked to see a strange "goatman" like creature walking under her pecan tree while her dogs steadily nipped at its heels. The creature was about 7 ft tall and was standing upright like a man with slightly curved shoulders, with the horns and hooves of a goat. Its hands were slightly curled with some very nasty looking gray fingernails. His skin was a yellowish-green color with sparse hair all about the body. Its legs and body were that of a man.

190

She caught a glimpse of the side of his face, which was nearly the shape of a man's. The creature never turned to look at her and quickly walked away from the area and the dogs. Later from time to time she could hear the sound of a "goat" calling in the night. According to the witness there are no goats in the area.

HC addendum.
Source: http://paranormal.about.com   Type: E

* * * * * * * *

Location: Pyt-Yah, Nefteyugansk area, Tumen region, Russia.
Date: February 22, 1992.
Time: Night.

Local residents began noticing very strange phenomena in the night sky. A flying humanoid figure was seen several times peeping into the windows of houses, the entity emanated light and flew easily in the air. Strangest of all, a smaller entity was noticed sitting on larger entity's back, the small entity resembled a small girl that seemingly directed or "commanded" the mysterious flying man around.

A local man named N. attempted to get to the bottom of the situation and strategically hid in an area where it had been seen more frequently, near house #12, located in the first micro housing area, and waited. Finally on the above date, he noticed some flashing lights at second story level, the light then began to assume a humanoid shape. The light became a man-like humanoid, dressed in black pants, and with black hair. Soon after that a small window opened on the second story apartment and a small girl crawled out of it. The girl seemed to be quite ordinary. Most likely she was a resident in the tenement housing complex. The girl had light hair and was dressed in a short sheepskin cloth, but besides that she was very normal in appearance.

Unexpectedly she sat on the tall flying humanoid's back, which was hovering in mid-air in a horizontal position. She then said something to the humanoid and they started flying towards some nearby buildings. N. chased after them. He could hear the pair (girl and humanoid) talking about something as they ascended towards the fifth floor, peeped into one of the windows and then flew towards another building. After noticing their pursuit they easily gained air speed and vanished from sight.

The next day, N. went to the house, calculated the apartment where the girl had come from and knocked on the door. The very same girl door answered the door and she seemed to recognize him. N. attempted to ask the girl a question but she slammed the door on him. He ringed the bell again, but the residents inside threatened to call the militia if he

191

persisted. He then left. Who was the mysterious luminous flying man remains a mystery to this day.

HC addendum.
Source: Mikhail Gershtein citing 'Tumenskaya Pravda' newspaper, 'Anomaly' newspaper, Saint Petersburg, #18, 1997.   Type: E
Comments: This extremely high strangeness case reminds me of Middle Age witch lore in which witches and warlocks were said to ride on the back of flying "demons."

* * * * * * *

Location: Northern New Mexico.
Date: Spring, 1992.
Time: Late night.

The uncle of a local police chief claimed to have been driving into town late at night, when he saw a woman dressed in red walking along the road.
He stopped to offer her a ride into town. She climbed into the front seat of his pickup truck, and as he turned to ask her why she was walking in a deserted road, so late at night, he noticed that she had "hairy goat legs and hoofs." She then instantly de-materialized from the front seat of his truck.

HC addendum.
Source: Christopher O'Brien.   Type: E

* * * * * * *

Location: Riga anomalous zone, near Krustakrogs, Latvia.
Date: March, 1992.
Time: Unknown.

As a result of an apparent "dogfight" between two UFO factions, an extraterrestrial disk was damaged by some sort of alien beam weapon and crashed. Soviet military units (still present in that country at the time) obtained the report of the crashed alien disc-shaped object in the woods and mires approximately about 90-100km northeast of the city of Riga. The military arrived at the location and found a disc-shaped object partially embedded into the ground or swamp.
The object was about 4.5-5m in diameter and 3m high, convexo-convex with a large hemispheric cupola on top, slightly flattened on the very top. On the bottom, the disk had a protruding base. One side of the disk and the dome were damaged, with numerous dents inside the hull,

192

obviously as a result of the tremendous impact at high speed. Its surface was ideally smooth, seamless, with a flange connecting the dome with the rest of the hull. The disk had a number of round or oval structures around its perimeter, obviously lights. The object was metallic without any seams or rivets, evidently of alien origin.

A retrieval team was dispatched on three "Ural" trucks, but they could not approach the disk. The truck's engine and electrical power suddenly failed several dozen meters from the disk, and the men felt sick and dizzy. The perimeter of the craft was secured and the military positioned personnel at several dozen meters from the crash site and began observing the disk. The disk was apparently still active, indicating that any entities onboard were still alive and attempting to take off. Despite the fact that one side of the disk was seriously damaged by the strong impact, the object began emitting light and rotating, creating clouds of dust. Twelve members of the team that arrived at the crash site were dressed in protective suits. Two or three of the men that inadvertently approached to close to the disk had died as a result of the intensive electromagnetic radiation emanating from the craft. Apparently the bones on their bodies lost all the calcium and the bodies turned into a jelly-like substance. (!) The rest immediately moved away and hid behind a hill.

Finally, thirty minutes later, the disk stopped all activity and the light turned off, the military now felt safe in approaching the disk. The disk and the earth around it were still hot, so they waited until dawn when the disk grew cold and they were able to approach it. Then the disk was covered by a special anti-radiation foil and then by tarpaulin and loaded upon a flatbed truck or suspended below an MI-8 helicopter. The military team then moved the disk to a surface hangar at the Centralized Material Research Institute (CNII MV) in the space-military industrial complex in the town of Kaliningrad (now Korolyev) just north of Moscow. Metal alloys from the disk were properly studied at the CNII MV, for inner examination of the craft; laser equipment was used to open the disk. That was done in extreme difficulty, because the disk had no visible doors or openings.

Two alien bodies were found inside the disk's cabin near the control panel, both dead. The aliens were about 1.3-1.4m in height, with large hairless heads (with helmets) yellow-greenish brown color skin, with four webbed fingers, long thin arms, long thin legs, long neck and large slanted frog-like eyes covered by black lenses, with two small openings in place of the nose, and a small slit-like mouth, and tiny ears folded back to the back of their heads. Both were dressed in tight-fitting and very durable metallic silver suits. In general the beings were similar to those found in the disk that crashed near the Kapustin Yar range (both disks probably belonged to the same alien race).

In extreme secrecy the bodies were immediately removed from the disk, placed inside a hangar and isolated by a biomedical team. Later both alien bodies were transported to a special KGB/FSB biomedical laboratory outside the town of Solnechnogorsk northwest of Moscow where they were autopsied and hidden in an underground bunker by only four officers. During the autopsy a yellow greenish alien blood poured out of the bodies reacting quickly with the oxygen, it was apparently copper based. During examination it was found that the disk had three landing props hidden in the bottom and four windows on its dome, transparent only from inside, but absolutely invisible from the outside, the top of the disk's dome was also transparent. An antenna on top was broken by the impact. A cylinder-shaped device was found in the center of the control room, the origin of which was established as a holographic projector. The chairs for the crewmembers were deep, cot-like.

The power plant of the disk was damaged, but partially operational and was properly analyzed. Something rotated inside the power plant for a long time after the recovery. The disc was eventually transported to the island of Novaya Zemlya (former nuclear test State Central Range #6 in the Artic) inside the top secret military installation build inside the mountain code named "Lednik" (Glacier), like most of the other crashed alien discs in the ex-USSR.

HC addendum.
Source: Academician Lev Melnikov, K.E. Tsiolkovskiy Academy of Cosmonautics and "International UN Academy of Information' and Dr. Anton A. Anfalov.   Type: H

* * * * * * *

Location: El Cayul, Sierra Bermeja, Puerto Rico.
Date: March, 1992.
Time: Afternoon.

A man out testing a new video camera in an isolated wooded area, suddenly caught sight of a flash of light overhead. He hid behind some bushes as he saw a small silvery disc-shaped object land in a clearing on three leg-like supports. A section of the object resembling an elevator was lowered to the ground and a door opened.

Two short four-foot tall beings then emerged from inside the object. The beings had gray skin and had large heads and large black eyes. They wore gray colored one-piece suits. They looked around for a few moments then re-entered the object only to emerge a few minutes later this time accompanied by a tall human, very pale and thin. He had short platinum-blond hair and wore a pair of dark sunglasses. He also wore a new black suit and pants with a white shirt and a red tie.

The tall human looked around and then walked towards a nearby path. There he was met by two soldiers in a military jeep. He sat in the jeep and it then drove away, disappearing into the woods. The two short humanoids then entered the disc-shaped object, which then shot, away into the sky at high speed.

HC addendum.
Source: Jorge Martin, Evidencia OVNI #1, and Diego Segarra.   Type: B

* * * * * * *

Location: Whitewood, Saskatchewan, Canada.
Date: March, 1992.
Time: 9:30 p.m.

The witness, a long distance trucker, was parked at a truck-stop overnight. He went to sleep around 21:30 and shortly after, found himself aboard a craft that was white with a blue stripe. There were windows on both sides but he doesn't remember seeing any passengers from outside. He was within twenty feet of it. It was shaped like a passenger jet, complete with a rudder from the side but no wings when viewed from the ground underneath the craft. He then somehow went inside. Inside he was then inside a different craft, square-shaped, like a 'platform.' There were many beings inside, some looked very human but others were quite pale. They were of below normal height, all under 5'6" he thinks. They all communicated telepathically. They were friendly. He knew this just because they appeared friendly but he could communicate openly with their 'minds,' or at least the mind of the one he assumed was the leader. He was the one that communicated with the witness.

He never did remember everything that happened. He does remember that he had the propulsion system explained to him in some detail. This craft was apparently powered by some form of 'hydrogen.' In the fog they could run forever without fuel by taking in water from the air. They showed him two fuel tanks that appeared to be made out of white polyester. They were around two and a half gallons. They told him how far they could go on one of these tanks of water, it was very impressive but he doesn't remember the distance. They put on a display of maneuverability for him as he stood outside his truck; the large object performed 'figure eights' in the sky as he watched. His next memory was of sitting in the cab of his truck on the edge of his bunk. It was around 3:30 a.m.

HC addendum. Source: NUFORC.   Type: G

Location: Palhano, Ceara, Brazil.
Date: March 5, 1992.
Time: 6:30 p.m.

    Military police officer Luis Ribeiro de Oliveira and his friend Pedro Rodrigues da Silva had gone hunting for wild duck in an isolated area when in the Rio Palhano area both men observed what appeared to be a "star" descending at high speed towards the earth. Suddenly a bright light enveloped both men and Pedro ran and hid behind some nearby bushes. Luis ran towards town with the light chasing him close behind. He could see that the light now resembled a luminous wheel-shaped object the size of a bus.

    Soon he felt as he was being sucked up into the object. At the same time Pedro watched in terror as he saw Luis being taken up into the light. Pedro saw Luis enter the round light and it suddenly vanished in plain sight. Terrified, Pedro armed himself with a shotgun and searched the area but was unable to find Luis. Pedro then ran towards town and entered a local bar telling everyone present what had just happened. But later on Luis suddenly appeared in town and related to Pedro a weird story. He remembers running and his legs suddenly becoming numb.

    He then came to hearing strange foreign sounding voices, looking up; he saw five strange beings standing in front of him. Frightened he asked the beings what was going on, he received the following answer, "Don't be afraid, we won't harm you, we are Catadorians from Catadorius Decnius. Our civilization originated from another higher civilization that lived on the earth 353,000 years ago." They pointed to a small pyramid shaped object and told Luis that it was a model of their "temple." The aliens told Luis that they were here on Earth looking for remnants and descendants of that lost civilization that they claimed lived in underground caves and tunnels worldwide.

    Luis was then placed inside what appeared to be a gas-filled sphere in the center of the room. He saw in front of him a panel with multicolored lights and heard what appeared to be radio transmissions. Around him stood five humanoids about 1.50 meters in height that spoke in a strange language. However their apparent leader communicated with the witness telepathically in perfect Portuguese. Soon the leader returned to speak with the other aliens and Luis lost consciousness.

When he woke up he found himself in the same place where the UFO had originally picked him up. Feeling a little dizzy he searched for Pedro and his shotgun and then walked back to town. Luis described the humanoids as short with gray skin, with black eyes lacking any pupils or eyelashes, large heads, wide shoulders, wearing tight fitting clothing with boots and gloves. Their heads and bodies were completely hairless. Their speech was measured and their breathing was heavy and labored. Every time their leader spoke to the others, Luis felt a sharp pain in the head. All the humanoids were identical to each other; he could not find any difference among them.

HC addendum.
Source: UBPDV 1992, Painel Ovni.   Type: G

* * * * * * *

Location: Kaposvar, Hungary.
Date: March 7, 1992.
Time: Night.

A worker at the local railroad station had stepped outside the buildings to feed and check the dogs. As he walked one of the larger dogs in the direction of a nearby container, the animal suddenly began to snarl savagely. He first thought that it must be a cat but when he looked in the direction where the dog was staring at he suddenly realized that it was something else. He noticed movement near some of the smaller containers and decided to approach with two of the dogs.

As he got even closer he saw a small man-like figure, prowling near the container. The largest of the dogs quickly approached the figure but stopped just short of it, the smaller animal remained behind with the witness in a seemingly protective mode. The worker stopped and thought that he was seeing some type of projection as the figure was surrounded by some type of silvery glow. But soon the witness realized that the glow came from the tight-fitting silvery outfit that the figure was wearing.

The shocked railway worker just stared as an eerie silence seemed to reign in the area. The figure briefly looked at the witness and the dogs and the witness saw that its eyes emitted strange reddish phosphorescent. The witness was distracted for a second and when he looked back the strange figure had vanished.

Accompanied by his dogs he searched the area behind the containers but did not find anything.

HC addendum.
Source: Kriston Endre RYUFOR Foundation Hungary.   Type: E

* * * * * * *

Location: Bellomonte, Guaynabo, Puerto Rico.
Date: March 11, 1992.
Time: 6:30 p.m.

The witness who had previously experienced a vision and telepathic communication with unknown entities, was sitting alone on her rocking chair in the rear patio area of her home, when suddenly she felt a strong presence near her, she looked and nearby stood two very tall muscular light skinned men wearing black tight-fitting outfits that covered everything except their faces. They told the witness via telepathy to remain calm; these two men were accompanied by two shorter humanoids with large egg-shaped heads, yellowish skin, wide lipless mouths, and eyes resembling two large dark slits. These wore brown loose-fitting outfits.

The two short beings appeared to be in charge of the situation and were intent on inspecting terrain and plants, constantly murmuring between themselves, in a strange language. The tall human-like beings communicated to the witness that the shorter humanoids wanted her to plant different, specific types of trees and flowers in her garden. The witness said that she had felt more comfortable dealing with the human-like beings than with the short creatures. But there appeared to be a definite cooperation between the two types of beings.

HC addendum.
Source: Jorge Martin, Enigma 52-53.   Type: E

Location: Hamar, Norway.
Date: March 9, 1992.
Time: 10:00 p.m.

Two women were walking home when they began hearing a low frequency sound that seemed to surround them, it resembled a cross between a train and a car engine on idle. Suddenly a very bright light appeared, blinding them and hurting their eyes.

They then saw an object 15 meters away and hovering two meters above the ground. The craft had a triangular bottom, with a transparent dome on top and a light at each apex of the triangular section. The light suddenly went off and now they could see two moving figures within the dome.

One of the women walked towards the object and saw that one of the figures inside the object was holding something resembling a steering wheel; he seemed to have long hair and large black slanted eyes, with black pupils that had a cold penetrating evil look. The object suddenly disappeared without the witnesses noticing how.

Later back in the house they heard a loud similar sound and it felt like an earthquake was going through their house and bodies. They both experienced nosebleeds and ear numbness after the incident.

HC addendum.
Source: Ole Jonny Braene, UFO Norge.   Type: A
Comments: Classic entity case from Norway.

Location: Town near Sea of Azov, Russia.
Date: Summer, 1992.
Time: Late evening.

Mr. Veniamin Kurochkin, involved in a previous contact in the spring of 1990, was again visited by three humanoids in his hotel room. As in the previous case, the trio penetrated into his room directly through the wall. The alien bodies were seemingly transparent. The visit ended when a bluish mist enveloped the witness and he lost consciousness.

Just before the aliens left, the witness had a "short talk" with them, which was accompanied by a demonstration of several "images." This time Kurochkin felt neither fear nor any psychological discomfort. This was apparently as a result of some invisible influence on the part of the aliens, which blocked his sense of fear. Veniamin saw a huge pipe inside a screen, with two "energy streams" curving into a spiral moving one in front of the other. There were huge oval-shaped windows in the walls of the pipe and behind them some mysterious buildings were visible.

This screen was floating in mid-air to the left of the semi-transparent alien trio and several steps from Kurochkin's bed. Looking at the image the witness asked the aliens if it was a "time travel machine." (?) One of the aliens, which appeared to have been about fifty years of age and dressed in a smoky gray tight-fitting suit answered, *"Your understanding of time is incorrect. This is something similar in the nature of a time travel machine."*

The witness then asked how did the machine work? The alien answered, *"There are several ways to travel through time. For example there are corridors in space, that humanity is not aware of. Do you see those spiral (helical) streams in the pipe rushing towards one another?"* The witness answered affirmative. The alien continued, *"They hold a great future for your civilization. They can be used for the benefit of humans."* The alien then added, *"Anyway even if I give you additional details you will not understand. Take our advice, stop wearing your wrist watch."* (!)

The witness was visibly confused and was told that, *"the rhythm of the Universe does not coincide with terrestrial time, it (the false concept of time) is one of the reasons for the many unnecessary problems on Earth."* Kurochkin then muttered, *"Well is this all connected with my watch?"* The alien answered, *"Take your watch off your wrist and keep it in your pocket. A watch on the wrist could be harmful; it "jams" the rhythms of the universe, partially penetrating into the temporal field of Earth and into the biorhythms of your personal biological time. Besides that stop drinking alcohol, (!) would you remember what we told you today?"* "Yes," answered Kurochkin. At this point the blue mist covered the witness and the aliens vanished.

HC addendum.
Source: Alexey K. Priyma, 'Unknown Worlds,' Moscow, 1996.   Type: E
Comments: Complicated and interesting case, were these visitors really time travelers? I must admit I always felt "discomfort" wearing a wristwatch, but I am not sure if I could stop drinking completely.

* * * * * * *

Location: Villota Ranch, near Medina de Pomar, Burgos, Spain.
Date: Summer, 1992.
Time: 3:00 a.m.

The witness Maria Palacios, had stepped out into the yard of her home to pick up some laundry she had out hanging, when she suddenly saw a very bright white light which bothered her eyes as she stared at it. The light flew over the house. Maria called out for her son-in-law Manuel Alvarez so he could also see the light. He was able to see how the light, which flew at about eighty meters in altitude, apparently was emitted by an object shaped like a half egg. The object was seen to descend on a nearby hill. Later accompanied by his nephews Manuel finds an area of flattened grass on the hill.

The next morning around 3:00 a.m Maria was in the bathroom and was suddenly surprised as to how bright the moon light was. Looking out the bathroom window, she was able to see inside the nearby equipment corral, also where two large guard dogs slept. Two strange beings were walking parallel to each other, both about three meters in height. Their heads were shaped like an inverted pear, and they had very long arms. She could not distinguish any facial features. The beings appeared to 'slide' just above the ground. She saw then entering the area where the dogs and the tractor were located. The dogs did not even bark.

Terrified she hid until the morning. Searching the corral area she fails to find any tracks or footprints, however the dogs seemed to be more aggressive than normal. That same night she again saw the object descend towards the hill, this time emitting a weaker strobe-like light.

Finally the object ascended and disappeared towards the village of La Cerca. Upon investigating in the morning she found an area of flattened grass.

HC addendum.
Source:http://www.looculto.26omb.com/ovnisenespana/ovnisenespan a.htm   Type: D?

Location: Montecito Heights, California.
Date: June, 1992.
Time: Night.

The witness, Rene Barrios, had checked all the doors and windows of his house to make sure everything was locked and had gone to bed. Three minutes later he heard a noise like an electrical saw, coming from behind the bathroom, in the patio near an orange tree. He tried to stand up but he could not move at all. He felt frozen against his bed.

Suddenly three persons entered his room. They were wearing acrylic blue and silver uniforms, with a "Zeus" logo or sign on the right side of the chest. There were two men and a woman. The woman then performed a medical examination on the witness and then had sexual intercourse with him. One of the men had dark skin and was doing all the talking the other one did not seem to move at all. The man spoke very softly, and spoke about a "son" and told the witness that he will not be able to remember anything that had transpired. The man removed a glove and put his hand on the witness's forehead, the witness immediately went to sleep.

Next morning at breakfast with two friends that had stayed overnight at his home in a guest room the two friends spoke excitedly about what they had heard. They felt afraid as they heard a noise but felt drained of strength to see what it was. His two friends also described the noise like that of an electrical saw.

HC addendum.
Source: http://www.mufoncms.com   Type: E

*   *   *   *   *   *   *

Location: Scottsdale, Arizona.
Date: June, 1992.
Time: 11:30 p.m.

The witness Kate (involved in previous encounters as a youngster), was working now as nurse on a cardiac intensive unit at a local hospital and had just finished the evening shift at the hospital. Normally, she would take the streets to walk to her apartment, but that evening she had a strong impulse to cross a field (a shortcut), but it was pretty dark and isolated. The moon was almost full that night, so she figured it would be safe since it was quite bright out. She slid under the fence and started walking through the field. It was about a mile long and she wasn't sure who owned it.

She carried a small flashlight in her purse and took it out to see where she was going because there were many holes and she didn't want to sprain or break an ankle. She was halfway through the field when three deer came out of the brush to her right; they were walking as if they were drugged and they just collapsed on the ground. Then several birds dropped from the sky and fell to her left and right, they appeared to be dead. At that moment several rabbits ran by her and one of them rolled over on the ground and looked like it was having a "convulsion."

She then heard this loud humming sound, and a yellow ball of light appeared in the air several feet above the ground. She was quite startled and stopped on her tracks, since whatever this was, it affected the animals and could possibly hurt her. She felt strange, like when she was a child and would have nighttime visits with a silver colored robot called *"Leenal."* The only difference this time was that she was still able to move, but didn't because she was so scared. She just stood there transfixed looking at the light.

After several seconds, a mist shot out of the light with a loud 'swoosh.' The mist then swirled into a shape that turned into *"Leenal."* He looked just like she remembered him, tall (maybe eight feet) and all silver with a helmet and visor-like thing where his eyes should have been. He then spoke, *"Hello Kate, I told you I would be back."* It was quite upsetting for Kate to see this being again because she had convinced herself that those childhood experiences were not real and just dreams. She yelled, *"Why are you bothering me now? It's been twenty years!"* Leenal said that time had no meaning to his people and that he had to show her his world. He waved his hand and she felt herself go numb and fall to the ground.

She opened her eyes and was in a different place that didn't seem like planet Earth. The sky was red and a fog was all around her. Leenal was standing in front of her and started to change shape, first into a horrible creature that looked like a *"devil."* When she turned away and screamed, he turned into a tall, handsome young man with long blonde hair, very pale white skin and the greenest eyes she had ever seen. He said he could take any form and be anything or anybody she wanted him to be. He told her they were in his world and he had to bring her there to establish a 'permanent connection' with her mind.

Leenal explained that he was part of a very ancient race that existed before mankind and that many of his people were trying to establish mental links with selected humans, so his race could come into our world. He then turned back into the tall silver robot-like form and put his hand on her head. Once again, her body went numb, but this time she didn't feel herself falling to the ground, she kind of floated. When she opened her eyes she was in the field and it was daytime. She looked at her watch, it was 6:25 am. The passage of time felt weird because it only seemed like she was in Leenal's world for under an hour, yet at least five hours had passed.

She went home, opened her door and found her apartment a mess. Furniture was overturned and all her dresser and kitchen drawers were pulled out and emptied. She thought at first that she had been robbed, but her jewelry, money, television, stereo and other valuables were still there. She asked her neighbors and the people who lived above her if anyone had heard or seen anything, but no one did.

Although Leenal never appeared again to Kate since that summer night in 1992, she continued to have paranormal experiences in the form of poltergeists and saw shadow-like beings in her home and at the hospital when she worked the night shift. She would later have a bizarre experience in 2005.

HC addendum.
Source: Phillip J. Imbrogno, 'Files from the Edge,' pp. 84-86.   Type: G

* * * * * * *

Location: Near Kingston, New York.
Date: July, 1992.
Time: Afternoon.

Whitley Strieber was walking about half a mile behind the cabin when he noticed what looked like about a twelve-year-old sitting against a big tree. He had something between his fingers, and Strieber assumed it was a local kid out sneaking a smoke. The woods were very quiet and he strolled over and said, *"Better be sure you put that out when you're finished."* Then he realized that the "boy" was wearing a tan jumpsuit. His eyes were deep set, and his skin was old. And it wasn't a cigarette he was holding; it was a little silver wand.

At this point Strieber felt scared. He opened his mouth slightly. Still looking straight ahead, he growled. Terrified Strieber ran away from the area and did not see the humanoid depart.

HC addendum.
Source: Whitley Strieber, 'Breakthrough; the Next Step.'   Type: E

* * * * * * *

Location: Klimovsk, Tula region, Russia.
Date: July, 1992.
Time: Unknown.

77-year old invalid Nikolay Vasilievich Astahov, veteran of the Second World War (Patriotic War) reported encountering human-like extraterrestrials and visiting their planet. He reported two contacts and refused to go with them on a third.

He stated that the aliens are similar to humans. He reported there were many humans living among the aliens, people who have disappeared without a trace, men, women and children.

HC addendum.
Source: Valeriy Rudenko, 'Oracle,' Moscow and 'Tulskiy Courier' newspaper. Type: G
Comments: Unfortunately there is no additional information on this fascinating case.

* * * * * * *

Location: Springfield, Missouri.
Date: July, 1992.
Time: Evening.

A Springfield woman reported two robed creatures in a vacant field near her home. The creatures had glowing amber eyes and appeared to be carrying a computer-like apparatus, (like modern day laptops) which one of them was operating. The creatures glided over the ground without apparent effort.

HC addendum.
Source: UFO Intelligence Newsletter. Type: E
Comments: Aliens carrying laptops?

* * * * * * *

Location: Brzozki, Poland.
Date: July, 1992.
Time: 4:00 a.m.

The witness, Ryszard P. was driving on a road between Krosno Odrzanskie and Gubin near the German border. The sun was coming up it was a warm and misty morning. After a long and exhausting trip he decided to take a break so he stopped by the roadside in the vicinity of the bridge on the River Bobr. He exited the vehicle and went for a stroll in the nearby forest. After walking for about thirty meters he heard a strange, unidentified sound and on the bank of the river he saw a very peculiar object.

The object was dish-shaped and gray or greenish in color. The witness noticed an odor resembling "burning chocolate". Ryszard hid in the thick bushes and observed several humanoid entities bustling about

205

around the object. He also noticed several entities onboard the object. The witness saw about fifteen entities which resembled "mummies" about 135cm tall. Their trunks were rather corpulent and similar to "stuffed sacks." The entities were unipeds or had both legs somehow joined together. The witness didn't notice any heels. Their arms were very flexible and seemed joint-less. The palms were also visible, but the witness does not remember the number of fingers on each hand. The entities faces were covered by whitish plates resembling the surface of a mirror and remained invisible. The way the moved resembled that of kangaroos (hopping?).

It didn't seem that the entities communicated among each other. They were examining local plants using utensils resembling tubes. Ryszard was probably seen by the entities but they ignored him. But after a minute he suddenly coughed and immediately lost consciousness. He recovered after an hour and found himself standing. The craft and entities had disappeared.

HC addendum.
Source: direct from woe_@vp.pl   Type: A & C

* * * * * * *

Location: Los Angeles, California.
Date: July, 1992.
Time: 6:30 p.m.

Reuben Taylor was driving on the freeway Hollywood 101 by Echo Park, accompanying him were his mother and son. His mother first saw the craft and called his attention to look as she dipped her head and covered her face. He immediately looked outside of her direction to the right and saw what at first he thought was the world's biggest Ferris wheel sitting about 100ft off the ground. It was approximately 300ft in diameter, golden bronze with colored windows and a glare that stretched out 50 to 100ft.

As he watched, it began to maneuver and assumed a more saucer-shaped form. The witness felt "a great surge of power" and a connection to the object as it came closer. Soon he was able to see in detail numerous human-like figures looking down at him smiling, from behind the center ring of windows. He also saw what appeared to be writing on the top of the craft, which resembled Hebrew or ancient Egyptian. Suddenly as quickly as it had appeared, the craft went straight up and disappeared into space.

HC addendum.
Source: http://www.ufoevidence.org   Type: A

Location: Paltanavichus, Lithuania.
Date: July, 1992.
Time: 11:00 p.m.

Rimas, a 50-year old Lithuanian rural priest, was at home when he heard the sounds of motors and foreign voices outside in the courtyard. He looked out the window and saw a large disc-shaped object descending quickly into the yard. As it approached the ground, a door opened and a rope-type ladder was lowered to the ground. Around the center of the object, the witness could see a dozen round-lighted windows.

Curious, the witness stepped out into the courtyard and climbed up the rope ladder. As he entered the hatch, he was greeted by two, silvery clad human-like figures, complete with helmets and antennas on top. Inside he saw numerous panels with buttons and estimated that the disc was about fifty meters in diameter.

Soon he heard a sound resembling that of a dynamo and the disc rocked and climbed up. Looking out a window he saw what appeared to be the earth moving slowly away, he did not see any stars only a dark blue firmament. Soon they landed, presumably on the alien's planet (or moon) where he saw low, one story dwellings with windows. He also saw trees and grass, which possessed striking colors. The aliens or inhabitants of the "planet," were human like, about 1.6 meters in height and were all youthful in appearance. They wore simply clothing and the women had their hair picked up in a bun, they wore no cosmetics.

The planet was very warm. He was given a juice that tasted like mango to drink. They aliens spoke neither English nor German but the witness somehow understood everything that was being said to him, he thought that maybe they communicated telepathically. He did not see any forms of electricity or lighting. He then asked the aliens if they believed in God or in a God. He was told yes. He was taken to a building, which he was told was a place of worship, which, in no way resembled a church. Inside he hardly saw any images except for that of a man with a belt and beard, which he was told was their superior "being."

He was told that there were other planets in their system populated by tall dark skinned aliens, three meters in height. He described the aliens as having beautiful gray eyes and light colored hair, most wore light colored coveralls and the women wore multicolored dresses. He remembered seeing beautiful fields of flowers and flat topped hills and mountains. He did not see any clouds but noticed that the sun was very hot.

After a while he was taken back to the disc shaped object and climbed again up the rope ladder. He was eventually brought back to his home. The aliens did not tell the witness if they would return.

HC addendum.
Source: Sergey Shpakovskiy, quoting Lithuania Television channel
Tele-3, 1992.   Type: G

* * * * * * *

Location: Sedona, Arizona.
Date: July, 1992.
Time: Late night.

The witness, a well-known local psychic, professional artist, and channel was suddenly awakened by voices talking in her bedroom. Looking up she saw several beautiful human-like figures wearing white sparkling uniforms, standing at the foot of her bed. The figures had blue upside-down triangle insignias on the breast area of their uniforms. Another figure with flowing blond hair and wearing a two-piece uniform with gold braided epaulets and a large gold triangular emblem on his chest appeared to be the leader.

A sort of light illuminated him and he smiled at the witness. He reassured her and a peaceful feeling came over her. The next day she was also visited by numerous entities including a blond young woman wearing a shiny white uniform with a golden upside-down triangular insignia on her breast area.

HC addendum.
Source: Helga Morrow, the Missing Link #125.   Type: E

* * * * * * *

Location: Nagornyi, Karabach Caucasus, Russia.
Date: August, 1992.
Time: Unknown.

During the military battles on the frontier between Azerbaijan and Armenia in which different types of weapons were used, a mass alien landing reportedly occurred. The beings observed by the different combatants were generally humanoid and robotic in nature, metallic and stocky in appearance. UFOs were also seen on several occasions. The humanoids were apparently attempting to appease both sides of the conflict, making their appearance in battles amid explosions and fire. As a result both sides were seized with fear and hid in their shelters and foxholes withholding their fire on several occasions.

According to some of the rumors one or two such bio-robots were damaged as a result of mortar fire and parts of the destroyed robots were taken to a special hospital either in Baku or Yerevan, where electronic specialists studied them. Reportedly it was found that the beings appeared to be biomechanical organisms or cyborgs.

HC addendum.
Source: Special issue of 'Oracle,' Moscow, 'Anomalies & Phenomena.'
Type: H?

* * * * * * *

Location: Obninsk, Kaluga Region, Russia.
Date: August, 1992.
Time: Evening.

Larissa N a local resident, was walking along a grass-covered gully when she suddenly noticed four semi-transparent human-shaped figures standing in a distance. When she looked closer, she noticed a strange apparatus standing 15 meters away on a slope. The figures were taking water from a nearby brook. The strangers were occupied with their business and had not noticed her. They were inserting the water as well as soil samples into some kind of packets.

As she watched in amazement, she suddenly realized that she could approach and speak to the aliens and they would not cause her any harm. Using telepathy she asked them why they needed the samples they were collecting. She received a telepathic response telling her that it was for examination purposes. She was told that Earth humans have a minimum twenty and a maximum eighty years left to survive. (!) She asked them where were they from and the response was "Planet LIKA," located in the Sagittarius Constellation.

She was then invited to go with them. Larissa agreed and walked to the craft. The alien spacecraft was slightly tilted and had vertical elongated windows and a double antenna on top, resembling like feelers on a butterfly. All entered the object and there she met the fifth member of the crew. She noticed an unusual and soft light inside the craft, and numerous control panels filled with multitude of instruments. All five aliens wore thin tight-fighting overalls, having the same color of their identical faces. Under the soft light she could see that the aliens were of

209

the same height, possessed the same rhythm of movements and had expressionless eyes, same hair, same voices, almost like "twins" or "clones."

"How long will the flight take?" Asked Larissa. *"Three hours and thirty minutes, using your time measure,"* was their answer. Larissa was placed on a chair in the middle as the rest of the crewmembers sat in the corner armchairs. The alien leader stood up in the middle, and suddenly all of the aliens became immovable and appeared frozen to the floor. Larissa had the sudden thought that they were "robotic" systems. Some kind of control lever was rose up from the floor and in a moment Larissa saw a screen that showed the outside of the craft. Everything became dark as she zoomed into space in just seconds.

The witness was taken to Planet LIKA near their Sun-like yellow star (G3v spectral class). There, she learned that the real aliens on Lika were thin tall humanoids with large closely set eyes, small mouth, long noses, and very powerful auras. Their language was very unusual, resembling melodic singing. Larissa learned that she had communicated with their biological robots, which they frequently used for various space missions, but the real aliens also piloted the crafts.

After the trip to Lika, Larissa was brought back to the same location where she was originally picked up. Another witness, F Kim from St Petersburg also reportedly being in telepathic contact with the inhabitants of the planet Lika, and that some of the authentic inhabitants of the planet resembled tall furry animals. (?)

HC addendum.
Source: Obninsk UFO Group, published in Aura Magazine # 3-37, 1994, Anton Anfalov.   Type: G

* * * * * * *

Location: Los Bateles, Spain.
Date: August, 1992.
Time: Late evening.

The main witness Luis S., and a friend, Ramon, were lying on the beach front alone, when suddenly an uncanny silence invaded the area, the birds who had been singing seconds before, were now completely quiet. Moments later, the witnesses noticed two very tall thin figures approaching in their direction no more than 10-12m away. The figures were very thin, about 2.2m in height and seemed to be moving in incredibly synchronized movements. Both figures were moving their arms and legs at the same time, and according to the witnesses they didn't appear to be touching the ground, but they couldn't be sure. The strange figures were moving at a speed of someone riding a bicycle at

210

moderate speed. Both witnesses stared at the strange humanoids in amazement without moving.

As the humanoids "jogged" by, the witnesses noticed that they wore shiny pearly gray coveralls. Their heads were very strange, a bit larger than normal, totally hairless, and with two huge black inexpressive slanted eyes. They also had a barely noticeable nose, very pointy chins and very pale almost gray colored skin. The two humanoids did not seem to notice the witnesses as they passed at about 15m in front of the witnesses. The two humanoids quickly disappeared into the distance, following a straight trajectory along the shoreline, never slowing down or without ever turning their heads.

Luis remembers that his friend Ramon was very nervous and wanted to leave, but both decided to stay. However minutes later Ramon fell into a profound sleep and Luis was unable to sleep at all. Later that night around midnight, Luis observed a strange yellowish light flying at a low altitude between the lighthouse and Cabo Roche. The light eventually faded from sight. Luis then fell immediately sleep and experienced a strange "nightmare" in his dream both were on the beach when suddenly 7-8 humanoids, similar to the ones they had seen before, appeared on the beach. The humanoids took both Luis and Ramon and separated them; Luis was then taken into a strange room bright yellowish in color. He suddenly 'woke up' and was not able to sleep for the rest of the night.

HC addendum.
Source: http://caravaca.blogspot.com   Type: E?
Comments: Translation by Albert S. Rosales.

* * * * * * *

Location: Kamchatka Peninsula, Far East Russia.
Date: August, 1992.
Time: Night.

A UFO research expedition was organized to this isolated region. Organizers of the expedition were led by telepathic instructions of an alien civilization, allegedly from the Planet DOTUMI in the Lyra constellation, as they stated. Detailed information about this alien civilization was received and then the aliens invited the participants to visit the region of their base or the place, which they frequently visited on Earth.

Through telepathic channels, the aliens detailed a list of names of persons they wish to be part of the "visit," plus they gave the exact time and place of the contact. By using a photo camera, several pictures were taken of a group of humanoid entities, semi-transparent in nature (apparently because they were surrounded by an energy shield or an

211

aura). The entities moved in groups, one after the other, among the mountain slopes, the last alien pair portrayed in the photos were holding each other's hands.

There was no direct contact, apparently because the aliens were apprehensive to the possibility of damage to the humans because of their high bio-energy field. After the photographs were taken, several members of the group entered into telepathic contact with the aliens and extensive information about their planet and its inhabitants was obtained.

HC addendum.
Source: G Soboleva, Y. Rychkova, and O Miheenkova,
'Mysteries of Extraterrestrial Civilizations.'   Type: E and F

* * * * * * *

Location: Dedestapolcsany, Hungary.
Date: August 11, 1992.
Time: Late night.

Awakened by a bright light from outside their home, several family members looked out to see an astonishing sight. A large bright spherical object was hovering over an adjacent construction site. The craft appeared to have several luminous oval shaped openings and was shining a beam of light from a circular opening on its lower half. Inside this beam the witnesses saw several small humanoid figures that flew in the air within the beam towards a nearby apple tree.

The beings were described as thin, with featureless heads, long thing arms, and wearing short robe like tunics, no legs were seen. The beings carried small containers and flew around the apple tree collecting as many of the fruit as possible. Soon they flew back into the craft via the same light beam. The luminous object then left the area. No other information.

HC addendum.
Source: Kriston Endre, Hungarian UFO Magazine 8/93.   Type: B

Location: Colinas Del Yunque, Puerto Rico.
Date: Middle of August, 1992.
Time: 5:00 p.m.

At least six independent witnesses, saw in broad daylight, two short beings walking side by side on the middle of the roadway. The beings were described as four-foot tall with shiny light-green skin, very thin long arms, and heads somewhat larger than normal and covered with a stringy light-brown hair. They appeared to be only wearing a pair of white shorts with a red stripe on the side.

The witnesses followed the short beings for a short distance until they entered a wooded slope and disappeared. One of the witnesses claims that one of the beings gave her the two finger "peace" sign as he walked by.

HC addendum.
Source: Jorge Martin, Enigma #60.   Type: E

* * * * * * *

Location: Tver, Russia.
Date: Autumn, 1992.
Time: Night.

A local woman named Nika Tverskaya (a pseudonym) claimed to have entered into telepathic and physical contact with an extraterrestrial civilization from a planet called "URU." Reportedly two tall humanoid figures suddenly appeared inside her apartment, located in a multistoried complex, while she was alone at home. The humanoid figures approached her and began communicating with her. They invited her to come with them and she agreed.

The two humanoids then accompanied her to a landed craft. Each humanoid was very tall, about three meters in height, and she soon learned that they were actually biological robots. Both "robots" were dressed in light colored coveralls. They had dim eyes that flashed at certain times. The robots communicated with her via telepathy. The alien craft had landed on the outskirts of the city. When they came to the craft she saw that it resembled a saucer with brightly lit "windows" or portholes on its sides. Suddenly at one location on the hull of the craft, a rounded wall of the craft "moved aside" creating an opening. To her surprise, Nika did not walk in, but zoomed into the air and flew into the opening. The robots also levitated into the opening that in moments, closed behind them.

The space within the craft was filled by a delicate vibration, as if the air was vibrating (a similar feeling when her face was exposed to a hair dryer). Moments later Nika lost consciousness and when came to, she found herself lying in a deep armchair in a large round room, probably in the center of the alien craft. She could see buttons and numerous sophisticated instruments all around her. The walls inside the craft were greenish, white and phosphorescent in nature. Close to her Nika saw three humanoid figures in tight fitting silver coveralls, a woman about three meters in height and two "bio robots." The alien woman began communicating with Nika telepathically. She explained that while Nika was "sleeping" they took samples of her "genetic memory" and they were convinced that she was useful and interesting to them.

It seemed that the aliens were interested in finding the reasons how humans were able to survive in difficult conditions. The alien woman was very well built and slender. The alien woman had beautiful long fingers, dark shiny hair, and wore a sort of "hoop" around her forehead. Her eyes were unusually expressive. The she then introduced herself and said that her name was "FA." She added that it was a "conditional" name. In general, it seemed that the aliens did not possess any names at all; instead each individual had its own bio-energy spectrum (aura?) FA's spectrum was white and violet in color. FA's clothing tightly fit around her body, but seemed very comfortable and did not hinder her movements and maintaining a constant temperature.

Nika also found out that the furniture in the room would easily change shape just from a single touch from the body. She then began asking questions. Nika asked, *"Where are we flying to?"*

According to FA, they were going to their dimension but that she would be brought back to her home earlier than when she was taken (!) since they had the ability to stop and reverse time, apparently the "stop-time" mode was already activated and the time was running in reverse. FA told Nika about an energetic connection of the human aura with that of the Sun and other planets. She also mentioned that about 3,000 years ago, a civilization on Earth had ceased to exist (Atlantis?) and that humanity was currently in a very dangerous situation as well.

During her experience, Nika received large volumes of information from the aliens. They told her that the name of their planet was URU. They added that the rotational axis of their planet was positioned at the appropriate angle to the ecliptic that provided an almost eternal summer season and the average temperature was from +15 to +35 degrees centigrade. Also, there was a second artificial Sun near their planet that help to light it. The planet URU made one full rotation around its axis much slower than Earth, taking approximately 24 terrestrial days. So the alien planet evidently had a much lower gravity. Relative to the Earth, the planet is located somewhere near the Orion constellation. Atmospheric pressure is stronger than that on Earth and the level of radioactivity is higher everywhere.

214

Their bodies are also radioactive and could harm humans if they did not use protective suits (heard this from other cases). They did not possess huge factories on their planet. And they also didn't have large cities. All of their settlements were well adjusted and implanted or built into the natural surface of their planet, probably partially under the surface or underground. They "create" buildings, instead of building them; they "grow" them remotely like plants, using a special process. The houses are at first soft, but then they harden, assuming their programmed shape.

Their average life span in one physical body is about 800 terrestrial years. They can easily change their bodies, implanting their souls from the old bodies to the new ones. So their "physical suit (or envelope) can be changed several times during their life span, perhaps lasting several thousands of years, with the entire memory preserved. Their medicine had reached an incredible level. They can replace not only the entire body but also the inner organs. Copies of the organs can be created by using holograms, after scanning the original and then artificially grown and implanted. They are vegetarians, and eat specially grown plants and artificial albumens. They cook their special pastes from plants; they harvest their plants in special tube-like devices (hydroponics?). They have love and sex, but not like that on Earth. If desired, all memories about their ex-lovers can be erased from memory. Like humans, the aliens have children, but they do not "waste" time in impregnation, birth and growing. The children can be "grown" inside special incubators with all the necessary conditions to develop. They give part of their soul to their children and then they are occupied in upbringing them. As soon as a child is born he or she is encased in a special "informational" coverall. While growing, the coveralls are exchanged with larger ones.

The children are unrestricted and have free access to go anywhere. The children study in incredible schools, totally different to the schools on Earth. In those schools they are taught not to learn mathematics, grammar, physics, etc, but are taught to take information directly from energetic and information fields. They also teach their children telepathic clairvoyance, creative imaginative thinking and the ability to forecast events. All the information can be taken from two energy (invisible) rings which surround their planet. There are no books at school; information is easily obtained from holograms.

From a young age the children are taught the ability to levitate and not to be afraid of flight. Their organisms contains numerous magnetic cells, and their race is close to the creation of an eternal artificial body, which can be disassembled to atoms and molecules and then reassembled again, while preserving all previous functions. Besides their natural ability to levitate, Urusians have the ability to teleport and to walk through material obstacles. Their spacecrafts can also fly through dense substances.

Their souls can also live in other biological bodies. The necessary bodies can be grown from the donor's cells by the method of artificial acceleration. The main different between the aliens and the bio-robots is that the robots cannot perform creative work and can't synthesize the biological energy. Aliens on the planet URU as FA told Nika are a race of creators and 'energy donors.' All Urusians are telepathic clairvoyants and can levitate in the air and teleport, and possess other "supernatural" abilities. Their spacecrafts can be controlled by mental impulses, and the new models of their craft can change their shapes and can take a variety of forms since they are made of something like liquid programmed metal.

The aliens also informed Nika that they have been on Earth for several million years, but now they are only observers, because humanity is developed enough to independently make a choice for the direction of its development. They added that they represented, "the Immortality group of the Universe," kind of an "evolutionary squadron."

When the spacecraft returned back to Earth, it remained hovering in midair at about 100 meters about the ground, then the floor in the craft's cabin trembled and became transparent, like a fog or mist had been dispersed. Nika was able to see the pipes and boiler rooms through the walls of multistoried apartments. Then Nika moved inside a beam of light and descended straight to the balcony of her apartment.

HC addendum.
Source: Belyaev F. "Civilization UR," Volzhskiy Currier newspaper, Tver, 1994, 'The Immortality group of the Universe,' Volzhskiy Currier newspaper, Tver, 1994, Pavel Khailov.   Type: G

* * * * * * *

Location: Yorkeys Knob, Cairns, Queensland, Australia.
Date: September, 1992.
Time: 4:30 a.m.

A retired woman saw a strange creature on a paddock; it was the size of a man but resembled a giant "bee." In the background she could see an object. Telepathic communication occurred over quite a lengthy period.

She went to the window where she saw an unusual object in the sky, it resembled a square within a square and bright white in color. At the same time she saw jets over the area.

HC addendum.
Source: Vlad Godic.   Type: C

216

Location: El Palmar, Conil de la Frontera, Spain.
Date: September 4, 1992.
Time: 12:30 a.m.

The two witnesses, Luis and Ramon had just finished celebrating the local festivities, when they decided to have supper and sleep on the beach. While resting peacefully on the sand they suddenly noticed two figures quickly approaching their location. Thinking the figures were joggers, they sat up to look at them, but as the two "joggers" passed near the witnesses, they immediately realized that these "joggers" were not normal humans.

According to the witnesses, everything became suddenly very quiet, not even the sea birds sang. As the figures passed to within 10-12 meters of the two men they noticed that these were very tall thin humanoids at least 2.2m in height, which seemed to move in quick synchronized movements. They both seemed to move their arms and legs and the same time and the witnesses were not sure if they were touching the ground but were moving at a very quick pace, as if they were on "bicycles."

Luis was convinced that the two strangers were not human and noticed that both wore shiny gray loose fitting coveralls. The heads were larger than humans and they were completely bald. Both had large black slanted eyes completely devoid of any expression. The nose was very small; however their chins were very pointy. The skin was pale and gray. Along with their coveralls, they wore a short "cape" on their backs and boots. Both humanoids continued on a parallel course along the beach and at no time did they turned their heads to look at the witnesses.

Later on Ramon, who had been very nervous during the encounter, fell into a deep sleep and Luis who had been very calm throughout the encounter, was not able to sleep. He later saw a bright yellowish light hovering above some fishing vessels in the water. He then fell asleep and suffered a terrible "nightmare" in which the strange humanoids had returned but this time accompanied by seven or eight more humanoids. The humanoids then grabbed Luis and Ramon and separated them; Luis remembers being taken into a room filled with a brilliant yellow light. The next day they left the area.

HC addendum.
Source: Jose Antonio Caravaca jacaravaca@gmail.com   Type: E or G?

Location: Near Budapest, Hungary.
Date: September 4, 1992.
Time: Evening.

The witness S. G., a local salesman, was on his way home in his car when he noticed a strange luminous object in the sky. He was so engrossed with the spectacle that he almost collided with an oncoming vehicle. He then stopped his vehicle on the side of the road and watched the object, wondering what it was.

A few moments later, he noticed a pulsating light from the nearby forest, about five hundred meters away and noticed what appeared to be a 'spacecraft' hovering just above the ground. Unable to overcome his curiosity, he ventured closer to the craft and noticed several short figures moving around the object. He felt no fear and was rather, flooded by an inner warmth. As if possessed by an ethereal lightness, he was suddenly floating in the air.

His next memory was of waking up, lying on the middle of a field, feeling very cold and surrounded by snow. He noticed that it was daytime and saw his car in the distance, parked on the side of the road. He eventually arrived home, where his worried and at the same time suspicious wife asked him where had he been in the last 24 hours. He was stunned when he realized that he had lost 24 hours for which he could not account for. His wife did not believe his story. He suspected that his memories had been blocked. He suffered from terrible nightmares in which he saw himself in some sort of foreign environment or world.

Then in June of 1993, S. G. was involved in a serious car accident but survived. This somehow triggered memories of the lost 24 hours. He recalled the aliens giving him a thorough medical examination onboard their spacecraft and giving him a 'tour' of the inside of their ship. They communicated by using telepathy but refused to tell the witness exactly where they came from and only told him that they came from an enormous distance traveling through "hyperspace."

He also learned that our planet was part of a "cosmic experiment," but they did not elaborate. The aliens were short, with huge eyes, small nostrils, tiny mouths and wore large helmets. However the witness somehow felt that "this was only a mask or disguise." He asked them to reveal their true nature or appearance, but received no answer. He was then shown an "imaginary space journey," where locations of several planets were shown to him.

HC addendum.
Source: Remtortenet FB Page.   Type: G

Location: Tansen, Nepal.
Date: September 17, 1992.
Time: Night.

At least two people saw a large bright light, which they took to be an angel, descend rapidly from the sky and fly in the direction of the local church.

The same evening, over a hundred others saw a vision in the sky of a man wearing a loincloth, with arms outstretched and head bowed, attached to a large cross. This stayed in the sky for over an hour and many people were very moved by it. Most of saw this vision were not Christians.

HC addendum.
Source: Paul Whitehead, FSR Vol. 39 #4.   Type: F?

* * * * * * *

Location: Sentul, West Persekutuan, Malaysia.
Date: September 22, 1992.
Time: Daytime.

A 13-year old student, Law Wai Chow, claimed to have encountered a strange tiny entity. He described it as having eyes like those of humans but red in color and with no eyebrows. The creature had pointed ears.

A group of children playing kites also saw the tiny being, which they described as human-like in appearance but measuring only 15cm tall. The body was reported to be greenish in color and shiny. They said that the hands had only three fingers. On seeing the witnesses, the tiny creature scurried away into the housing project, which was still under construction.

Mohd Najib Rasli, went to the site where the creatures were reportedly seen. He spent nearly an hour searching for the creatures in the area. Finally at 3:00 p.m. he spotted the tiny being near a hole. He tried to catch it but it immediately ran away and was lost from view.

HC addendum.
Source: Ahmad Jamaluddin.   Type: E

Location: Huaika Tabio, Colombia.
Date: September 22, 1992.
Time: 8:00 p.m.

About 15 members of an international UFO group had gone to the scene of previous encounters and were waiting around for any type of unusual phenomena. Soon they saw a large, orange colored sphere descend from the mountain and land about 300 meters away from the group.

Five of the group approached the object and watched a beam of white light strike the ground ahead of them, on the ground it became a half moon shaped light, blue in color. Smoke was then seen rising around the object then a tall blond haired Nordic looking individual emerged from the smoke, he walked around briefly then was seen entering the half-moon shaped light. Everything then seemed to disappear.

The next morning, after a heavy downpour the same group involved in the previous incident watched a large orange spherical light descend from the mountain and come close to the ground on the road close to their location on the farm. Three minutes later, several tall, human like silhouettes became visible, these ranged from 1.8 meters to 2.3 meters in height and seemed to be enveloped in a bluish mist.

Four members of the group attempted to approach the figures but they suddenly became invisible.

HC addendum.
Source: Alexander Beltran, Colombia.   Type: C

* * * * * * *

Location: Castellammare, Italy.
Date: October 21, 1992.
Time: Close to midnight.

A woman standing on her balcony, reported seeing three giant, white colored humanoid figures with large cone-shaped heads, moving over a nearby field, apparently levitating, suspended just above the ground. The giants disappeared from sight behind some bushes.

HC addendum.
Source: Notizie UFO #40, Denys Breysse Project Becassine.   Type: E

Location: Hardangervidda, Odda, Norway.
Date: October/November, 1992.
Time: Evening.

A strange object was seen landing near a cabin at a place located 20km southeast of Odda, just at the outskirts of Hardangervidda, 700-800 meters above sea level. The observer Torbjorn Reinsnos, saw the object land about 100 meters from his cabin. He estimated it at 6-8 meters long, trapezoid in shape with rounded corners.

After a short while, he saw two human-like beings (estimated height 1.2m and 1.4m) come out of the object. They appeared to have been dressed in silvery clothing and some sort of helmets on their heads. They also seemed to be carrying something, possibly a tool of some kind, but it was not possible to tell exactly what it was.

Torbjorn Reinsnos had ample time to observe the craft and the humanoids, using a pair of binoculars. He soon became very frightened though, and fired off a few warning shots from his shotgun toward the beings. These returned to and disappeared into the object, which took off and shot into the distance at a high rate of speed.

HC addendum.
Source: Ole Jonny Braenne, UFO Norge.   Type: B

Location: Ilager, West Virginia.
Date: Late November, 1992.
Time: Night.

During a spate of UFO sightings over the area a young man using a pair of binoculars saw a metallic craft flying above some trees and shining a beam of light towards the ground.

The object had large windows and inside he was able to see several tall muscular men with light hair and wearing silvery outfits. The craft drifted slowly away from the area.

HC addendum.
Source: Bob Teets, 'West Virginia UFOS: Close Encounters in the Mountain State.'   Type: A

Location: Devil's Punchbowl, near Hindhead, Surrey, England.
Date: December, 1992.
Time: Evening.

Brian Birch and his son Andrew (involved in previous encounters at the same location) were revisiting the Punchbowl for a night skywatch. They were close to the car park on the far side of the Punchbowl. There were some steep steps down from the car park which led to an area with an uninterrupted view. When they walked down these steps, they noticed another man there of slender build wearing a dark colored suit. He was openly staring at them both. After this had gone on for a short while, Brian became annoyed and approached the man to ask what he was looking at. As he got near he realized that the man's face looked horribly disfigured, like he had been in some kind of accident. Brian's anger turned to pity and he walked past the man without confronting him. He stopped and stared at the view. Soon Andrew walked over to join him.

Next a woman walked on by pushing a pram. She passed extremely close to the man in the suit and paid him absolutely no attention. Nor did she look at either Brian or Andrew. A short while later a second man turned up. He looked like a construction worker and appeared quite strong. He walked right up to the man in the suit, who was about 15-20 feet away from them. Then both men suddenly began "conversing." But they weren't talking normally, they began screaming at each other almost like two animals. Both Brian and Andrew were stunned by what was taking place. The men continued to scream at one another and gesticulate with their hands. Then abruptly they stopped. The man in the suit walked towards the steps, while the other man headed towards some tall bushes. Brian was intrigued by these two men so he asked Andrew to follow the man in the suit up the steps, while he followed after the other man who had disappeared into the bushes. The bushes were extremely thick, seemingly too overgrown to even walk through. It was like the man had completely vanished. He ran around the edge of the bushes to see if the man was walking up onto the A3 but there was no sign of him.

It was a complete mystery. He returned to Andrew to tell him about what had happened. Andrew informed his father that exactly the same thing had happened to him. He had only been a short distance behind the man on the steps but when he reached the top he was nowhere in sight, despite the wide open car park. It was absolutely bizarre. Later on after dark, Brian and Andrew were sitting in their car when they suddenly began to feel extremely uneasy. They decided to get out of there before the strange men made an unwelcome reappearance.

HC addendum.
Source: Dave Hodrien, Birmingham UFO Group report.   Type: E

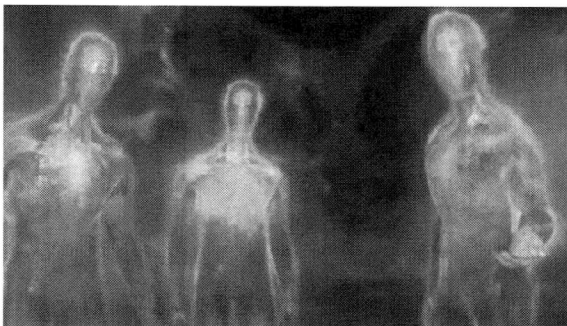

Location: Cape Vincent, New York.
Date: December 24, 1992.
Time: Late night.

 The witness had stayed up late on Christmas Eve, sewing Christmas stockings for her nieces. Her husband was in bed and only her sewing machine light and the hall light were on. She went to the kitchen and saw a huge glowing light and movement in a farm field directly across the street. She went into the bedroom to wake her husband and look out the bedroom window. Her husband awoke and remembers seeing the lights but could not stay awake. She was aggravated as he always had been interested in the unknown, but could not stay awake.

 She continued looking out the window, only to see an entity that appeared to have a masculine type human form, very tall, 7-8 feet tall. The only way he could describe it was like a form surrounded by a glow. The entity was standing by a light pole directly across from the end of her driveway. She then became frightened, and prayed for God not to let whatever it was to bother them.

HC addendum.
Source: Mufon CMS, Ken Pfeifer, Mufon NJ &
www.worldufophotos.org.   Type: E

1993

Location: Pinaya, Peru.
Date: 1993.
Time: 7:00 p.m.

Peasants in the village reported seeing two very tall humanoid beings dressed in shiny gold colored metallic suits enter the village and walk around the Plaza. The beings were very athletic looking and had glowing yellow skin. They took short steps as they walked and moved their arms. At one point both entered the local church, looked around briefly then left towards a nearby hill.

HC addendum.
Source: Carlos Paz Garcia Corrochano, Intl. UFO Library Magazine.
Type: E

* * * * * * *

Location: Finca Del Duque, Tenerife, Canary Islands, Spain.
Date: 1993.
Time: Late evening.

Albert Dieppa and some friends drove to the remote location simply to enjoy the surroundings and ride. The group remained within the car with the dome light on, chatting late into the evening, when they suddenly became aware of six or seven presences outside their vehicle, staring at them intently. Dieppa turned on the headlights, and was surprised to see several little child-like figures with adult faces. The beings appeared to be naked, at least form the waist up and they had dark, olive green skin and intense red eyes. The car's occupants remained in stunned, paralyzed, silence until one of them began screaming hysterically, causing the driver to set the car in motion and abandon the

225

area as quickly as possible. Dieppa added that the little men did not try to block their way; they just seemed to vanish as soon as he touched the ignition key.

HC addendum.
Source: Scott Corrales, Uncensored UFO Reports #1.   Type: E

* * * * * * *

Location: Near Sim, Chelyabinsk Region, Ural mountains, Russia.
Date: 1993.
Time: Late evening.

The female witness Madesta Antina Stonke (involved in a previous encounter), was born in Lithuania and had moved to this mountainous region in the Urals. The day before her encounter while driving her car she observed a yellow egg-shaped UFO glowing and hovering in the sky near the road. The object emitted a beam of light towards her vehicle. The engine of her car stalled and in a short period of time the UFO departed.

The next evening she was spending time in the company of her friend an FSB (Federal Security Board) ex-KGB General (name cannot be divulged) and was sitting, talking and drinking wine. The General had told her on a previous occasion that, he worked in a top-secret location in the area, a base located in the mountains. On this evening, the General invited Stonke to come with him, since he wanted to show her the secret installation.

They drove in his car with two other military officers, on a dirt road some 10-12 kilometers from the town of Sim in the mountains. Soon the General said that they were approaching the secret installation and one of the officers put cloth over her eyes to prevent her from seeing the exact entrance to the location. She did not resist and accepted the "rules of the game." She was told that if she resisted, everything would be "over" for her. The only thing she was able to see before she was blindfolded was a strange bluish light descending from the sky.

When they removed the blindfold, she could see that they were in an underground cave or chamber. They proceeded to an elevator-like shaft and entered the elevator. The cabin dropped down at lighting speed and she felt fear for the first time. When the elevator finally stopped to a depth estimated to have been no less than a kilometer and they stepped out, she was stunned by what she saw. They were in what appeared to be some kind of transfer point. She saw a huge and brightly lit tunnel. The General told her that the tunnel connected the towns of Sim and Karaidel via underground passages a distance of about 100km.

The General also added that there existed similar tunnels all along the Ural Mountains, and they were all connected. They boarded a special vehicle that moved along the tunnels, resembling a bus. Then it traveled to the underground equivalent of Sim. She saw numerous underground cavities and equipment.

What stunned her the most was the human-looking entities she noticed, but these were definitely not human. They were small, about 1.5 to 1.6 meters in height, with yellow skin. They were at all times silent and working, loading some gelatinous substance, black in color into metal containers. The General told her that these were zombie-like creatures, basically slaves of the extraterrestrials. And the strange gelatinous substance was an alien weapon. (!) *"Those entities,"* said the General, *"are descendants of humans."* They were some kind of human hybrids. Some of the missing children and others in Russia ended up at this location, said the General. Madesta was completely stunned, she wanted to spend more time at the location, but the General grabbed her and moved her out quickly, explaining that, if the aliens see them, especially her, they will face inevitable death. So they ascended back to the surface, they blindfolded her again and drove her back to town; she was warned not to talk about what had occurred. She suffered from nightmares after the incident.

HC addendum.
Source: Igor Kolomiets, Rostov-on-Don, Anton Anfalov.   Type: G?

*   *   *   *   *   *   *

Location: Panama City, Panama.
Date: 1993.
Time: 11:00 p.m.

The witness was sitting on a chair resting in his third floor balcony when he suddenly was overcome by a feeling of well-being. Soon he found himself flying through space; he could see the buildings below him become smaller. He was accompanied by two tall beings, one at each side, these were man-like, and were wearing shiny silvery tight fitting outfits, silvery boots, and a belt that had different apparatus hanging from it.

They soon approached a huge silvery oval shaped craft, smooth with no apparent openings or seams. A hatch suddenly opened and he was conducted inside. There he saw a huge metallic sphere on the floor that seemed to be the source of the beings communications. He heard their voices inside his head. Human-like aliens who communicated with him extensively met him. He was told many different things about the nature of the universe and the creation of humanity. Apparently about the same time our universe was created an identical dark universe, or anti-universe sprung into being also. This particular group of aliens belonged to some kind of Space Federation that included many different species.

Later he was taken to a larger space station that was called "Arkeum," there he saw many different types of beings, but most were human-like. He was warned that beings from the so-called anti-universe were visiting our universe at an increasing rate. He was eventually brought back to his apartment, apparently by the same means of travel.

HC addendum.
Source: Juan Valdez Ibanez.   Type: G

* * * * * * *

Location: Bradwell, Norfolk, England.
Date: 1993.
Time: Night.

The witness was told to check an area on a suburban road at a passage that bisects a blocks of houses near his house, because of reported apparitions in the area.

One night as he stared at a fence about 20ft away, a humanoid suddenly came into view. It was described as at least seven feet tall and wearing dark heavy clothing. It had a white, pear shaped head with two dark, eye sockets as its only facial features. The head was topped by tight orange hair, flat on top that gave the face the appearance of being an upside down triangle. Its arms were very long and almost touched the ground and it appeared to be carrying a black doctor's bag in one of its gloved hands.

Despite its malignant appearance, the witness was not afraid and watched as it repeatedly took one step forward and then returned to its position. It seemed to fade away after about ten minutes.

HC addendum.
Source: Karl Thornley, Fortean Times 4-98.   Type: E
Comments: This being appeared to have some type of inter-dimensional travel capability. Or maybe some type of hologram?

Location: Medveditskaya, Volgograd Region, Russia.
Date: 1993.
Time: Late night.

Local resident and chief of the local collective farm Mr. Ivan Yurov, while driving his truck, quite accidentally stumbled upon a landed UFO that was sitting in the middle of the road. The engine of his truck immediately cut off. He opened the door of the cabin and saw the UFO, which was allegedly disc-shaped; he was able to catch a glimpse of several humanoid beings that were moving about in a strange manner.

The beings were tall and slender and wore slightly luminous suits, the humanoid's heads were hairless and they wore helmets with strange devices resembling antennas jutting out of it. Seized with fear, the witness quickly fled the area. A strange feature noted later was that the witness forgot all details of the incident for five years.

HC addendum.
Source: Vadim A Chernobrov, 'Cosmosearch,' Moscow.   Type: C
Comments: Noted aftereffects; temporal amnesia. There is no information if hypnotic regression was attempted on the witness.

*   *   *   *   *   *   *

Location: Togliatti, Russia.
Date: 1993.
Time: Late night.

A 55-year old woman was lying on her couch when she saw on the glass of the balcony door what appeared to be a fluorescent tunnel forming. It resembled a corridor of light. Directly from the tunnel, a strange humanoid figure stepped out. The humanoid was about 1.5m in height with grayish-green skin, a large hairless, oval shaped head, with a narrow chin and very large staring eyes. The being wore a tight-fitting diving suit gray-blue in color. He moved very smoothly as if floating just above the floor.

As he approached the woman, she fell into a state of shock and was unable to move. Her vision became cloudy and she apparently passed out. Soon after the visit the woman began experiencing all the signs of being pregnant this was of course impossible. She visited a local gynecologist and it was indeed confirmed that she was carrying a fetus.

Three months later as she slept on the sofa, she experienced the feeling of immobility once again, but she remained awake as she saw the same humanoid appear and slowly approach her. As he stood leaning over her, in smooth, careful swoops of his hand he would somehow introduce his hand into the woman's stomach and appear to make

229

scooping motions, after performing this task for a while, the alien walked back down the light corridor and disappeared through the window. Her pregnancy disappeared after this visit.

HC addendum.
Source: Gennadi Stepanovich, Russia.   Type: E
Comments: This type of report, although apparently common in the US and other westernized countries is almost unheard of in Russia and other eastern European countries. It appears to involve some form of genetic manipulation.

*   *   *   *   *   *   *

Location: Transylvania, Louisiana.
Date: Early 1993.
Time: 2-3.00 a.m.

The main witness and her boyfriend were on their way to their new home in southeastern Louisiana to the above town located on Hwy. US 65 about 44 miles northwest of Vicksburg Mississippi. There are cotton fields all around in this region. They had their car loaded down and their dog (Barky) was sleeping in the back seat.

As they rolled into the sleepy town of Transylvania. They quickly noticed the huge water tower with the black bat and the name, "Transylvania." They cracked a few jokes about the spooky water tower, but other than the unusual name for a seemingly normal small southern town, the place was not eerie until they came upon something very incredible.

It appeared there was a man, a very tall man walking in the road ahead of them. It was a little foggy so, she thought she might have been imagining it. As they came closer, they noticed that this was no 'man.' It appeared to be some kind of creature she had never seen; it looked like some mythical creature, part human, and part buffalo. Its coloring was brown and patchy, and she could see right through it. Suddenly as they came within ten feet of it, the creature stepped directly in the path of their moving vehicle (they were probably going about 55 mph). Her boyfriend slammed on his brakes and the dog went flying into the back of his eat and yelped. The beast slowly and nonchalantly turned its head sideways and looked at them intensely with despondent hollow eyes, yet in an almost scolding look, then vanished. She got the definite feeling that this 'thing' very purposely walked in front of them with every intention of making them wreck their vehicle.

About a month later, her boyfriend was traveling the same highway at night with a friend, whom he had told not a thing about the creepy supernatural beast they had seen before. When they came into

Transylvania, they saw the same creature walking on the side of the highway.

HC addendum.
Source: http://www.yourghoststories.com/ghost-stories-categories.php?category=4&page=2 Type: E?

* * * * * * *

Location: Passa Tempo, Minas Gerais, Brazil.
Date: January, 1993.
Time: Night.

David Pereira saw a glowing object that was on the ground and next to it two humanoid figures were seeing moving around. Light from the object illuminated the figures, causing an X-ray like effect, apparently causing them to become transparent. The witness watched them, hidden from on top of a nearby tree. Soon the humanoids apparently noticed his presence and re-boarded the object, which then took off at high speed. No other information.

HC addendum.
Source: GEPUC Brazil. Type: C
Comments: Additional report again describing the transparency factor on some of the humanoids.

* * * * * * *

Location: Bella Vista, Itapua, Paraguay.
Date: Middle of March, 1993.
Time: Night.

The family of 67-year-old farmer Pedro Aguilera, has reported encountering on several occasions, a short dark hairy dwarf-like creature that usually hides in some woods near the house. Paranormal activity has also been reported that includes levitation of household items.
During one incident, a machete jumped on its own accord into the air striking a young girl on her face wounding her. Several family members have also been hit by flying stones.

HC addendum.
Source: Fabio Picasso Type: E
Comments: This dark hairy dwarf appeared to have possessed some type of paranormal properties. But why the apparent violent reaction towards the young girl?

231

Location: Catemaco, Mexico.
Date: March 20, 1993.
Time: 5:00 a.m.

Mr. Julio Chagala, was sleeping at home when suddenly a bright-blue light entered through his window and woke him up. Everything seemed to be very still and all the surroundings were enveloped in that strange blue light.

Looking out the window he saw a gold colored disc-shaped object, about fifteen meters in diameter, land in a nearby field. The craft was totally silent. A hatch opened and several "huge" figures came out. These were about 2.5 meters in height, human like and wearing tight-fitting silvery diver's outfits. They had long arms, pale complexions, large blue slanted eyes and long golden-blond hair. The witness at this time had walked over to the craft. The visitors saluted him with a gloved hand wave and then invited him inside the craft.

Once inside, the witness noticed that the humanoids also had long pointed ears. He saw numerous consoles and what appeared to be comfortable seats. He also saw a metallic table with several different instruments. One of the humanoids showed him a screen where he saw scenes of war, destruction, and ecological collapse.

After an undetermined amount of time, the craft then landed in an unknown beautiful city, filled with humans of all ages. A large golden sun illuminated the city. He was taken to a crystalline waterfall that was surrounded by beautiful colored stones. There the humanoids explained to Mr. Chagala that his destiny was that of caring and healing his fellow human beings. He was also told that the humanoids had several bases in his area, including one at the Laguna Nixtamalapan.

Chagala was also warned of a different type of humanoid that also visited earth and were the ones responsible for the reported animal mutilations. These were described by his hosts as the short large headed humanoids with huge black eyes, with four fingered hands and protruding stomachs that mostly wore tight fitting maroon outfits and traveled in small flying craft with ball landing gear.

Mr. Chagala was eventually returned to his home. He reported a drastic loss of weight soon after the incident but recovered. Other locals reported low flying lighted objects over the area about the same time. Currently Mr. Chagala is a known healer that uses natural herbs and remedies.

HC addendum.
Source: Grupo Cassiopeia, Mexico.   Type: G
Comments: Direct communication and interaction with aliens. Travel to unknown location. Very high strangeness case. What location did the witness indeed travel to? Why did he obtain healing abilities after the

encounter? Who are the short large headed humanoids these aliens warned him about? The grays?

* * * * * * *

Location: Kadima, Israel.
Date: March 20, 1993
Time: 6:30 a.m.

Ziporet Carmel woke up earlier than usual and went to her kitchen. As she got there, she noticed that the room was bathed in a strange light. Curious, she stepped outside to check the grounds and as she walked around the storage shed, she noticed what appeared to be a large fruit silo on a nearby field. As she took a closer look, she noticed that the silo-like object was silver colored and square in shape. It had what appeared to be eighteen glowing square windows along its side. Five huge beams of a powerful light shone from its top, high into the sky.

Suddenly, what appeared to be a second section of the object just materialized close-by. Then, a seven-foot tall, man-like figure, appeared near the object. The dogs reacted in a violent manner upon seeing the figure. The being wore a metallic overall and what appeared to be a sombrero-like headgear with a veil that covered his face completely. The figure and the witness then stared at each other for about thirty seconds. Ziporet then quietly whispered, *"Why don't you take off your hat so I can see your face."* She then heard a clear voice inside her head that spoke in Hebrew telling her that "that's how things were." The witness then felt compelled to go back inside.

Later during a search of the field numerous ground traces were found an unknown smelly substance that made people sick with nausea, was also found.

HC addendum.
Source: Barry Chamish, UFO Universe, spring, 1995.   Type: C
Comments: The beginning of a wave of bizarre encounters and contacts in Israel. It must be noted that the alien used telepathy in this case.

* * * * * * *

Location: Kadima, Israel.
Date: March 30, 1993.
Time: 3:00 a.m.

On this night the witness, Aviva C, fled drawn to leave her bed and go outside. There she witnessed a silver craft land in two stages; first the front touched down, then the rear. She estimated the size and shape of

233

the craft to be similar to an "orange storage tank" or a fruit silo, about sixty feet in circumference.

She approached the craft to investigate and from about twenty feet away saw one of the crew. He was 2.5 meters tall and wore silver foil coveralls that clung to the body like a second skin. He wore a helmet but its tinted visor prevented her from seeing the face, the next day Carmel ventured into her backyard and saw the imprint of the craft. It was a circle twenty-two feet in diameter, formed of living vegetation. Plant life outside the imprint had died.

The following night, the neighbor of the previous witness felt her house tremble during the night. When she opened her eyes, she saw a bald giant, seven to eight-feet tall, with round, yellow eyes and a small flat nose, dressed in gray metallic, overalls, standing next to her bed.

"Don't be afraid. I will not harm you," she heard in her mind, and saw the being gliding through the room. The next morning, two more circles were found, twenty and eleven feet in diameter that appeared to be "pressed down by a centrifugal force."

HC addendum.
Source: Michael Hesemann, 'UFOs: The secret history.'   Type: D

* * * * * * *

Location: Kadima, Israel.
Date: Late March, 1993.
Time: Night.

A woman named Ophra reported being lifted into a hovering "spacecraft" by a ray of light. She could not struggle or resist in any way. She was lifted up and brought into a room entirely composed of a brilliant crystalline material.

She communicated in English, telepathically with a crew of three, one of whom was clearly the leader. The three were tall, very fair, blond and handsome; looking something like "Nordic Gods" or "Californian Surfers." No other information.

HC addendum.
Source: Barry Chamish, Flying Saucer Review, Vol. 39 #4.   Type: G

News Tribune illustration from a sketch by Dave Kiele

The 'Batsquatch': Brian Canfield describes a winged creature about 9 feet tall with claws, blue-tinted fur, yellowish eyes, sharp teeth and tufted ears.

Location: Mount Rainier, Washington.
Date: April 19, 1993.
Time: 9:30 p.m.

Brian Canfield was driving his truck along the foothills of Mount Rainier when suddenly he experienced total engine failure and its headlights went out. Then a nine-foot tall, broad-shouldered, winged creature landed about thirty feet away.

The being had a large mouth with sharp teeth, yellow eyes, a wolf-like face and was covered with bluish fur. After a few minutes, the creature turned his head and looked at the witness and started flapping its wings. The creature then took off towards Mount Rainier. The witness then was able to start his truck and drive away. A later search of the area failed to locate anything.

HC addendum.
Source: Strange Magazine #14.   Type: E

Location: Vila Peri, Fortaleza, Brazil.
Date: April 23, 1993.
Time: Unknown.

During a period of heavy concentration of UFO sightings in the area, a man named Jose Ernani claimed to have encountered a being of light during prayer at a local grotto. He described the being as a female, about 19-years old, with finely chiseled features, pink complexion, heart shaped mouth, and long brown wavy hair. Her eyes were of a "penetrating" blue color. She wore a silky dress with a sash about four inches wide. On the sash, he could see two ingrained faces, one a bearded man (interpreted as Jesus), and the other what appeared to be a white dove. Ernani interpreted the being as "the Virgin Mary."

HC addendum.
Source: Reginaldo de Athyayde, FSR.   Type: D
Comments: Interpreted as a "Marian" apparition.

* * * * * * *

Location: Rishon-le-Zion, Israel.
Date: May, 1993.
Time: Night.

Batya Shimon reported encountering an eight-foot tall humanoid with "fascinating blue eyes," dressed in silver coveralls that appeared in her bedroom and glided through her apartment. The incident repeated itself the next night, when Batya followed the creature and saw a "mushroom shaped craft, surrounded by searchlights," hovering outside. A hatch opened which looked like dark glass, and two beings stepped out.

The next thing she felt was a pressure on her shoulders. She was then blinded by the bright light, and found herself back on her bed, with one of the giants standing next to her, the other one further away. *"Don't be afraid,"* she heard inside her head. She could not reply, since she was paralyzed. Her husband was sleeping deeply next to her. The beings glided, surrounded by fluorescent light, out of her bedroom window, back to their craft. The next morning, Batya found a powder that was found to contain mainly cadmium on the floor of her flat.

On another occasion later that same month, Batya had another experience where she saw a large mushroom shaped object with a clear door, approaching from the sky. A light was then directed at her shoulder and it felt like a strong punch.

Her next memory was of being back in bed watching a tall humanoid wave his hand slowly above her husband's head. He telepathically told her to calm down. He told her they were not there to harm her. While the visitor was in the bedroom, another was touring the rest of the house, not so much on foot as floating upright, its legs did not even move. The beings face was covered in a thin haze that obscured the details somewhat, but Batya recognized both humanoids as the same race of guests that she had seen previously. This time, however, she noted more details. Their hands were human-like, but their skin was as light as an albino's. Their clothes were also white but they "shone like neon and were skin-tight."

Suddenly the second visitor appeared opposite her bedroom door, just inside her son's bedroom. He gestured his comrade to come and have a look at what he had found. The first being floated to the boy's room and both stared transfixed at the boy's aquarium. The visit lasted just a couple of minutes, when a light shone through the kitchen window and they disappeared into it. The next morning all the doors were again opened and a sand like material (previously found), this time described as smelling like sulfur, was spread over the shelves.

HC addendum.
Source: Michael Hesemann, 'UFOS: The Secret History,' and Barry Chamish, 'Return of the Giants.'   Type: B

* * * * * * *

Location: Aragon, Spain.
Date: May, 1993.
Time: Afternoon.

Six woodcutters were working high up in the mountains, when one of them, Miguel Cazcarra, came upon a strange being, some five and a half feet tall that emitted loud screams and squeals.   -

The rest of the men came up to see what had happened and saw the hairy humanoid climb a woodpile, clutching a branch with both arms and legs. Later that week someone or something broke into Cazcarras's Landrover, leaving unknown footprints nearby.

HC addendum.
Source: Mike Dash, Borderlands.   Type: E

Location: Chekikah State Park, Dade County, Florida.
Date: Middle of May, 1993.
Time: 2:30 a.m.

Four men traveling on an isolated road at the edge of the State park, were stopped on the side of the road, when they suddenly felt a strong energy surge through their bodies. The witnesses screamed as they saw a glowing green, man-shaped figure, standing nearby in the middle of the road. It began walking towards the men, who ran to their vehicle and began driving away west on the road. The strange energy force apparently began getting stronger and all felt numb.

They then noticed a bright green light in a nearby field; the light was estimated to be as large as a football field. Figures of unknown description could be seen moving back and forth in front of the light. The driver then turned the vehicle around and began to drive away; he was then urged by the others to return to the site. He drove back and at this point, two of the men saw two figures with white faces and large bug-like eyes standing behind a wire fence on the nearby field.

The panicked witnesses now drove away from the area again; as they left, they saw two maneuvering lights over the area that at one point shone several long white beams of light towards the ground.

HC addendum.
Source: Timothy Good, Mel Tennis.   Type: C

* * * * * * *

Location: Bourgata, Israel.
Date: May 30, 1993.
Time: 3:00 a.m.

Hannah Somech woke up when she heard her dog barking. She went downstairs from her bedroom to the kitchen and looked out the garden through the glass door, when she saw her dog literally flying through the air and slam against a wall.

Shocked and terrified she bravely opened the door but was confronted by an invisible wall; she could not go any further. Then she was surprised to see an eight-foot tall giant in bright coveralls. A thief, she thought. *"You think I am a thief?"* she heard inside her head. *"What did you do with my dog,"* she asked furiously. *"He disturbed me, as you do now,"* the giant spoke telepathically, without moving his lips. *"I could crush you, but I don't want to. Just leave me alone, I am busy."*

The witness then ran back to the bedroom to wake up her husband, but when both returned, the giant had disappeared. In the garden, they found huge footprints; one foot, four inches in length. Later, circles appeared too covered by a reddish cadmium based liquid. After the encounter, Hannah suffered severely from fatigue, headaches and muscle pain.

HC addendum.
Source: Michael Hesemann, 'UFOS: The Secret History.'   Type: E
Comments: Bizarre encounter. Did the dog attack the humanoid and was repelled?

* * * * * * *

Location: Bella Vista, California.
Date: Summer, 1993.
Time: 1:00 a.m.

The main witness and a friend were relaxing at his remote cabin, outside of Bella Vista. They had just moved some furniture from Mt. Shasta and were relaxing, before heading back to his house in Redding.

His intuition told him to look out the window, and he saw a mist forming across the road about twenty yards away. It was a warm summer night so this was unusual. Over the course of about ten minutes, he looked twice more and the mist had thickened and expanded to about 3' x 5' up on a dry grassy knoll at tree line. It was not a full moon but the moon was bright that night.

They decided to leave and when they went outside the mist had now transformed into a chrome or steel colored, metallic, robotic-looking, humanoid form. It appeared to be sitting Indian-style in the grass. Sitting, it was 5' tall. It had a barrel-like torso but not as round. It had a head and a face, but its face lacked definite features.

The main witness, "immediately knew it didn't belong there and freaked out." He yelled at it, and told it that it had better leave. He threatened with violence. He was too terrified to run inside and grab his shotgun, so they jumped in the old GMC pickup truck, he yelled at this friend, "Let's get out of here."

His friend started up the truck and they sped down the driveway, which turned right along the grassy knoll. His friend told him that he could see "others" on the other side of the truck. They looked back and the robotic entity at the knoll was now levitating in its Indian-style position towards them. It made lurching, lunging actions towards them but never raised any arms or anything; but its face had turned into a terrifying metallic 'scowl.'

He was yelling as he watched the strange entity through the passenger side window. Telling his friend, *"It's after us! Haul ass!"* He stepped on the gas but the truck kept lurching towards the deep ditch on the side of the road. It took everything they had to fight the wheel and keep the truck in the road. They stopped the truck to make sure it wasn't a broken tie rod or something. He inspected under the truck and found nothing wrong. They continued to Highway 299 and finally headed towards Redding. Strangely, the sun was now coming up as the sky turned from night. They had apparently lost five to six hours within a frenzied five mile drive down the dirt road through the woods.

The next day his girlfriend accused him of having a 'hickey' on his abdomen just above the waist line. The strange mark resembling a birth mark about an inch wide by two inches long faded after a few days. His buddy refused to ever talk about that night again.

HC addendum.
Source: NUFORC.   Type: E or G?

* * * * * * *

Location: Zernograd, Rostov region, North Caucasus, Russia.
Date: Summer, 1993.
Time: Late evening.

Local resident, Alexey Ivanovich had gone into the porch of his home in an attempt to get some relief from the terrific summer heat when suddenly he noticed a globe-shaped object in the sky, which emitted a beam of white light, projecting it towards the ground, apparently scanning the area.

Two years later, the witness began to remember additional details of that night, his memory partially returning. He recalled being taken onboard the UFO and then to a base located on the moon. (!)

He remembered a humanoid alien woman which showed him various special laboratories which contained huge glass containers and inside of each one numerous human bodies in an apparent state of suspended animation. He also saw many "non-human bodies" and was told that these were "representatives from other worlds."

After the tour, the alien woman gave Alexey some strange food (not described) and then returned him back home to Earth. The woman was basically human in appearance; however she was taller than most Earth humans and possessed "unearthly beauty," beyond that of terrestrial women. She was dressed in a blue, tight-fitting one-piece suit.

HC addendum.
Source: Igor Kolomiets, ENIO Research Center, Rostov-on-Don, quoted in the 'Encyclopedia of Mysterious Places in Russia,' by Y. Suprunenko and Irina Shlionskaya, Moscow, 2006.   Type: G

* * * * * * *

Location: Near Allentown, Pennsylvania.
Date: Summer, 1993.
Time: Night.

A witness saw a six-foot Bigfoot-type creature near Baker's Point. As he watched, the creature spread a pair of huge wings and took flight, quickly disappearing from the sight. No other information.

HC addendum.
Source: Lena Griffith, New Jersey MUFON.   Type: E

* * * * * * *

Location: Kfar Saba, Israel.
Date: June, 1993.
Time: Late night.

The witness had gone into her bedroom to sleep when she encountered what appeared to be a three dimensional entity standing less than a meter from her. The being was very tall and was wearing a silver/green "space suit." It emitted white beams of light from its waist area. The witness felt an intense energy emanating from the beams of light, which traversed her whole body. She described it as a joyful feeling. The being then took several small steps and vanished.

HC addendum.
Source: Barry Chamish.   Type: E

241

Location: Conero, Ancona, Italy.
Date: June, 1993.
Time: Afternoon.

Several anglers came upon, sitting on top of a throne like rock on the ocean, a very short dwarf-like man that appeared to have huge feet. It suddenly levitated up into the air and disappeared into the distance over the sea. No other information.

HC addendum.
Source: Notizieufo, X-File #7.   Type: E

* * * * * * *

Location: Lirio, Italy.
Date: July 8, 1993.
Time: 8:00 a.m.

While working in the fields, farmer Domenico C, saw a two meter tall humanoid. He described it as having a metallic scaly body, robot-like, and gray in color. It had a large round head and two round holes for eyes, from which it emitted red beams of light. From two round holes on its abdomen area it also emitted a beam of blue light. Its whole body appeared to be encased in a yellow glow.

Frightened at the sight of the figure, the witness ran home to get his rifle. Upon returning it was gone but later while riding on his tractor, he saw the strange figure again, which suddenly rose up into the air in a vertical flight without emitting any noise. It disappeared in twenty seconds.

HC addendum.
Source: CISU.   Type: E

242

Location: Between Dhaka & Chittagong, Bangladesh.
Date: July 19, 1993.
Time: Unknown.

A passenger onboard flight TG919 from London Heathrow to Hong Kong via Bangkok, witnessed a very bright object which he believed was stationary or moving slowly. Through a transparent cockpit he could see three occupants in line facing a large screen. The occupants were very tall and thin. They had no clothes on, and their bodies were red (like they were sunburned).

HC addendum.
Source: MOD Files Released February, 2010.   Type: A
Comments: Rare report of occupied UFO seen by witnesses from onboard an aircraft (there are several of these on record).

*   *   *   *   *   *   *

Location: Dunajska Streda, Slovakia.
Date: August 5, 1993.
Time: 10:30 p.m.

About ten children saw in a field, two strange looking humanoids with large cucumber-like heads, and wearing all silver clothing. They glided over the field and disappeared from sight. No other information.

HC addendum.
Source: Dr. Milos Jesensky.   Type: E

Location: Narre Warren North, Victoria, Australia.
Date: August 8, 1993.
Time: 1:00 a.m.

Three carloads of people, including the principal witnesses, 27-year old Kelly Cahill, her husband and three children encountered a huge round object hovering low above the roadway. It had what appeared to be orange-lighted windows around its bottom. Humanoid figures were seen moving inside.

Their next conscious memory was seeing the object suddenly shoot away at high speed, and later as they approached their home, they saw a tall dark figure standing on the side of the road. Later they were able to recall how they had stopped their vehicle and walked out. To their surprise, they noticed another car stopped on the side of the road.

As they walked down toward the craft, they suddenly saw a seven-foot tall black figure with huge fiery red eyes appeared on a nearby field. The figure began moving slowly towards them apparently gliding. The main witness panicked and began yelling hysterically *"they have no souls!"*

Suddenly dozens of similar beings appeared and began moving quickly towards the group of witnesses. The aliens were out there in the field, beneath the immense flying craft. The beings seem to congregate in small groups, and one group glided toward Kelly and her husband, covering a hundred yards in a mere few seconds. Another group was approaching the other car, which sat motionless near the hovering craft. Kelly had a sense that the creatures were evil. She clung to her husband, fighting the feeling of blacking out.

At this point the witnesses blacked out and the next conscious recall was being in their vehicle watching the object shoot away. The occupants

244

of the other vehicle would come forward and tell almost an exact story, a story of abduction, mind control, and embarrassing procedures. Kelly recalled through dreams the black aliens stooping over her helpless, nude body like he was kissing her navel.

From all indications of the descriptions of the aliens, they were intruding into our dimension taking space in our universe. That night as Kelly undressed for bed, she noticed a strange triangular mark on her navel, a mark she had never seen before. Kelly suffered from general malaise for the next two weeks, and was taken to the hospital on two occasions, one for severe stomach pains, and another for a uterine infection. There was an almost two hour time lapsed reported.

A few weeks later, Kelly was sleeping when suddenly she experienced a strange sensation as if something was being taken from her. She woke up and was confronted by a tall black figure wearing a floor length hooded cloak. The being was about seven-foot tall and had glowing red eyes. She screamed and the being vanished.

HC addendum.
Source: Bill Chalker, IUR Vol. 19 #5.   Type: C or G? & E

* * * * * * *

Location: Huerfano County, Colorado.
Date: September, 1993.
Time: Unknown.

An elderly hermit living in a remote ranch on the eastern slopes of the Sangre de Cristo Mountains, reported seeing a "ship" land near his cabin. Two bearded human looking beings came out of the craft and floated towards his cabin, shining a very bright spotlight at it.

The hermit claimed that when they pointed the light at the cabin it went right through the wall. Holding a gun, he was blinded and paralyzed as the light illuminated the inside of his cabin.

HC addendum.
Source: Christopher O'Brien, Enter the Valley.   Type: B

* * * * * * *

Location: Belish, near Troyan, Bulgaria.
Date: September 6, 1993.
Time: 4:00 p.m.

79-year old farmer Petko Chavdarov had gone out to his fields to tend to his cows when he noticed someone apparently "ransacking" his potato field. At first he thought it was a thief gathering food for the winter, but then he noticed that the figure was wearing a black monk-like outfit.

When he came closer to the figure, it silently rose up into the air and flew out of sight in the horizon. Moments later he saw a 40cm fiery ball rushing past the yard of his neighbor Dimitar Kanchev.

HC addendum.
Source: Miroslav Minchev, Bulgaria.   Type: E

* * * * * * *

Location: Victoria, Entre Rios, Argentina.
Date: October, 1993.
Time: 7:00 p.m.

Jose M. a worker at the new bridge project in the river, was approaching the area in a small boat in the river when he noticed a glow on the water up ahead near the bridge site. As he approached he saw what appeared to be a glowing man-like figure about 80cm in height that seemed to be walking on the water. Terrified, he turned the launch around and left the area at high speed. Others in the area have reported similar encounters.

HC addendum.
Source: Vision Ovni, Victoria.   Type: E

* * * * * * *

Location: Near Atascadero, California.
Date: October, 1993.
Time: 20:45

Nick M. was watching TV when he saw a flash of light in the window shining through the curtains. Jumping up to get a better look, he saw this glowing red light on the hillside in the trees. From his back door he could see a ship sitting on the ground in the trees. The door of the craft opened suddenly and two Bigfoot like creatures came out and took some soil samples, and went back into the ship. It then shot up into the sky and vanished. After they left, he check the area but found nothing.

HC addendum.
Source: WBS Alien Report Vol. 2 #5.   Type: B

246

Location: Salisbury Plain, England.
Date: October 6, 1993.
Time: Night.

The witness was camping near the famed and ancient Stonehenge site, when she spotted odd colored storm clouds forming over her head and a ball of electric blue light that flew towards her. When it touched her, she blacked out.

When she awoke, she was lying on a bed or cot that was really hard in texture. She was in what appeared to be an examining room. She remembered seeing a strange light over her, which was soft and kind of comforting. Soon a tall beautiful woman entered the room, approached the witness and spoke to her in a soft voice, although the witness could not understand her, somehow she knew that the woman was telling her that she was not going to hurt her. The woman then proceeded to perform tests on the witness with hard to describe instruments. When she was finished, she waved her hand over the instruments and they seemed to vanish.

At this point a male alien entered the room. He was described as tall, somewhat pixie-like but in human proportions. The being led her through a lighted corridor and to a door. He touched her lightly on her forehead and she blacked out again. When she woke up she was back near Stonehenge and the sun was already rising.

HC addendum.
Source: I Was Abducted.com.   Type: G

* * * * * * *

Location: Near Hemet, California.
Date: Late October, 1993.
Time: Sunset.

A senior forest service employee was in his backyard when he heard a noise. He turned to his right and saw a five-foot tall, hairy, upright, flat-faced creature, standing and staring at him. The witness ran and was able to see the creature running at very high speed through the brush towards the west.

Prior to this incident, there had been some other peculiar happenings around the witness' home, including heavy footfalls and motion activated yard lights that switched on at all hours of the night.

HC addendum.
Source: B. Hanlyn, Peter Guttilla, & Bigfoot Co-op Vol. 14 2-94. Type: E

Location: Elkhorn, Wisconsin.
Date: Winter, 1993.
Time: Night.

Lorianne Endrizzi was driving down Bray Road when she saw what she at first thought was a man crouching at the side of the road. Curious she slowed down to take a closer look. Within the next few moments, she was astonished to see that the being spotlighted in the beams of her headlights was covered with fur, had a long, wolf-like snout, fangs, pointed ears, and eyes that had a yellowish glow. The creature's arms were jointed like a human's and it had hands with human-like fingers that were tipped with pointed claws. Frightened, Lorianne sped off.

HC addendum.
Source: Brad Steiger, Out of the Dark.   Type: E
Comments: The Wisconsin werewolf.

* * * * * * *

Location: Siracusa, Sicily, Italy.
Date: November, 1993.
Time: 9:00 a.m.

At least ten people living in the vicinity of Viale Teracati spotted a short humanoid that appeared to be levitating along, at a height of 30cms or so off the ground. The humanoid measured about 1m 20cm in height, was in an area that the road was under construction. It was wearing a green one-piece garment, a yellow cap, and silver colored boots.

Two witnesses, Maria Lo Bello and her son, Mimino Cassia, watched it with a pair of binoculars as it now floated five meters above the ground. Finally around 9:15 a.m., the little humanoid took off. He shot straight up into the air, and in a few seconds he was merely a black dot in the sky.

HC addendum.
Source: Roberto Pinotti CUN, FSR Vol. 40, #2.   Type: E

* * * * * * *

Location: San Luis Valley, Colorado.
Date: December, 1993.
Time: Evening.

A distraught mother and son claimed to have been driving back from the mountains, when they rounded a curve in the road and came face to face with what they described as a tall, dark, hairy creature with large pointed ears and large glowing eyes. The creature had long arms that dangled well below the knees.

They put the car in reverse and turned around. This evidently startled the creature, which suddenly dropped down on all fours and ran away like a dog. They reported their encounter to local authorities.

HC addendum.
Source: Christopher O'Brien.   Type: E

*   *   *   *   *   *   *

Location: Caibarien, Las Villas, Cuba.
Date: December 21, 1993.
Time: Evening.

Several local anglers had gone to one of the offshore keys, apparently involved in black market fishing operations. While there, the men noticed a very strong light coming from over some nearby dunes. Some of the men went to investigate and reported seeing a hovering disc-shaped object and next to it, several 'winged humanoids' moving about. The entities apparently saw the men but completely ignored them. Afraid, the group immediately left the area, and soon observed the arrival of several Cuban Coast guard units to the area.

Around the same time there were many other reports of anomalous events in both Las Villas and Matanzas provinces. Another report very similar to this event, alleges that several elderly vacationers had been taken on an excursion to one of the cays when they also saw a hovering disc accompanied by several winged 'men.'

HC addendum.
Source: Hugo Parrado Francos.   Type: C

1994

Location: La Coruña, Spain.
Date: 1994.
Time: Evening.

After receiving telepathic messages, a retired technician saw in a secluded area, a landed disc shaped craft, ten meters from his position. Two beings exited the object, one a tall blond male of Nordic appearance wearing a white robe, and a shorter creature resembling a robot.

The two figures briefly approached the witness but did not communicate with him. They both walked back into the object, which took off at high speed.

HC addendum.
Source: Jose Lesta & Miguel Pedrero.   Type: F and B
Comments: date is approximate; I have been waiting for additional details on this case for a while now.

* * * * * * *

Location: Central northern Guadalcanal, Solomon Islands.
Date: 1994.
Time: Evening.

Two government officials were on a long drive up 'Gold Ridge' to survey the area of a proposed gold mine, the road was slippery and the twin cab Toyota Hilux 4WD vehicle slipped off the road and got stuck in the mud. They walked back to the last village they had passed and brought back about thirty helpers.

To their great surprise, when they returned, the vehicle was back on the road and standing beside it were two giant men, one at each end of the vehicle. In fear they all turned and ran. Half an hour later when they cautiously returned, the giants had gone. From examining the footprints it was apparent that the giants had each picked up the 4WD by placing one leg on the road and the other near the vehicle. The "men" were estimated at about 15ft tall (unfortunately there is no description of their clothing).

HC addendum.
Source:http://www.wunderkabinett.co.uk/emporium/index.php?topic =1140.0   Type: E
Comments: Date is approximate.

* * * * * * *

Location: Naryan-Mar, Nenets Autonomous region, Russia.
Date: 1994.
Time: Afternoon.

　　Several deer herders watched a large metallic, disc-shaped object descend and land among a herd of deer. Immediately from the craft emerged several short humanoid figures. Ignoring the stunned herders, they began to conduct on the seemingly paralyzed animals what appeared to be 'surgical operations.'
　　One of the shepherds approached the group of aliens, intending to drive them away. However the other men then watched as he apparently came under the same hypnotic control that had affected the herd. Without trying to escape he approached the aliens and 'voluntarily gave himself to them.'
　　His body was found the next day, completely drained of blood. His genitalia removed along with the prostrate and pancreas; also several pieces of skin were removed on other parts of the body.

HC addendum.
Source: Igor Voloznev Anomaly news 2010 http://anomalia.kulichki.net
Type: X

* * * * * * *

Location: Cirebon, Indonesia.
Date: 1994.
Time: Evening.

　　The witness was walking through a sugar cane field along with a friend when he became separated due to the thick foliage. Suddenly he spotted several small, child-like creatures that were crowded around some sugarcane stalks. The creatures were shorter than the witness and very thin, with huge heads and silvery gray bodies, a bit dull in nature. Surprised, the witness stopped and then the creatures noticed him. He turned to run but suddenly felt heat on the back of his head, and a silvery blue light engulfed him and he passed out.

When the witness woke up, he was lying on the ground close to the Pinggir River near the sugar plantation. He walked home feeling a very sharp pain in his upper abdomen area. The pain lasted for about a week after the incident. When his family saw him they were very surprised and told him that he had been gone for about two weeks. The witness also reported that on several occasions after defecating, he has found aluminum or bright blue colored oval shaped objects inside the waste which are flexible and act like a magnet. After 48 hours they disintegrate leaving a burn mark on the ground or floor.

HC addendum.
Source: BETA UFO Indonesia.   Type: G

* * * * * * *

Location: Melbourne, Australia.
Date: January, 1994.
Time: Late night.

The witness, Kelly Cahill (involved in previous encounters), was sleeping when she felt a presence in the room and something grabbed her right hand. She woke up and was confronted by a tall dark creature, wearing a black robe. It disappeared or became invisible suddenly. The witness then realized that the bathroom light had apparently blown and that two rings were missing from her right hand.

HC addendum.
Source: Bill Chalker, IUR Vol. 19 #5.   Type: E

* * * * * * *

Location: Tronville en Barrios, Meuse, Lorraine, France.
Date: January 4, 1994.
Time: 12:05 a.m.

A family of four was getting ready to go to bed when they noticed a bright light shining on the road between two nearby fields. The light became dimmer and an object with two yellow lights and several flashing red lights became visible. The object was shaped like a bowl and had a transparent dome on top. Inside the object three human shaped figures could be seen, they were of average height. The one in the middle appeared to have a larger head and the one on the right was shorter and heavy set. The figures wore shiny multi-colored outfits. The father went outside and woke up two neighbors who also watched the object.

A door on the left side of the object opened, making a slight noise and one of the humanoids stepped out. He was human-like and was carrying a bright torch that he shone towards the witnesses, moving it from side to side. The "torch" was described as square shaped. The humanoid then walked back into the object. The door then closed making a loud noise. The transparent dome became dark but the yellow lights stayed on. The object then took off, making a slight hissing sound and disappeared at high speed. Other residents in the area saw mysterious red flashing lights over the town.

HC addendum.
Source: Claude Raffy.   Type: A & B

* * * * * * *

Location: Carranza, Maule region, Chile.
Date: February, 1994.
Time: Morning.

Local laborer Florencio Arellano, was performing his morning chores and was sitting on his tractor preparing to go into the fields, when he suddenly he looked to the nearby trees and noticed a strange figure with its arms outstretched, staring at Arellano.

The figure was at least three meters and a half in height and wore a white tunic. It stood without moving staring at Arellano. The figure's clothing was very white and the entity seemed to have pale features. The witness sat stunned on his tractor and stared back at the figure for a few minutes, when it suddenly just vanished in plain sight. He took the encounter as a "sign from God."

HC addendum.
Source: Revista Revelacion Año 3 #23.   Type: E
Comments: Date is approximate. Translated by Albert S. Rosales.

Location: Near Toledo, Washington.
Date: February 16, 1994.
Time: Night.

Two women watched from a 2nd story window, a hovering disc shaped object right outside their upstairs window. They could see a hairy Bigfoot type creature inside the object through a large observation window. The craft was about 50 ft away from the house. When they yelled for their father to come and take a look, the saucer shot straight up and vanished.

HC addendum.
Source: WBS Alien Report, Vol. 2 #5.   Type: A

* * * * * * *

Location: Lomas de Poleo, Mexico.
Date: March, 1994.
Time: Night.

Around the same time that several farm fowl were found mutilated, missing their eyes and tongues, locals watched several lights maneuvering over the same area. Then a huge disc shaped object that descended to a low altitude.

A young girl Zaira Luna, encountered a short white-gray humanoid with large protruding ears near the place where the object hovered. Also, in a very bizarre development, a severed claw of an apparent polar bear was found at the site of the mutilations. (!)

HC addendum.
Source: OJIO, Mexico.   Type: D?

* * * * * * *

Location: Georgetown, Kentucky.
Date: April 11, 1994.
Time: 8:40 p.m.

On a farm in a rural area, a 37-year old man observed a 50-foot long triangle with a rounded apex. It had a bright white light at both ends of each apex.

In the front apex there were three windows and behind the window stood several short gray colored entities. The object also had a dim red light in the center and three white lights around its perimeter. It hovered at about 200 feet away and about 40-70 feet altitude.

255

No sound was heard.

HC addendum.
Source: Mufon Files in: http://www.ufodna.com   Type: A

* * * * * * *

Location: Edmonton, Alberta, Canada.
Date: April 22, 1994.
Time: 3:00 p.m.

A witness reported a large ball of light that landed nearby and transformed itself into a tall entity that ran into the woods and disappeared. No other information.

HC addendum.
Source: Gordon Kijek AUFOSG.   Type: E?

* * * * * * *

Location: Feijo, Acre, Brazil.
Date: May, 1994.
Time: Unknown.

An Indian chief in a remote Amazon area, reported that a huge hairy humanoid with sharp claws attacked and killed several of his men, apparently eating a couple of them.

Another Indian Chief, Joao Kampa, from the nearby Coco-Acu settlement, also reported an attack by a similar creature that killed two of his men.

The creature is reported to emit a strong defensive odor out of the center of its belly from some type of odor emitting gland located there, sometimes confused with a mouth. Locals call the creature "Mapinguary."

HC addendum.
Source: Pablo Villarrubia Mauso.   Type: E

*   *   *   *   *   *   *

Location: Near Flagstaff, Arizona.
Date: May, 1994.
Time: Late night.

A couple was camping in an isolated pine forest. During the very chilly night they built a campfire, but for some unknown reason the fire kept failing. The woman felt uneasy and scared for no apparent reason. As the temperature dropped, they sat in the car. Shortly thereafter the woman saw a bright star like object above the tree line. The light moved from side to side and up and down.

After about twenty minutes, they looked to the west and saw five more similar lights above the tree line. These appeared to be balls of light that danced around very quickly. As they watched, the original light descended down behind the tree line. While observing the lights a multi-colored craft came out of the distant northwest sky, it flew at incredible speed and then quickly went out of sight. Increasingly scared, both prayed. Soon the lights from the sky were gone, but an oblong bright white light illuminated the forest floor. Both then took a shotgun and a pistol and settled in the tent.

Soon they heard what seemed to be persons walking outside. They sat and listened to what sounded like six to ten people walking around in every direction with an occasional tap or prod to the tent. After an hour, a sound came over the tent while simultaneously the ground under the tent floor moved like waves of energy. The wife then looked up through the screened roof and saw a bright ball of white blue light in the sky, just about the tree line.

From this light came a large white colored beam of light shining into the tent. The number of "persons" or creatures outside the tent increased, sounding like quite a large group. Occasionally they heard a sound like whipping wind, along with what sounded like a yipping barking noise that gave them the creeps. At one point a pulsating orange white blue light glowed right next to the tent on the forest floor. It grew larger in size then just disappeared.

At daybreak, both left the tent and found strange footprints in the dirt and handprints on the dust of the car. The footprints "were toed

257

cloven hoofs" and larger three toed feet. The four-fingered handprints had a skeletal, very long thin look. Frightened, they left the area. Their families did not believe their story and they were told that they were "possessed."

HC addendum.
Source: Roger Bollinger.   Type: C?

* * * * * * *

Location: Long Beach, California.
Date: May 7, 1994.
Time: 8:00 p.m.

The witness was at Walnut Avenue & E 8th Street, standing next to his friend's car, smoking a cigarette on a clear night. At this point he noticed that approximately a quarter mile from his location, in all directions, there was a lot of helicopter activity. He wondered why they were just hovering. What caught his attention was the backyard of the house to his right, behind a large tree. He noticed a light first, and then he thought, another helicopter; he thought the rotors must be slamming into the tree.

He began approaching the area to get a better view and at that moment this craft slowly came around and began hovering above him, it then slightly descended no higher than between the telephone poles, perhaps ten feet above. From what he could tell the craft had no markings and no propellers and emitted a slight hum.

At first he was afraid as he noticed behind the thick glass of a canopy type section a being that was looking at him, but it bothered him that he could not see the being clearly. He thought to himself, *"to see clearly one must get past their technology."* Being a mechanic he focused his thoughts observing the craft's structure, he then looked at the canopy again and at that moment the being kind of leaned back with an almost surprised expression.

At that moment the witness pointed his hand at him and then pointed to the sky, the being then tilted its head to one side with a little smile. He could only see the being from the "chest" up, he didn't see any hair its face was a little longer than humans and appeared quite attractive. One interesting aspect that he noticed was the "eyes/expression/personality" characteristics of the being, resembled that of a 'cat.'

HC addendum.
Source: NUFORC.   Type: A

258

Location: Metan, Salta, Argentina.
Date: May 9, 1994.
Time: Night.

Jose Perez, a young hunter had become separated from two other hunting partners in a wooded area when suddenly he came face to face with a huge hairy creature over two meters tall. The gorilla-like creature, using incredible strength, lifted Jose up over his shoulders, carrying him over fifty meters towards a nearby cliff.

Suddenly out of the darkness, two dogs came running out and attacked the hairy humanoid, which dropped Perez to the ground and ran into the thick foliage quickly disappearing from sight. Perez attempted to shoot at the creature but it moved too fast.

HC addendum.
Source: Fabio Picasso.   Type: E

* * * * * * *

Location: Sagrado Corazon, Cosolapa, Mexico.
Date: May 10, 1994.
Time: 11:00 p.m.

A local villager watched a large white light descend from some nearby hills and land a few meters away. A short humanoid creature descended from the object. The humanoid was dressed in all white and had a shiny belt and helmet that changed colors constantly. Another villager attempted to approach the humanoid but it withdrew back into the object. Minutes later a boy threw a rock at the object, which then promptly dimmed and took off towards the hills at high speed quickly disappearing from sight.

HC addendum.
Source: Dr. R.A. Lara in Samizdat Vol.2 #4.   Type: B

* * * * * * *

Location: Frigole, Lecce, Italy.
Date: May 20, 1994.
Time: 12:05 a.m.

Soldier Claudio Mucignat, was making his rounds at a local Army installation when he noticed a small laser-like point of light near a nearby-parked armored vehicle. Thinking that it was a soldier smoking a cigarette he approached the area in his military vehicle.

As he neared the site, his vehicle headlights illuminated a two-meter tall, human-like form, wearing a dark, non-reflective outfit that appeared to move towards him in a strange undulating fashion. Terrified, he attempted to fire his weapon but it malfunctioned. Suddenly, a red beam of light shone on him, apparently causing instant paralysis. After about five to six minutes he recovered his senses, but the strange figure and lights had disappeared.

HC addendum.
Source: IL Giornale dei Misteri #296.   Type: E

* * * * * * *

Location: Near Waroona, Western Australia, Australia.
Date: May 21, 1994.
Time: Night.

Two strange beings walked out of a paddock and approached a vehicle with four passengers inside it. The people were just leaving a friend's house at the time, when the dark figures appeared. Beyond in the moonlight, the witnesses could see a dark object. A flashlight was shined onto the two figures when they approached the vehicle, and it was then that the passengers noticed that the beings were clothed in plastic-like, blue-gray body-clinging garments. They had thin necks and large heads for their five foot heights. Instantly when the flashlight beam hit them they turned and ran back into the paddock toward the object. As the people watched, it lit up and with a loud roar and "shot off" eastwards, gaining height and disappearing into the clouds.

HC addendum.
Source: Rex Gilroy, The Temple of Nim newsletter, November, 2006.
Type: C

* * * * * * *

Location: Near Santa Fe, New Mexico.
Date: Summer, 1994.
Time: 3:00 a.m.

Andrew W. Montoya and some friends were driving around an isolated area and soon the passenger sitting next to him fell asleep. Soon a strange feeling came over Montoya. He looked to the right and was astonished to see saw a white, ape-like creature running besides the car. He immediately woke up his friend who then saw the creature also. At that time the ape turned and looked at them. The ape's eyes were an

260

orange-red that seemed to glow as if there was a fire behind them. It kept up with the car for a little while and then turned off and ran into the mountains. The car had been going at approximately sixty mph.

HC addendum.
Source: Obi wan UFO-Free Paranormal page.   Type: E

* * * * * * *

Location: Arica, Chile.
Date: June, 1994.
Time: 1:30 a.m.
   Croatian national and electronic technician Ivan Bukvic was exploring the desert outside of Arica when he suddenly felt a strong electrical discharge through his body from head to toe. In front of him then appeared a humanoid figure about 1.8 meters in height, encased in a luminous glow. There was reported telepathic contact. No other information.

HC addendum.
Source: Luis Ramirez Reyes, 'Encuentros en todo el Mundo.'   Type: E?

* * * * * * *

Location: Near Harbin, China.
Date: June, 1994.
Time: Evening.

   At a local tree farm, Mong Zhao Guo and two other peasants saw a strange object on nearby Mount Phoenix. They climbed the mountain in order to investigate. As they approached the site, they could see that it was a round, white object with a scorpion-like tail. They attempted to approach the craft several times but were unable to since it apparently produced a very high-pitched sound that caused unbearable pain.
   The following day Guo and some co-workers again saw the object at the same location. Guo watched the craft with a pair of binoculars and saw a "being" with a raised arm standing next to the craft. At that point the being emitted a beam of light that burned Guo's forehead, he then fainted.

HC addendum.
Source: Shi Li in Fate Magazine September, 1997.   Type: C

Location: Nevada (exact location not given).
Date: June, 1994.
Time: Evening.

The witness and his wife were driving under a slight rain in an isolated area, when they saw what appeared to be an accident off to the side of the road. It looked like an accident because there were lots of flashing lights around the site. Curious the witness slowed down to see if he could help and as they came closer they saw what they thought was an ambulance but it turned up to be an object resembling a large soda can lying on its side and resting on three "legs." It was a weird, sort of creamy color, but with a bright red halo around it. Flashing lights could be seen around the object.

As they watched fascinated, his wife suddenly let out a blood-curling scream. The witness turned around and saw two "aliens" coming towards the car. These were described as bug-like, with their heads looking like praying mantises. They had humanoid-looking bodies, however, and wore bluish gray jumpsuits. The terrified witness, who was armed with a gun, pulled it out and fired two shots towards the road in front of the figures. This must have startled the humanoids, which suddenly ran back to their landed cylinder shaped object. At this point the witness began speeding away from the area; looking back, he saw additional similar appearing humanoids standing around the craft, about nine or ten of them. They did not see the object depart.

HC addendum.
Source: UFOs and Aliens Online.   Type: C

* * * * * * *

Location: Pacific Ocean near Tonga.
Date: June 5, 1994.
Time: Evening.

The catamaran 'Heart Light' was in a terrific storm that left half a dozen yachts sunk or abandoned. The owners of the Heart Light, Diviana and Darryl Wheeler, were on board with their son and daughter in-law. Wheeler reported how the Heart Light teetered at a 90 degree angle on one hull as it "careened down a 100-foot wave out of control."

Suddenly, the Heart Light was caught in a powerful "tractor" beam from a "spacecraft" hovering above them in the tempest. Wheeler's mind became inseparably linked with the occupants of the hovering craft. He was somewhat confused with their telepathic intelligence. The craft was crystalline in nature, lens shaped and surrounded by an etheric green glow.

Wheeler was certain the spaceship pilots had saved their lives (he called them, "Etherians"). Around the same time, there were reports of lights being seen and other odd occurrences. Paul Everett onboard the yacht 'Irresistible' heard foreign sounding voices and saw the figures of a man and a woman on his boat. People on other yachts and the navy ship 'Monowai,' also heard strange voices and saw odd lights in the sky.

HC addendum.
Source: Peter Hassall, The NZ Files.   Type: C or F?

* * * * * * * *

Location: Near Padova, Italy.
Date: June 8, 1994.
Time: Midnight.

In a farm area, a robot-like entity with lights approached a witness. It communicated by using telepathy, warning the witness that he could not hurt him since there were fourteen others just like him, hiding in nearby woods. It then lifted vertically and flew away.

HC addendum.
Source: LDLN #329.   Type: E
Comments: Telepathic robot?

* * * * * * * *

Location: Seuzach, Switzerland.
Date: June 27, 1994.
Time: 9:10 p.m.

A family out in a field together, were astounded to see something coming from the Southwest and headed on a Northeast direction at about 250-300 meters altitude. As it got closer overhead, they could see that it was a man-shaped figure, wearing all dark, standing on top of an object resembling a "surfboard."
It flew silently in a horizontal position and was in sight for about fifty to sixty seconds. They described it as a tall man in black, standing on top of a flat, board-like object. There were several witnesses.

HC addendum.
Source: Greyhunter Site, Germany.   Type: E?

Location: Arad, Romania.
Date: June 27, 1994.
Time: 4:00 a.m.

At least five witnesses heard a loud hissing sound when a nearby wheat field became illuminated by a very bright light. A flattened circular area of wheat was found at the site.

One of the witnesses, 48-year-old Traian Crisan, a shepherd, approached the site and saw the light gliding towards the field. He ran to his hut and watched from inside, but then the walls and roof began to shake. He then ran outside and was confronted by a strong wind.

He noticed a round hovering object and through a small opening he could see two short men that appeared to be holding a tube. Both men were bearded; one with a long white beard and both had slanted eyes. The men each wore a device resembling headphones and had instruments in their hands. The nearby sheep panicked and ran, as a blue flame shot out from the bottom of the craft and it accelerated straight up into the sky and disappeared.

HC addendum.
Source: Michael Hesemann in 'The Cosmic Connection.'   Type: A
Comments: This case appears to be a direct connection between UFOs, humanoids and Crop Circles.

* * * * * * *

Location: Castelo do Piaui, Piaui, Brazil.
Date: July, 1994.
Time: 1:00 a.m.

A young night-watchman, standing guard at the Municipal City hall located next to a church, noticed a sudden flash. Afraid and thinking it was a "malignant Chupa light," the guard saw a luminous globe-shaped object descend slowly onto the church's patio. He could then see that the globe was bronze-aluminum in color and had a revolving light on its perimeter.

His surprise tripled as he witnessed a small door open on the globe and two one meter tall humanoids exited the craft. He could only describe them as "purple" in color and wearing large helmets that covered their faces. The two beings then headed directly towards the witness.

Terrified, the witness ran to a nearby square where he found another guard and told him what he had just seen. The other guard did not believe him and upon returning to the church's patio the object and beings were now gone.

According to the source, the witness was ridiculed for reporting the incident.

HC addendum.
Source: Reinaldo Coutinho in 'Apovni,' Portugal.   Type: B

* * * * * * *

Location: Silbury Hill, near Avebury, Wiltshire, England.
Date: July, 1994.
Time: 2:00 a.m.

Three people climbed England's Silbury Hill and planned to spend the night, atop the 131-foot high mound, to watch for possible crop circle activity. The three people (two men and a woman) were soon met by two other friends, but the two friends left shortly before dark. A group of five teenagers were also on the summit of the mount at the same time. The teenagers fell asleep around midnight as fog began to encircle the mound and they appeared to be "frozen" or deeply asleep, when the strangeness began to unfold.

Around 1:00 a.m, the three witnesses heard what they thought were the sounds of someone ascending the hill by coming straight up the side, not by using the spiral path that leads up and around the hill. Looking over the side of the steep mound, they thought they could see small dark forms moving around, forms resembling children, but their attention was immediately grabbed by the sight of an orange fireball appearing about a mile away, slowly floating above the ground. When all three

265

witnesses looked at the orange fiery orb, another fireball immediately appeared beside the first. At that distance the witnesses described them as looking like flaming, orange torches. They smelled sulfur and something like burning rubber and could hear dogs in the distance barking wildly.

The fireballs floated quickly toward the three witnesses. When the orbs were about 170 yards away from the mound, one of the witnesses turned on a flashlight. Immediately the orange orbs stopped moving. The witnesses then could clearly see a "structured form" hanging below each of the orange orbs. The balls of orange fire appeared to be about two-feet in diameter, but the objects below each were larger. The objects under the orbs were tetrahedron shaped, a three-sided pyramid, and floating above the ground.

When the flashlight was turned off, the floating lights continued moving toward them. They then observed what looked like electrical discharges that occasionally flashed to the ground from the orbs. When the forms got closer, the witnesses were stunned by what they saw.

Inside both of the now translucent pyramid-shaped objects, they could see a small being sitting with crossed legs and hands clasped on their laps. The beings were glowing orange colored and were estimated to have been four to five feet tall. The female witness, for reasons she could not explain, blurted out, *"They're little people."* The fireballs floated higher and eventually elevated to about ten feet above the hill and about 15-20 feet away from the witnesses. At that point everything seemed to move in slow motion. They heard a cracking sound and what seemed to be whispering.

One of the witnesses believed that the creatures were somehow communicating with them. As the orange glow from the objects was reflected onto the surrounding trees and the hill, both fireballs silently expanded in a massive and blinding flash of light. The orbs and dangling pyramid shaped objects reappeared after the light flash subsided and then floated down the hill, they then joined together into a single fireball, and moved over a nearby road to an adjacent field. It was at this point that the most bizarre event occurred;

One of the humanoid beings slowly emerged from the fireball, but as it emerged it was holding the hand of the other humanoid, also pulling it out of the orb. Both of the orange, glowing beings floated next to the orb, hand-in-hand, and then they re-entered the fireball. At that moment from behind the object, several more orange orbs suddenly appeared, numbering from four. Below each of these, the witnesses could see a translucent tetrahedron with a small humanoid being sitting inside. The group of orange objects then moved away from Silbury Hill following a road toward the town of Marlborough, illuminating the road as they moved.

266

Unexpectedly, a car then appeared on the road, moving toward the lights. In response, the orange orbs merged into a single light and shrank to the size of a tennis ball and rapidly jumped off the road into a hedgerow. Then, all the witnesses saw the tennis-ball size light reappear and rapidly move toward Silbury Hill and spin around it. Shortly thereafter the witnesses saw what they described as a string of multi-colored lights moving up a nearby hill and over it out of sight. The three main witnesses decided to tell no one about their experience, but for years thereafter they were haunted by the experience. Nightmares, fear, changes in career, and various other emotional issues emerged.

HC addendum.
Source: Andrew Collins, 'Lightquest,' 2012.   Type: E & A

* * * * * * *

Location: Harrison County, West Virginia.
Date: July 3, 1994.
Time: Late night.

The witness was alone in his store when he suddenly saw lights around him and his body began to vibrate. Somehow he was able to see an object hovering above the building and was transported onboard the craft. He found himself in a room with a table and a light above it. There was a railing around the side of the room. He then saw a short gray skinned humanoid that appeared to be operating a control panel.
The short gray being communicated telepathically with the witness, supplying him with a wealth of information, including the fact that he has been implanted with some type of tracking device and also mentioned the Roswell incident, stating that it was not one of their craft.

HC addendum.
Source: Bob Teets in 'West Virginia UFOs: Close Encounters in the Mountain State.'   Type: G

* * * * * * *

Location: Near Caleufu, La Pampa, Argentina.
Date: July 20, 1994.
Time: 12:40 a.m.

34-year old Bernardino Cabrera was outdoors on an errand, when a powerful reddish light descended on him from above. Then a craft landed nearby and from it came two "gigantic" beings that took him aboard and laid him on a sort of "stretcher" and drew blood from him. There was no

267

spoken communication between them, but he says he understood what the beings were saying to him even though they did not move their lips and no sound was heard from them.

They told him that if he wanted to reveal the affair to the public, he could do so. Cabrera was then set down on the main square of the town, in front of the police station. He was later examined at a local hospital.

HC addendum.
Source: Jane Guma, FSR Vol. 42 #1.   Type: G
Comments: Unfortunately there is no additional description of the humanoids other than 'gigantic.'

* * * * * * *

Location: Vladivostok, Far East, Russia.
Date: July 20, 1994.
Time: Night.

A local 16-year old girl named Natasha (see previous contacts) disappeared for one week from her household. Her parents and police searched for her without any results. At the end of the week she returned and claimed that she had visited another planet with her extraterrestrial friends from space. Her parents did not believe her story and punished her. No further information.

HC addendum.
Source: Alexander Rempel, VAUFON in 'Gentry,' Vladivostok, #8, 1994.
Type: G

* * * * * * *

Location: Near Allende, Nuevo Leon, Mexico.
Date: July 25, 1994.
Time: Evening.

At a local ranch, a woman encountered a strange winged, half bird and half man humanoid, covered with gray feathers up to his shoulders and with a human head, claw like feet and huge wings on his back. No other information.

HC addendum.
Source: Marco A. Reynoso   Type: E

Location: Agreste, Pernambuco, Brazil.
Date: Late July, 1994.
Time: Late night.

Local farmers and ranchers reported seeing a monstrous creature that killed numerous cattle, goats, and other assorted farm animals. One man reported seeing a tall hairy dark figure, with a huge square, strong jaw. It ran away into the darkness. Many of the animals were found mutilated and partly eaten.

HC addendum.
Source: Recife Assombrado, Brazil.   Type: E

*   *   *   *   *   *   *

Location: Alton Barnes, Wiltshire, England.
Date: Early August, 1994.
Time: 4:00 p.m.

The primary witness, 53-year old Jenny, a retired teacher and a friend; 26-year old Steve, were traveling in their work van representing a Gourmet food company, when they came over the top of the hill by East Field and immediately saw crop circles. The crop circles in the golden wheat were a beautiful sight that neither witness had seen before. They pulled into a farmer's track at the side of the hill and drove up to the edge of the tramlines for a better look. They both immediately noticed six very tall figures in the nearest crop circle. The figures appeared to be wearing hooded cowls and appeared to be purposefully moving around in the circle. The witnesses were fascinated because the people were moving around the circle with their arms high above their heads and they appeared to be all, moving in a rhythmic way. They were moving from the center of the circle to the outer circumference. Jokingly Jenny exclaimed, *"Oh look we've caught them, they must have just made it."*
At this stage the figures were about a quarter of a mile away. Jenny decided to stay in the van and wait for the strangers since they had to walk right by them when they left the field by the tramline. The six figures walked up the tramline. The figures were all over six feet tall. The two male figures among the group of six were wearing their hooded cowls up even though it wasn't raining. The high hooded cowl worn by each of the figure resembled in profile the shape made by a penguin with its head down. These men also wore long brown capes down to ground level. The hooded cowls revealed these two males to have very large blue eyes, very high cheekbones and long pallid faces. The four females all had the same identical blond hair and very large faces. All their hair had been cut in a medieval Pageboy style, to shoulder length and parted in the center. All

of them had blue eyes. Two of the females wore green cowls, and the two others wore one red and one yellow cowl. The colors of the textiles were muted and matte in color. The females had more oval faces and deep-set eyes than the males, however, they all looked so near identical it was uncanny. The females had all let their hoods down, to rest elegantly upon their shoulders, revealing their fine blond hair. What was most noticeable was their eyes; they remained both limpid and expressionless throughout. They appeared almost resigned, a grave expressionless air emanated from them that made the witnesses uneasy. One of the females had crimped hair and a straight fringe. It was this person that came forward to Jenny at first as she passed by them, the others gathered around on her side of the van. She felt compelled to stay in the van. As she looked at the strangers she saw no limbs other than their booted feet, their bodies remaining completely covered.

Jenny spoke through the van window to the first female as she approached her, with a mischievous twinkle in her eye she said, *"Are they freshly made?"* The woman answered, *"Oh yes they are freshly made,"* in a part Germanic and part Dutch accent. In awe, Jenny asked, *"Ah, have you seen these before?"* *"Oh yes!"* was the reply. *"Where are you from?"* Asked Jenny, while she thought in her head that they were not of this world. The surprising answer was, *"We are from Holland,"* said the blond female. Jenny then asked the woman if they had seen crop circles in Holland and they reply was in the affirmative. Jenny then asked, *"Why do circles only seem to appear in cereal crops?"* She was told that circles and patterns appear in vegetables, in cabbages, and spinach, circles in the trees, in the sand and in the ice. Jenny received no reply when she asked how they had arrived in Alton Barnes. She then asked the group what they were doing in the field. They each replied randomly from where they stood, *"We are testing the circles for vibrations."* *"We were dowsing with metal rods."* *"We could feel the energy under our feet."* *"They have just been made."* *"We make a study of these circles."*

Although the strangers said they had dowsing rods, they were not in evidence. Jenny then asked, *"What happens when dowsing rods are used?"* The answer was, *"When they are held in front, the rods violently swing in opposite directions. The left to the left and the right to the right."* At this point, two of the other females had just gone, Jenny checked for them in the wing mirrors, but could not see a trace of them. The woman with the crimped hair now appeared to dig her still covered arm deep inside her cape. *"I have something to show you,"* She told Jenny. Jenny put her hand out of the van window pinching her finger and thumb in anticipation to pick up whatever she was about to receive.

"No, open your palm," came the reply. She obediently opened her hand revealing her palm. Quickly the stranger's hand darted out of her sleeve as she pulled something out from within her cloak. It was a very rapid darting movement, but in that time she noticed that the fingers

were extremely long and without an obvious thumb. A piece of metal about twice the size of the British 50 pence piece now lay on Jenny's palm. It was about a quarter of an inch thick. It fitted close to her skin, almost as if the metal had something, soft and molten about it. This was the rounded side, underneath the object. The metal looked like new pewter, and the shape tapered at one end. The top surface had hundreds of little facets cut like diamonds. On top of this, there was a little cut motif. It was rather like the shape of a fern leaf but with fractal like detail, similar to that found with ice on a frozen windowpane. There were also many tiny holes, similar to the tiny holes found in an old piece of driftwood. It was beautiful and Jenny looked at the strange object for two minutes without saying anything. She gave it to Steve so he could hold it and he exclaimed how light it was. Jenny turned to the female at the window and went to plant the object where she expected her hand to be, but was told, *"Put out your hand out flat."* Again her hand without a visible thumb shot out rapidly and took the object back. Jenny was told that they had found the object in a crop circle in Holland and that scientists had examined it and said that it was not from the Earth, that it came from outer space.

"We must go now," said the woman, as she began to move behind the van with the other remaining female. Again Jenny looked back and they did not go up the path and they did not go up the bank. They just vanished. Now the two male hooded figures remained behind, which up to now had been quietly watching the witnesses. They then stepped forward silently. Jenny turned to them and said, *"Well what do you think this all means then?"* Again came a reply in heavy Dutch German accents, and once more the men took it in turns to speak. They looked like twins and sounded the same. *"They are trying to tell us something, we will not listen."* Jenny questioned them on their statement. They each answered again in turns, *"Earth's resources are finite."* *"We must stop pillaging the earth."* *"We must stop exploiting each other and stop killing each other or God will be very angry."*

Then one of them said, *"Did you know that the DNA of the wheat that has been flattened is different from the wheat that is standing next to it?"* Jenny told the men that she had heard that before, they seemed surprised at this. Then they said, *"We must go now."* Then they proceeded to pass the van and with a step toward the road they vanished. They disappeared just like the others. Both witnesses then proceeded to explore the crop circles; they found blackened sections in the center of the circles.

HC addendum.
Source: Harry Challenger, FSR.   Type: E
Comments: A clear-cut case, apparently directly connecting crop circle activity with "alien" humanoids.

Location: Pacajus, Ceara, Brazil.
Date: August, 1994.
Time: Late evening.

A 28-year-old peasant woman, Joaquina Nogueira, was coming back to town when she saw a very powerful light in a nearby grove of cashew trees. She stopped and watched. Suddenly out of nowhere, two luminous beings appeared in front of her. The beings were tall and human-like, wearing phosphorescent tight-fitting clothing. They stood there looking at her from about ten meters away. They came closer and the witness could see that one was a woman the other a man.

The man was very tall and powerfully built. He had black fluffy hair combed back, dark slanted eyes and arched eyebrows, his ears were larger than humans and slightly pointed, he had a prominent chin and darkish skin. He assured her, telling her not to be afraid, to keep calm. His lips moved but she heard the words in her mind. The being went on to tell her that he was "Karran" that he had been here before. The woman also said something that the witness was unable to understand; the woman also had combed back black hair. She had a sculptural looking body and wore tight-fitting clothes, revealing a well-delineated silhouette, she smiled and appeared gentle.

The woman stepped back and drew something out of the wide belt she wore. The object began to click, and she put it to the witness right ear then said a few strange words. At the same time, louder sounds came from the device. The man then took something from his belt and gave it to Joaquina, gesturing to her to raise it to her mouth. She did and it tasted sour. Her mouth quickly filled with saliva and she began to feel nauseated and spat several times. She felt herself dominated by the eyes of the male being that came closer to her and put something into her ear.

At the same moment the witness' brother was approaching their location. The two beings then withdrew the device from the witness ear and then turning away with their backs to the witness they vanished in plain sight. The witness brother was also able to see the two tall beings from a distance.

HC addendum.
Source: Reginaldo de Athyayde in FSR.   Type: E
Comments: A humanoid claiming to be "Karran," or similar name reputedly was encountered in Brazil in 1976 and 1977.

Location: San Juan De Rio, Queretaro, Mexico.
Date: September, 1994.
Time: Evening.

A Mr. Olmos, saw a small figure walking on a path near his home. It seemed to be of normal proportions, except for its arms; that seemed to be somewhat short. It was wearing a green-colored inflated outfit. It walked under a barb-wired fence and seemedthat to be carrying in his right hand a glowing object. It wore a helmet with a glass visor that reflected the light from a nearby lamppost. The top of the helmet ended in a sharp point, resembling an antenna, from which a green flame emerged. From each side of its helmet protruded a large pointy ear. Mr. Olmos instructed his young daughter to turn the porch light on.

At that same moment the humanoid put his hands on his waist and a light came on, on an object on his back resembling a rucksack. Red and blue lights came on and the witness then heard a buzzing sound. The humanoid then rose up in the air about three to four meters and disappeared from sight. As it did the witness was able to notice duck-like feet on the humanoid. That same night, neighbors of Mr. Olmos reported animal disturbances among the cattle and dogs.

HC addendum.
Source: Contacto Ovni & Fabio Picasso.   Type: E
Comments: Sounds suspiciously like a 1977 Puerto Rican case.

* * * * * * *

Location: Marathon County, Wisconsin.
Date: September, 1994.
Time: 11:00 p.m.

A woman was driving home when she suffered a flat tire. Upon preparing to exit the vehicle to fix the tires, a large beast appeared in front of her. She described the creature as being about 6.5 ft tall with large pointed ears, very yellow eyes, huge curved fangs, very hairy and walking upright. The creature made a lunge for her, causing her extreme terror. She immediately slammed and locked the door and made a bolt for home on her flat tire. When leaving she said that the creature howled like a wolf and took off across a field. To this date she will not travel down this road at night.

HC addendum.
Source: W Files, http://w-files.com/   Type: E
Comments: Nightmarish encounter indeed, what would have occurred if the creature had succeeded in grabbing the witness?

273

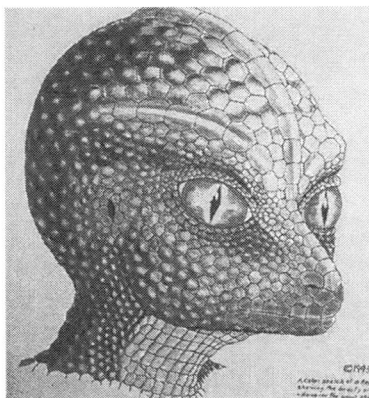

Location: Framingham, Massachusetts.
Date: September 1, 1994.
Time: 3:15 a.m.

Mona Kempka was suddenly awakened by a "hand" pressing firmly with great force on her hand. Looking up she was stunned to see a reptilian entity materialize in front of her. She described the entity as breathtaking in appearance, very tall, covered with scales that were congruent to its frame, with smaller scales around the elbows and knees. Its torso put the most proficient bodybuilder to shame, its legs were like giant frog's legs only more developed muscularly, there was a mist covering its face, so she could not see it. As this event was taking place the whole room took on a pinkish hue, the entity repeatedly stated that his name was "ZOZO" to her telepathically.

As this was occurring Mona became hysterical standing straight up in her bed and screaming. The reptoid was greenish in color and highly developed in musculature, with intimidating claws, rather talon-like. It then dematerialized again in front of the witness. She claims that six months later a gray-type entity appeared in her room. The witness further claims that before the first encounter, she had been in contact with an entity calling itself "ZOZO" by means of an Ouija Board.

HC addendum.
Source: webmaster@ufoinfo.com   Type: E

Location: Ruwa, Zimbabwe.
Date: September 16, 1994.
Time: 10:15 a.m.

Some 62 children were playing in a field of the local 'Ariel' primary school when they saw three silvery balls in the sky over the school. These disappeared with a flash of light then reappeared at another location. This happened three times then they began descending towards the school. One of the objects then landed or hovered over a section of rough ground composed of trees, thorn bushes, and grass. Moments later a small man about one meter in height appeared on top of the object. He then walked a little way across the rough ground, became aware of the children, and disappeared. He then reappeared back at the object, which took off very rapidly and disappeared.

The little man was dressed in a tight fitting black suit, which was "shiny." He had a long scrawny neck and huge eyes, with a pale face and long black hair coming below his shoulders. The smaller children were very frightened and cried for help. They believed that the little man was a demon who would eat them.

African children have heard legends of "tokoloshis;" demons that eat children. The children ran to the snack shop operator, but she did not want to leave the shop unattended and so did not go. Curiously, the older students said that they felt that the creatures communicated with them somehow, sending the message that we humans are destroying our planet, polluting the environment in ways that will have dire consequences.

According to some sources, UFOs had been seen in the skies over Zimbabwe for two days before the incident occurred. One witness described the object as resembling a perfectly shaped oval granite rock on the virgin African bush that seemed to be glittering.

HC addendum.
Source: Cynthia Hind in MUFON Journal #320.   Type: C

* * * * * * *

Location: Rocchetta Sant'Antonio, Italy.
Date: October 14, 1994.
Time: 11:15 a.m.

While walking along the countryside M. F. noticed at about 500 meters away next to an oak tree a short human like figure or form that appeared to be picking something up from the ground. The figure was silvery in color, with the top section blue in color. It was about 50cm in height. The witness hid behind some bushes to watch the figure. The figure suddenly rose up in the area and hovered above a tree. At this point the witness noticed an antenna like protrusion on the top portion of the figure. The figure then shot up into the sky and vanished.

HC addendum.
Source: C.I.S.U Puglia.   Type: E

* * * * * * *

Location: Near Karatau, Kazakhstan.
Date: November, 1994.
Time: Late night.

A night watchman at a relay station was roused late at night when his dog suddenly rushed outside, barking at "a huge, globe shaped, luminous machine" standing about fifty meters away. A number of creatures, slightly resembling human beings and wearing skin-tight silver suits, disembarked from the object through an invisible door, and the dog "gallantly" attacked them. However, one of the humanoids stretched out his hand to the dog, and a thin blue ray shot out of his hand and touched the animal. The dog immediately froze and fell to the ground noiselessly. The guard had only time to call the Karatau police station by telephone and urge to come over, before the same humanoid appeared in the doorway, and the same blue ray knocked the guard to the floor.

The police were stranded when their car engine cut out about a kilometer from the relay station. This also happened to the back-up car, and all efforts to start the engines failed. Both cars unexpectedly started up again an hour later. The police brought the guard out of his "strange quasi narcotic coma," and he recounted the incident to them. A perfect circle of carbonized rock was left at the place where the UFO had landed. The unfortunate dog never did wake up.

HC addendum.
Source: FRS Vol. 40 #1.   Type: B

* * * * * * *

Location: Berceto, Italy.
Date: November 17, 1994.
Time: 1:30 a.m.

A luminous point in the sky descended and became a humanoid figure. After about ten minutes of hovering around, it left the area at high speed.

HC addendum.
Source: CUN.   Type: E
Comments: Flying humanoid report. These reports became more and more common towards the end of the 90's and the advent of the new millennium.

* * * * * * *

Location: Tiete, Sao Paolo, Brazil.
Date: December 11, 1994.
Time: 11:00 p.m.

Two observers watched a luminous green sphere land nearby. Two humanoid figures appeared next to the object. One of the witnesses shined a flashlight at the figures and a beam of light from the object immediately disabled it. The beings and the object then departed.
The beings were described as about 1.2 meters in height, very pale skin and with four fingered hands, large staring eyes, and two small holes for a nose. Crushed grass was found at the scene. No other information.

HC addendum.
Source: Brazilian UFO Report Vol. 1 #1.   Type: C

Location: Las Mitres, Monterrey, Mexico.
Date: December 13, 1994.
Time: 1:00 a.m.

A CSETI team led by Dr. Steven Greer was camped out in this mountain region hoping to establish some sort of "contact" with aliens/UFOs. At around 22:30 the group had observed a very bright light that appeared in the zenith of the sky, traveling rapidly in an upward arc that terminated in the center of the constellation Orion. Soon very dense clouds materialized within a minute on parts of the sheer mountain cliffs. At 1:00 a.m. Dr. Greer and another team member were standing slightly down the gravel road when they observed a bright, strobe-like white light appear at the edge of the mountain.

At about the same time Shari Adamiak had gotten up and walked closer towards the brush at the base of the mountain. As they stood there, another round light came rolling down the side of the steep slope. Adamiak felt some type of invisible energy that felt as it was gently pulling her deeper into the brush. Both she and Greer felt that there was a presence nearby that, from past experience, led them to feel that there was a spacecraft and extraterrestrial beings very close-by.

Just then, Adamiak began to perceive small, square-shouldered beings in the brush around them. They could be dimly seen, but a clear view of them wasn't possible. The little beings were extremely shy and reticent. They would scurry close to the witnesses, and then backtrack quickly into the brush. They could not hear any brush moving or footsteps but they could dimly see them. The aliens seemed to have been wearing uniforms that covered their body and legs that were a dull orange-rust color. They were very short, just up to the Adamiak's knees (she was 5'7").

She soon became aware of a telepathic message. They were concerned about the video camera, behind, to the witness' right. She send back a telepathic message to them, advising them not to worry, that the camera was not on and no one was going to touch it. They seemed to trust her assurance, as the event continues to unfold.

Dr. Greer went back to the other three members and instructed them to stay where they were unless he called them forward. Adamiak could mentally "hear" concerned conversation going on amongst the small beings. They eventually conveyed to her the message, again mentally that they were having difficulty adjusting "our" energies in preparation for a meeting because her physical energy was concentrated in her stomach, trying to digest some food (just before the encounter, Adamiak had eaten an energy bar). Mentally she conveyed to the aliens a message giving them permission to remove it from their body. Suddenly she felt as if someone were standing some distance away with a fishing line whose hook was inside her stomach. It felt as if someone was slowly reeling in the line as the food came back out the way it went in. After this purging procedure her energy felt softer, with less intense vibration.

Soon the little beings sent both Dr. Greer and her the message that if they removed their glasses, they would be able to see them better. They did as they were told. At this point, they could feel a harmonious flow of energy between them, the little beings and some other unseen source. At this point, the small life forms disappeared. Shafts of golden light began to come from an unknown, unseen source and lay across the bushes in front of them. They learned later that the three other team members behind them were able to see that as well although they had been unable to perceive the small beings. Adamiak could feel one of these shafts of light approach her and fill her torso with a warm, golden glow. After the light beams faded, a large oval of bluish fog began to form about ten feet in front of them.

As the bluish mist began to coalesce, Dr. Greer and Adamiak became aware of a being within it. Although again they could only see him dimly, he appeared very humanoid, tall, with long and straight silvery hair. He appeared to be clothed in a light blue and silver uniform. They learned later that one team member saw a tendril of the blue fog travel along the ground towards her. It frightened her a little until the mist reached her foot and began to send wisps around her feet. She later said that she felt a gentle kindness about the fog and all her misgivings vanished. Another witness, who was not an actual team member, became very frightened by the golden light and blue fog.

It is important and interesting to note that both Dr. Greer and Adamiak received nearly identical mental messages each time there was a communication from the extraterrestrial. Greer and Adamiak consulted each other and decided to send a joint message. They told the tall being that if they could not come to us, it was okay if they could take them to where they were. They could sense this was being discussed with a "central command control" or his more senior members. Soon Greer and Adamiak saw a copper gold sphere, ten to twelve feet in diameter, begin to coalesce to the left of the tall being. It never reached material solidity but soon began to disperse. Finally after what seemed like a few moments, the tall being sent them a message that they would not be able to manifest fully in the physical this night. But they sent an additional message, "soon again, soon again." At this point Greer went back to meet with the other team members.

The next night the members saw a gigantic brilliant round beam of light that shot light down the entire mountainside. During this lengthy encounter the members sent signals to the craft. The craft would then signal back to them in the exact sequence. Then its lights would extinguish. This went on and on. Twice during this time period they saw the shadows of beings walking in front of the blinding beam. At times the beam would rotate upon itself, appearing to the left of its original position, then back where it was, once the light seemed to turn over on itself, illuminating the sparsely forested slope behind it. This was one of times when figures were seen to move in the beam.

HC addendum.
Source: Shari Adamiak, CSETI.   Type: C & F

About the author

Albert S. Rosales, was born in Cuba on January 3, 1958. After living for some time in Spain, in 1967, his family moved to New York City before ultimately settling down in Miami where Albert became a US citizen and attended school. Albert had many strange incidents as a child and developed an interest in UFOs and unusual events from the time he was in high school.

He joined the United States Navy after high school and traveled the world. Later on, after being honorably discharged from the Navy, Albert went into the jewelry business with his father. After his father passed on, Albert joined a local law enforcement agency in Miami and has now been there for over 30 years. Albert is married, with five grown children, one girl and four boys.

For over 40 years, Albert has been studying UFOs, and since 1993, has been regularly updating his Humanoid Encounter catalogue. Albert's efforts are a continuation of the work of pioneers like Ted Bloecher, David Webb and others. You can forward your own humanoid encounters to Albert at:

garuda79@att.net

Made in the USA
San Bernardino, CA
26 February 2016